COUNSELING TOWARD SOLUTIONS

A Practical Solution-Focused Program for Working with Students, Teachers, and Parents

LINDA METCALF

A Center for Change
Arlington, Texas

Illustrations by Ryan Metcalf

**THE CENTER FOR APPLIED
RESEARCH IN EDUCATION**
West Nyack, New York 10994

10 9 8 7 6 5 4 3 2 1

Library of Congress Cataloging-in-Publication Data

Metcalf, Linda.
  Counseling toward solutions : a practical solution-focused program for
working with students, teachers, and parents / Linda Metcalf.
    p.   cm.
  Includes bibliographical references.
  ISBN 0-87628-267-2
  1. Educational counseling—United States. 2. Education counseling—
United States—Case studies. 3. Solution-focused therapy—United States.
4. Solution-focused therapy—United States—Case studies. I. Title.
LB1027.5.M445   1995
371.4—dc20   94-36512
                                                                CIP

ISBN 0-87628-267-2

**The Center for Applied
Research in Education**
Career & Personal Development
A division of Simon & Schuster
Englewood Cliffs, New Jersey 07632

Printed in the United States of America

This book is dedicated to my children Ryan, Kelli, Roger Jr.,
and my husband Roger.

ACKNOWLEDGMENTS

To Ryan, my ten-year-old son (diagnosed with Attention Deficit Disorder [ADD] five years ago), thanks for doing the illustrations for this manual. From the very beginning, you have proved you are a winner! To Roger Jr., for your excellent computer skills—without you, many of these reproducible sheets would be plain...you are incredible! To Kelli, your editing of the classroom guidance chapter helped me see what was "cool" to do. Many students will benefit from your wisdom. To my husband, thanks for your constant support, encouragement, belief in me and keen ability to know when I needed a break. Thank you for always being there and telling me I could finish this book. Finally to my parents, especially my dad, who told me when I was very young that I should be a teacher and helped me achieve that. Thanks.

Thanks a thousand times to Connie Kallback and Win Huppuch of Simon & Schuster for offering me the opportunity to express my ideas in this manual. You have made my dream of educators learning these ideas come true.

Many other wonderful and creative people made contributions to this manual: Thanks to Brian Cade for writing an original case study; Michael Durrant for his constant support, comments and preliminary editing; Bill O'Hanlon for his contributions of informational sheets which helped reinforce his wonderful ideas about task development and working with sexual abuse survivors; John Walter and Jane Peller for sharing "Jack's" story; Stephen Chilton for his creative ideas and collaborative way of working that helped to produce marvelous classroom guidance ideas; and Frank Thomas, a professor who intoduced me to Solution-Focused Brief Therapy and changed the way I think about working with people. Thanks to Michael White and David Epston for their generosity in allowing me to print extensively what I found helpful. I appreciate their work immensely and their "down under" hospitality in sharing their wonderful ideas. Finally, thanks to the many teachers, counselors, administrators and students who expressed their appreciation of my ideas and encouraged me to write this manual. You made writing this a pleasure.

Many thanks to the following educators who gave of their time in long phone conversations and in writing up successful cases: Terry Walkup, Charlie Thomas, Ellen Boehmer, Peggy Dowell, Jean Cadell, Tricia Long, Charles Thompson, Nan Lovelace, Ella Starnes, Kay Woodard, and Geri Kellogg.

ABOUT THIS BOOK

Counseling Toward Solutions is a handbook written for teachers, administrators and school counselors who would like to approach school populations with a more positive, solution-focused approach. The ideas developed in this book are based on the principles of solution-focused brief therapy and other competency-based models that address solutions rather than problems. The approach makes interventions in the school setting more efficient and less stressful for students and school staff, since the focus is not on understanding the "why" of a problem. The program described in the book stresses noticing "exceptions" to when problems *do not occur*, instead of *when they occur*. The book utilizes exercises and tasks for school staff, to encourage them to look into their own lives and apply firsthand some of the ideas presented. The result is a better understanding of why focusing on exceptions instead of problems can indeed make a difference in one's perception of himself/herself.

Chapter 1 describes the major Guidelines and philosophies of solution-focused brief therapy as suggested by Michelle Weiner-Davis and William O'Hanlon (1989) and adapts them to the school setting. These guidelines are further explained through actual case examples from school settings. This chapter also serves as a personal introduction to SFBT ideas through a self-evaluation exercise which invites the staff member to look into his/her personal life successes and professional successes.

Chapter 2 utilizes the power of language in making problems more solvable when they are described in a more "normal" context. "If in our world, language plays a very central part in those activities that define and construct persons...then a redescription of persons is called for." (Epston, 1989). As problems are "redescribed" into language that emits possibilities, success seems more eminent. For example, a teacher may complain of a child who is angry all the time. The SFBT school person may reflect back to the teacher that the child is *bothered by anger at times*. This externalizing of problems, (White, 1989) as if they were outside influences, stops people from seeing *themselves* as the problem. The school person can go a step further and ask both the teacher and the student to notice when the anger does not bother the student as much. This approach encourages the teacher to perceive the student differently and the student to become *conscious* of anger so that he/she can take on a new behavior. Narrative approaches, or, writing notes of competency to students, teachers, and administrators are part of this chapter's contents and serve as a marvelous way of communicating through language that people are noticed in successful contexts. In addition, two case studies are included which illustrate examples of interventions for children and adolescents that led to efficient and quick resolutions. Questions and guidelines are included in the form of worksheets, suggestions for notes, and conversations.

Chapter 3 begins to describe specific questions and the basic process of helping students, teachers, and parents identify "exceptions" to the problems which intrude in their lives. A case study offers an example of actual application of SFBT ideas. Developing and defining goals is a major part of this chapter, since success depends on one's ability to accomplish tasks. The integral part of SFBT is that of asking school populations to attempt the possible, not the uncontrollable. For example, a school counselor cannot stop parents from fighting or divorcing, and neither can the student. However, the student can define and list to the counselor how he/she has coped with the situation before, even though it has been difficult. The actual counseling session is itself an exception! How did the student know to come to the counselor? How did he/she open up and discuss troubles so efficiently? These simple and minute actions are exceptions to when the *problem is in control*. A worksheet for teacher-student case conversations is included for duplication in this chapter which serves two purposes: to provide documentation on the spot for the counselor who is required to do this, and make a *contractual agreement* with the student. The notes are taken during the time the student and counselor meet, a copy is made, and the student takes his/her strategies home as a reminder.

Chapter 4 outlines an actual school program resulting from a collaboration of guidelines, questions, and application of SFBT to the school setting. The chapter begins with suggestions for the teacher who refers a student for counseling. In many school settings, the counselor is looked to and sought out to "fix" students. While this is a compliment, school counselors and administrators today have less and less time to take on a full load of counseling students and thinking up solutions. The school program based on SFBT places more responsibility on the referring teacher and student, requiring minimal involvement by the counselor after the initial meeting. In addition, recommendations for parent conferences, or teacher-student conferences that employ a solution-focused approach is provided in the form of excerpts from actual conversations, in worksheet format. Special attention for special education programs and diagnostic meetings is given so that these sensitive situations open up possibilities for improvement instead of diagnosing and suggesting failure.

Chapter 5 offers ideas and suggestions for recognizing and developing small group dynamics within the school setting. Counselors who have little experience with groups can effectively run groups with the guidelines suggested from other school counselors who have applied SFBT ideas to group situations. Ideas are given for involving teachers and students in the process of group development so that the groups are run most effectively and cooperatively. The counselor in today's schools is faced with traumatic problems as well as simple concerns from students and parents. This chapter addresses how to assist the student who is coping with trauma to designate them as *survivors*. Suggestions for groups dealing with sexual abuse, anger, sibling rivalries, death, divorce, and lack of school success is given in the form of worksheets.

Chapter 6 offers suggestions for dealing with students in difficult situations such as loss and death, divorce, suicidal ideation, depression, violence in school situations, physical abuse and sexual abuse. These topics begin to seem less threatening when SFBT principles and questions are applied to them since the focus is on *when the problem has the lesser impact on the student's life* and *he/she is in control*. Ideas in the form of case studies are given that have proven effective in identifying exceptions, especially in crisis situations.

Chapter 7 gives suggestions for classroom guidance children and adolescents, often for a requirement in many school districts. Many of the ideas suggested in this chapter are examples developed by school counselors currently in school situations. Whether the topic is AIDS information and prevention, drug abuse, relationships, or motivation, this chapter will assist the teacher or counselor in developing strategies in a manner that involves kids to the maximum. Special attention is devoted to specific ways of beginning a topic so kids can learn to identify their abilities to deal with certain situations and apply them to others.

Chapter 8 helps those administrators and teachers within the school setting to set the stage for competence, beginning with discipline. The chapter outlines methods for noncounseling staff members to use, which lessen defensiveness and open possibilities to solving problems. Role-play dialogues are given from actual student-administrator (teacher) conversations which illustrate how SFBT can lessen defensiveness and promote responsibility. Ideas for consequences other than D-Hall or in-school suspension give the administrator another avenue when such strategies fail time and time again. Implementing programs where kids notice what teachers do well is a part of this chapter as well as seeking out troubled or repeat offenders and commenting on their staying out of trouble.

Chapter 9 seeks to offer ways of empowering the very important population of school staff members. How administrators and counselors approach teachers can make or break relationships between the hierarchy. Looking into classrooms and pointing out a teacher's competency can go a long way to encouraging their cooperation with other school staff members and students. This chapter offers ideas about school-wide recognition of "exceptional teachers," reproducible training pages, and directions for staff development.

The Appendix contains additional cartoons, quotations, and ideas suitable for classroom bulletin boards, certificates for success and note-writing examples for teachers, students, and parents.

About the Author

Linda Metcalf, Ph.D., a licensed marriage and family therapist, is a former junior high school teacher, elementary school counselor, and currently a lecturer at the University of Texas at Arlington in the Department of Education. She is the author of several articles on brief therapy with adolescents and children, and has presented at The Texas Association for School Counselors as well as the Texas Association for Marriage and Family Therapists and the American Association for Marriage and Family Therapy conferences on brief therapy.

Dr. Metcalf is in private practice in Arlington, Texas, where she works extensively with school systems as a consultant in Solution-Focused Brief Therapy and also with children and adolescents on school and family issues.

FOREWORD

If you are a teacher, school administrator, or school counselor/psychologist, you probably remember the sense of excitement you had when you first decided to pursue your career. For some of you it was a teacher who touched something inside you that inspired your choice. For others it was a sense that you had something you could contribute to kids and this was a way to do it. But as you acquired more education, training, or experience, some of you might have lost touch with that original excitement or sense of possibility. You may even have become cynical and decided that kids were more unmotivated than you initially thought or that parents weren't that interested in their children's education or that school personnel were being asked to fix society's problems.

This book by Linda Metcalf is a powerful way to reconnect with your sense of energy and possibilities even in the face of serious challenges in schools. Reading this book can be like a massive injection of vitamins and minerals full of hope and solutions for you.

Without minimizing the serious problems teachers, school counselors/psychologists, parents, and students face in today's schools, she gives a practical roadmap for rapidly solving these problems. This roadmap doesn't require massive infusions of federal funding or new students or any other pie-in-the-sky solutions. Instead, it relies on strengths and resources that are already available and dormant within students, parents, and the school.

A revolution is going on in the mental health field, which has for so long been a mental *illness* field. We are finally focusing on health. We have seen dramatic and moving changes in the people we counsel with the techniques and philosophies used in this book. School is a natural place to use these ideas. Teachers, administrators, and school counselors/psychologists don't have time to do psychoanalysis with troubled students. Brief, pragmatic and effective interventions are required. This book has more of those than you need. I got so excited when I read it that I requested one for my son's third-grade teacher and the new principal at his school. I'll bet you'll get so excited, you'll end up buying and recommending this book to your friends and colleagues. But here's a warning: This book could be dangerous to your sense of burnout and discouragement. Reading it could cause persistent episodes of hope and enthusiasm in you and your students. Now you've been warned. Proceed at your own risk

Bill O'Hanlon, M.S.
Author/coauthor of *In Search of Solutions, A Brief Guide to Brief Therapy, Love Is a Verb, Rewriting Love Stories* and others.

CONTENTS

CHAPTER 3   69
COMPETENCY-BASED CONVERSATIONS

CHAPTER 4

THE "EXCEPTIONAL" SCHOOL PROGRAM
(THINKING ABOUT STUDENTS DIFFERENTLY)

CHAPTER 5

COMBINING YOUR RESOURCES (GROUP COUNSELING)

Chapter 6   171
TURNING IMPOSSIBILITIES INTO POSSIBILITIES:
IDEAS FOR DIFFICULT SITUATIONS

Chapter 9   245
A SOLUTION-FOCUSED SCHOOL STAFF:
Creating the Atmosphere

APPENDIX   265

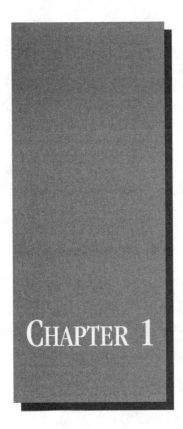

CHAPTER 1 CHANGING OUR THINKING TO A SOLUTION FOCUS

Just for a moment...*imagine*. For a few minutes, look back over the past week and recall your best day at school. Try to remember the lesson plan that really worked, the conversation with a colleague that stimulated your interests, the behavioral intervention that made a difference with a resistant student, the explanation in class that seemed to enlighten your students—the activity which captured their imaginations. How did you do that? Now, imagine that you could create more "good days" such as this one, simply by identifying "what works." Would you be willing to do so? Imagine what your days would be like if you began to focus more energy on *solutions* instead of problems. Imagine how your students might react if you complimented their small successes and stopped commenting on their problems. Imagine if you gave in to your own resources as well, integrating your own interests into guidance programs, administrative duties, and classroom creativities.

The ideas in this manual are based on ideas from *competency-based and solution-focused therapy*, brief and efficient ways of approaching problems by concentrating on "exceptions" or times when the problem does *not* exist.

Chapter 1 Focus:

- New ways of thinking differently about problems
- Noticing students with a solution focus—lessen resistance, encourage responsibility
- Introductory case study: "Easing the Tension." A family attacks a school problem
- Guidelines for using solution-focused brief therapy
- Self-esteem Building

Learning to Think Differently about Students Means Learning to Think Differently about Ourselves

You cannot solve a problem with the same thinking that created it.

Albert Einstein

I recall a day as a young teacher years ago, when I sat in the teacher's lounge listening to teachers label and classify kids. I remember finding myself depressed and frustrated with some of the negative behaviors my junior high students were exhibiting. I expressed my frustration to several experienced teachers in search of help or advice. I received many empathetic statements such as "yes, he's in my class and he's a terror there, too," and "her mother has refused to answer my phone calls...one of those families." While I am certain these statements were meant to be supportive, they offered little help.

Fortunately, I recalled a professor from one of my college education classes who once stated that the most helpful thing a new teacher or any teacher could do for themselves and their students was to *stay out of the teacher's lounge— less you become prejudiced against your students!* With this in mind and frustrated that I was not getting anywhere talking to equally frustrated teachers, I 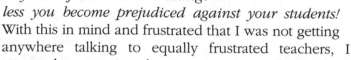 retreated to my Art classroom on a regular basis with another teacher for lunch and conference periods. We soon found that our more positive conversations at lunch time were refreshing as we talked about personal issues and productive lesson plans. I noticed how I began to feel differently about my students without the labeling from fellow teachers. Thereafter, I also noticed how the students reacted more positively to me when I knew *less* about their behaviors in other classes.

This same way of thinking differently helped later as I became a counselor. Once, for example, I consulted with a Residential Treatment Center in Texas, whose staff was interested in applying SFBT principles to an already existing program based on a behavior modification program with psychiatric diagnoses. As I drove up to the psychiatric facility, I noticed children playing soccer in the play area. Watching them, I remember thinking how *typically* they were playing and reacting to each other. There were the usual squabbles that children who compete with each other experience, but there was also team work going on and lots of giggles and laughter.

I approached the director of the RTC, ready to compliment him and his assistant on creating such a fun environment for the children. He looked at me curiously and said, "tough bunch." I told him how impressed I was with watching their interactions; they seemed to be enjoying themselves and were playing quite typically of children their age. He then said to me: "You don't know what's wrong with them yet, do you?" He was right, I didn't. I saw their competencies and successes without the prejudice of labels. I can't help but wonder how the children would have reacted to me if I had approached them with an impression of their being "typical." I wonder what they would have told me was *their* reason for being there and what it was that they wanted to be different in their lives. I wonder how their perceptions might have differed with the staff members'.

Maybe It's Time to Change How We Think

Schools, counselors, and teachers today experience pressures to "*do something* about students and their problems," but in order to do this effectively, educators might need to consider learning about themselves, and noticing the times school works for themselves. Time is measured out in an educator's day so strictly that spending time analyzing problems is basically impossible. What is helpful about using SFBT is that analyzing and figuring out *why problems occur* is not necessary in order to be helpful. Why not examine times when school went well? Noticing when a consequential action with a challenging student went well, or a lesson plan captured the imaginations of students, when an assignment gave the teacher a break and turned the responsibility back to the students to learn, when the school nurse learned to cooperate with a child in need of attention, or when a pat on the back in the hallway closed the gap between administrator and student—these competency-based, solution-focused actions can and have made differences in school settings.

Thinking differently about what we do in our schools means looking beyond the negative behaviors, especially when they are diminished, and noticing times *when the negative behaviors are not dominating the student.* More importantly, it means catching ourselves in times of good experiences in school and noticing *What made this work today?* This way of thinking changes the context of the problem from: *"Jimmy, you're having a temper tantrum/anger outburst—get some control"* to *"The temper tantrum/anger outburst is in control again, Jimmy, how can you take over now?"* It takes noticing when Charlie sits in his seat, if only for 5 minutes, while other students are running around the room. It takes noticing that Charlie stayed on task slightly

longer today, even though Jonathan was having a tantrum. It may mean noticing that a poem in English class stirred a high school junior to ask a question for the first time this week. This new way of thinking dissolves resistance and opens the door for information to students. Isn't that what education was meant to do?

It's Time to Close the Book!

Perhaps in school settings, closing a book *is* more important, since it forces us to see our students differently: as competent people, more often. It is important for educators to identify their own personal competencies as well. What is your most valuable resource in working with your students? Are you a good listener, a creative teacher, a humorous administrator? Bradford Keeney encourages us to use *our* resources to reach students. Music, art, activities, sports, whatever your avenue, utilize it to stimulate yourself ! The ideas presented here are open to expansion and are most truly realized when educators use them with their own resourcefulness.

The ideas in SFBT contain suggestions for simplifying interactions between educators and students. As Walter and Peller mention in the following, suspending one's theories while examining this new way of thinking and responding is one way to try out the new ideas and let them work for you:

> *We suggest to those who may be learning this approach that in order to avoid the muddles that may occur while they are trying to believe several things at the same time, they suspend beliefs.... Later, after attaining some facility with this way of working, they can decide how much they want to incorporate in their work and in what way.*

Jumping Over the Barbed Wire Fence

Dr. Bradford Keeney says "diagnoses are like barbed wire fences," in that the labels we often place on people keep them stuck. A diagnosis does not give leads to solutions, but instead may help us to understand *why a behavior is occurring*. The media has supported the idea that celebrities who claim victimhood have reasons for their behavior and personal dilemmas. My concern about these survivors is that they do not see themselves as survivors. Instead, they need to look at who they are, what they have succeeded at accomplishing, and how they have overcome personal feats to rise to the top!

Recalling Times When Students Did Well

An adolescent boy who is hyperactive in junior high cannot be excused, for instance, from learning mathematics. His inability to focus in his junior high math class should not limit his competency to do better in a different context. Obviously, at one time he was able to learn simple math skills or he wouldn't be in secondary school. Our job as educators is to help assist him in identifying how he *did* perform before. His label of hyperactivity can be a true obstacle to him in taking responsibility for his learning. Instead of labeling him, let's *cooperate* with him. Let's ask him to tell us what worked before. Many energetic (a redescription of hyperactivity) children and adolescents are aware of their energy and are often as frustrated as their teachers. Framing the "energy" as such, and asking the student and ourselves to notice when he is not as energetic, will help educators to provide the appropriate context for him.

A very energetic seventh grade boy once discovered that the classes he did well in were the classes where he sat on the front row. I suggested, in response to his discovery, that he and his parents request a seating change for the remaining classes. He mentioned too, that his failure to turn in many homework assignments caused his grades to stay below the passing level. As he began to notice how he turned in *some* assignments, he found that he turned in all his papers when he put his homework in a book, then took the book to class. He said he had never been one for keeping an organized notebook, much to his parent's dismay, because he found it to be too much trouble. He turned to me in the session and said "I just need to put my homework in each of my books and carry them *all* to class." While this would not have occurred to me, it worked so well for him that his teachers called his parents to report his improvement in turning in his homework.

Discouraging Labels Encourages Possibilities

A solution-focused approach is not really new. Whittgenstein has said that:

> *The classifications made by philosophers and psychologists are like those that someone would give who tried to classify clouds by their shapes.*

Classifying students may give us a means to divide them into appropriate classes, but it also can make us participants in exacerbating problems. Jay Haley talks of such phenomena when he says:

> *To label a child as "delinquent" or as suffering from "minimal brain dysfunction"...means that one is participating in the creation of a problem in such a way the change is made more difficult...the way in which one labels a human dilemma can crystallize a problem and make it chronic.*

Where Do the Test Scores Fit?

The SFBT approach energizes students, parents, and teachers with cooperative, empowering statements instead of cornering them with "barbed wire fences." This is not to say that diagnostic tests are not helpful. Tests give us clues to where our concerns should be but they also identify strengths. I am more interested in higher test scores on standardized tests than the lower ones because they give direction for success. By noticing when, where, and how students do well, directions for more of the same can lead to better learning style information. Many diagnosticians who use SFBT like the idea of revealing diagnostic scores and then designing programs which focus on student competencies. The same goal is achieved, because by examining classroom situations in which students do well, clues for enhancing deficits become more clear. (Chapter 4 contains an *Individual Educational Program*, designed for review committees, with SFBT ideas added). Students approached with competency-based questions often become motivated to excel beyond their wildest dreams. The SFBT educator knows that *no one can have negative behaviors or poor academic skills 100% of the time.*

Gathering Around the Conference Table

I often visit the schools of my private clients and gather teachers, parents, and students into an informal conference. In a recent conference with an eighth grade boy who was struggling with paying attention and completing homework assignments, I asked all his teachers about the times he turned in work, paid attention, and performed with other positive behaviors. Four out of eight of his teachers said he turned in all of his work, and that paying attention was only a slight problem. The other four were adamant about his reluctance to turn in work and pay attention. I casually mentioned that I wondered what was going on in four of Tom's classes that encouraged him to participate and complete his work.

Needless to say, four of Tom's teachers became very quiet. They began to look in their grade books. One of the four teachers who had given positive reports said, "Let's ask Tom." Tom was reluctant to respond, but as he did so, he stated how some classes worked for him and some did not. I asked him to be very specific about what worked. I then asked him how he might use some of the strategies that worked in half of his classes in one or two of his others for just a week. He stated some very specific strategies:

- I sit in the front of the room.
- I complete the homework in class.
- The teacher asks me if I understand the assignment.
- My dad checks my assignments when I ask him.
- When I know dad will check with my teachers, I get with it.

I asked the teachers (who were adamant) if they would watch Tom for just a week and notice when he attempted to do things differently, and *tell him directly* when they noticed his new behaviors happening. I then asked Tom to "do whatever it takes to get your teachers to notice you." The dynamics that occurred were very powerful. The teachers who were quick to critique Tom's performance experienced peer pressure. Why was it that Tom succeeded in other classes *but not theirs?* The student, having stated his strategy in front of all eight teachers and his dad, committed himself to being watched and encouraged his dad's future participation and collegial competition! His school performance improved. An outline of this conference is provided at the end of this chapter.

Resourcefulness Encourages Resourcefulness

DR. BRADFORD KEENEY, 1994

Educators utilizing SFBT ideas have taught me that as they changed their thinking about students and themselves from a problem-oriented view to a solution-focused view, they changed their behavior, and so did the student! The following case study describes such a phenomenon:

GETTING THROUGH THE DAY WITHOUT CRYING—A CASE STUDY

Ms. Pat Peters, a fifth grade teacher specializing in English as a Second Language (ESL), came to therapy as a last resort before she resigned her teaching position. She had taught for twenty years in another city and had recently taken a job at an inner-city school. She told me she was experiencing a deep depression that affected her so deeply that merely walking into the school building in the morning caused her to burst into tears at the sight of her students.

The students, a majority of whom were dealing with severe problems at home such as neglect, abuse, poverty, and little supervision, would react violently in the classroom towards Ms. Peters when she tried to discipline them with conventional discipline plans set by the district. She had spoken to the principal, but received little support except for empathizing.

I began the first session by asking Ms. Peters how she had been able to stay in teaching for 20 years in what I considered to be a very challenging teaching position. She responded modestly, saying that she was a good teacher who loved her profession. She said there had been students over the years who had made it a very rewarding career. She said that was the difficult part, for these students were not *all* difficult.

I asked about the students she found less difficult and asked how she had made it in the present position for the past five months, in spite of the difficulties. She responded that there had always been one class in the morning at 10:00 A.M. that she looked forward to. The children in that class could not read when she began teaching them and now they were progressing. Many of the students were adolescents, and since they were nearing an age to drive a car, she had taught them to read a driver's license test booklet since she knew that subject would keep their interest. She smiled as she told me of one boy whom other teachers found very violent. She said initially she often placed her hand on his shoulder and he would wince. Now she could place her hand on his hand and he smiled at her.

I commended her spirit and caring for her students and her practical approach to gaining their interest in reading. While she was glad to be given the compliments, she still became sad as she mentioned the current difficulties at hand. I continued to commend and affirm her professionalism to seek out those who needed her and help them respond to her so warmly. Quietly, she took the affirmation, although reluctantly.

As the session ended, I asked her to do only one task until I met with her again:

Counselor: During the next week, I would like you to look at your students differently. Instead of seeing them as resisting you and fighting you, I would like you to see them as needing you but not knowing how to relate their needs. I'd like you to pick one student this week and do what you did for the student you told me about. I am asking you to do this for yourself, not just the student, because I can see the joy you receive when you touch a student and make a difference. It seems to work for you. Your smile told me so.

Reluctantly, Ms. Peters said she would try but did not expect to really do it. I told her I realized that this was a tremendous task for someone as sad as she described herself. This realization prompted me to write her a note and mail it the same day as the session:

Dear Pat,

I enjoyed meeting with you very much today. As I mentioned to you, I hold a special feeling for teachers, having been one for ten years. I admired your desire to talk to me about things that were bothering you at school and also your need to have better experiences in your classroom. This week I hope you will look at your students differently. I have a feeling that the magic you worked with (student name) made a tremendous difference in your life as a teacher. My hope for you this week is that you will do this for yourself once again with another student. I look forward to hearing about it!

Sincerely,

Linda Metcalf

Reminiscing: A Natural Tranquilizer

Merely focusing on Ms. Peters' problems would have done little to rid her of the frustrations and sadness she was experiencing. I sensed that it would be much more helpful to focus on her successes and help her fondly reminisce on times when school worked. Many of us enjoy looking through photo albums and recalling happy, joyful, and meaningful occasions. What does reminiscing do for us? It often changes our perception of life events, people, experiences, and even future events. It reminds us that there have been happier times. Most of all, it changes our focus from one of problem saturation to that of a time when problems seemed less dominant. Our successes are like badges of courage and we revel in our—or family members'—accomplishments. It was important that Ms. Peters recall her teaching successes at a time when she felt that there was little success.

When working with students, teachers, parents, and administrators, searching for more efficient, successful, happier times solicits solutions. Ms. Peters needed a reminder that she was indeed a teacher who made a difference, even in her current situation. She had become "problem saturated," noticing *only* the times when negative behaviors kept occurring, and her students readily responded to her perceptions! More importantly, her goal was to "get through the day without crying." If I had appealed to her that her students needed her and that she must give more of herself and put aside her feelings, I would have been giving advice, perpetuating the problem, and losing Ms. Peter's trust by not hearing her goal. Both the teacher and the students would have received a true disservice.

> *If therapy is to end properly, it must begin properly: by negotiating a solvable problem*
>
> HALEY, 1987

Ms. Peters sought relief from feeling depressed and frustrated. If her goal was "to be less depressed and frustrated," it would have been difficult to project how she would do so, especially since depression and frustration are entities that occur intermittently in many people's lives. In addition, being in the context of seeing herself depressed and frustrated left her feeling hopeless. She knew she had a tough population and simply wanted to make it through the day and then possibly make a difference to her students.

Never Ask a Person in Counseling To Do Something New

The task was designed from her previous successes so that she would receive some satisfaction as she had before. I make it a point when using SFBT ideas never to ask the person in counseling to do something they have not done before successfully. This means I will *always connect the task with a similar successful action* the person has taken previously. For example, Ms. Peters was successful with a student who often experienced violent situations. As I asked her to attempt with only *one student* what she had been successful in with another student, I asked her only to do what she had been successful at previously. If I had asked her to go out of her way and implement a new behavioral program, hug each of her students in spite of their behaviors, and smile when she felt like screaming, I couldn't have been as confident that she would succeed. In short, I cooperated with *her* goal. de Shazer is clear when he mentions that cooperating lessens resistance and encourages success.

One week later, Ms. Peters returned to therapy, smiling and reporting that her kids had been better that week. She thanked me for the note, commented on my taking the time to write her, and mentioned how much that had meant to her. She said she realized now that she had just been "thinking too negatively about the kids." I complimented her on this discovery. From that point on, she turned our conversations to other issues of concern in her life. Using the same approach throughout our remaining time together, Ms. Peters' depression and frustration lifted and therapy ended after six sessions.

THE FOCUS IS ON THE SOLUTION, NOT THE PROBLEM

The solution-focused brief therapy ideas presented in this manual offer a different way of thinking about school problems and assist both educators and counselors in dis-

covering solutions through exceptions that have already occurred previously. The ideas of SFBT encourage the student, parent, or teacher to step outside the problem for a moment and observe the influence of the problem on his/her life. From this observation and from identifying times when the problem is in less control, the student is able to develop his/her own tasks so that *he/she* is in more control. This approach is particularly helpful in work with parents and teachers, for it allows them to notice how they encourage and discourage problems with students. **When there is no centralized blame placed on a parent, student, or teacher, resistance is lessened and everyone's task is to simply** *solve the problem.* The result? Everyone becomes responsible and the problem becomes the enemy to be defeated!

AN INTRODUCTORY CASE: EASING THE "TENSION"

Joey, 16, a sophomore in high school, had been a star athlete for most of his school years. He had played baseball since preschool and had excelled at the sport until this year when he was dropped from the team for failing three classes. Depressed and rebellious at home, he came to counseling with his mother, step-dad, and brother at the request of the vice principal and school counselor. The school was concerned about Joey's failing grades and his tendency to engage in fights.

In my first meeting with Joey and his family, his mother expressed her concerns about his father's murder when Joey was two, Joey's violent outbursts towards her and school, and about her fear that he would fail his sophomore year. Joey's step-dad described his relationship with Joey as stable but was concerned that Joey had recently stopped talking to him and was choosing to stay out late with his friends instead of studying or being at home with the family.

As I listened to the family's description of the problem that they felt was bothering Joey, I watched him stare at the floor and sink deeper and deeper into the couch, as if succumbing to the "problem" and its claim on his life. The family was desperately concerned and their concern was burying Joey and creating a sense of hopelessness. The last thing I needed to do as a counselor was to help them create more of the same hopelessness by trying to probe or understand what was troubling Joey, thereby giving credence to the fact that there was indeed a terrible problem.

In an effort to help Joey and his family, I might have, a few years ago, examined educational assessment forms, cumulative folders, and test scores. I might have asked the parents about the consequences they were currently presenting to Joey in that he was failing three classes. I might have asked personal questions of the parents regarding their family life, searching for reasons why this problem was occurring, yet keeping my boundaries as an educator. In an attempt to get to the root of the problem, I might have looked for sequences in behaviors, interactional patterns that did not work, or sibling rivalry between the younger brother and Joey. I might have questioned the step-father/step-son relationship and asked more questions about Joey's biological, deceased father.

Instead, as I met with Joey, I refocused and tried to think differently about the situation, looking for something different. I looked for what Steve de Shazer describes as "exceptions" to when the problem occurs. Michael White also mentions the importance of looking for times when the problem is not as dominant and controlling, as if it were an entity in itself. I was more interested in searching for Joey's competencies rather than perpetuating the problem through probing for more understanding of what Joey was doing wrong. By Joey's sad appearance, he obviously knew enough about the problem that had brought him to counseling. In fact, by this point, he seemed to be feeling that *he was the problem!*

It's been my experience as a teacher, school counselor, and therapist that adolescents are a unique population who respond with rebellion, resistance, and sadness when blamed or criticized. I was interested in Joey's opinion and solutions to his school problems, and knew that to gain his cooperation in counseling, I needed to align heavily with him against the problem. I knew he was competent in at least part of his educational history, because he had in fact succeeded in school up to this point. He had also succeeded in doing well at a sport. Most importantly, he had come to counseling *willingly* with his *family.* With these exceptions in mind and an assumption that Joey wanted things to be different, I began the session by expressing my concern for the family's worries and then asked:

Counselor: How will you know when things are getting better for all of you?

After a few minutes of silence, the family replied:

Mom: Things will be better when I don't worry as much about Joey's grades, or his outbursts at school. I will receive fewer phone calls about Joey's behavior, and will feel confident to go to work without worrying.

Dad: The "tension" which seems to perpetuate the family life will be less prevalent and I'll be able to stay off Joey's back and do more things with Tommy (Joey's younger brother).

Tommy: I'll be able to play with Joey without being afraid that he will beat me up, and I'll have friends over more often, because there will be less yelling.

Joey: I don't know, I guess school will be better and everybody (family and school) will be off my back.

Listening to the family's description of the problem, I asked about the "tension" described by step-dad and how each of them kept this tension around. Speaking about the problem in an external way is what Michael White calls *externalizing the problem* and will be explained more completely in Chapter 3. Externalizing is an approach that encourages persons to *objectify their problems as outside of themselves.* In this process, the problem becomes separate from the person. I explained to the family that problems are often maintained through interactions and that persons influence the "life of the problem." With this in mind, I addressed each of the family members:

Counselor: I've often learned that problems are what I refer to as **maintained**. You know, that possibly people keep problems around by their behaviors with each other. Can you each tell me how you might possibly keep this tension in your family?

Mom: I badger Joey, I worry too much, I yell at Brian (step-dad) when I worry about Joey. I complain too much about his low grades. I get so frustrated that I keep nagging him to study, and of course, the more I nag, the more he refuses to study.

Step-Dad: I pick on Joey...my dad and I used to punch on each other and I used to think that playing around with him would lighten him up...wrong! I do let things get to me and then jump down Joey's throat.

Tommy: I yell back at Joey when he bugs me. I tell on Joey to dad and mom, he gets in trouble and then everybody yells. Then I guess I aggravate him when his friends are over—it's fun.

Joey: I don't do my school work, don't come home on time...yell back when they yell at me. I get mad pretty easy.

As each of the family members described how they contributed to the "tension," Joey began to look up at his family and myself instead of at the floor. He seemed to feel less blamed and the family backed off from blaming him as well. We continued to talk more about times when the "tension" was not as prevalent.

Counselor: Joey, take me back to a time when school was better, and the tension dad talked about wasn't in control of your life.

Joey: Last year. I passed all my classes last year.

Counselor: How did you do that?

Joey: They have this class at school called Academic Opportunity, where you go for help when you need it. I went when I needed to and I passed.

Counselor: Really! By the way, aren't you passing four classes now?

Joey: Yes.

Counselor: Tell me which ones...

Joey: Math, English, Home Economics, and Art.

Counselor: That's great! What's your secret to doing that?

Joey: I don't know...I do my work in class and just hand it in.

Joey brightened considerably and became more verbal instantly. He began to describe additional ways he had passed classes in the past and strategies he currently used to pass classes now. He recalled how a few years ago, his mom praised him and rewarded him with time spent together. He also mentioned that she had been reacting differently lately, not noticing his passing grades and barely giving him a pat on the back. According to Joey, mom was correct to be concerned about her badgering. Her efforts to encourage him had backfired.

Joey turned his attention to his step-dad and reminisced how he and his step-dad had at one time gone over work together before he turned it in. Step-dad admitted that he had become negligent in checking Joey's work recently, and recalled that he did enjoy checking Joey's work in the past. As Joey described his past successes, mom mentioned her concern about the violent outbursts at school. Joey admitted that he had a temper, but by this time in the session he too was changing his thinking as he mentioned that on more than one occasion since eighth grade, he had learned to curb his temper. I was curious about his ability to curb his temper, especially since that was an issue brought to my attention by the family and school, and asked him to describe how he did this:

Joey: One day at school, I was sitting with six of my friends at lunch. We got up to get some food and when we came back a bunch of guys had thrown our books on the floor and were sitting in our seats. It took about 15 seconds for me to clench my fists and get ready to fight.

Counselor: Did you fight?

Joey: No.

Counselor: How did you stop?

Joey: We asked them would you please move...and then I noticed the coach watching us. I slowed myself down.

Counselor: Wow, you asked them to move first?

Joey: Yeah.

Counselor: Has that helped in other situations?

Joey: Yeah, it has.

Counselor: That's incredible...tell me.

Joey: With my mom, once, she was yelling at me and grabbed me...I was mad but I kept my cool and didn't hit her.

Counselor: Amazing.

Joey: I would never hit my mom...I love her.

The initial session ended with a simple task. The family was asked to *focus on easing the tension.* White's ideas of refusing to cooperate with the requirements of the problem render it less effective. As the family discussed how they "maintained" the problem, they discovered what they might do to make the problem less effective in coming between their relationships. Joey had stated his specific strategies to control anger, pass some classes at school, and had expressed how important his mom was to him. He indeed had the resources he needed to escape from the tension. I expressed to him and his family that there were simply too many occasions when he did not allow the problem to influence his behavior for this not to be the case. The other family members, hearing the *exceptions* I solicited from Joey, agreed that the *tension* was the problem at hand. In an effort to assist the family in noticing more times when the tension was not interfering with their family life, I asked Joey and his family to do the following:

Counselor: During the next week, I'd like you all to notice times when, purposefully, you do not allow the tension to interfere with your family life.

Counselor: Joey, I'd like you to notice when school works, especially in the four classes you are passing, and notice specifically how you are doing that.

By offering a task to notice when the problem was less bothersome, Joey and his family were more likely to see relief and experience themselves as more competent. It was very important that Joey experience himself as competent, so as to lessen any dependency on his family and teachers to succeed in school, both behaviorally and academically. The ability to gain independence from the problem is clearly a self-esteem builder and motivating agent for change in adolescents.

Within a week, step-dad again began checking his step-son's work, and mom stopped badgering her son. After three weeks, Joey raised his grades to passing. The younger brother, Tommy, followed his parents' lead and bugged his brother less, resulting in more pleasant times together with Joey. Interestingly enough, in a future session mom said to me, "I started noticing *what* he passed instead of what he was *not* passing, and the times we got along instead of what went wrong that day." This was a nice outcome of the first session task, and since I only suggested that the family look for exceptions, mom's behavior change was her own decision. I made sure I gave her credit for such a nice way of relating differently to her son.

A SOLUTION-FOCUSED WAY OF THINKING

Problem

The ideas and questions that were used in Joey's situation were an example of using a *solution-focused way of thinking*. The family's world view of the tension that bothered the family was the problem. The problem statement should be encouraged to be stated in terms of what the individual needs to be changed in his/her life, not how he/she wants others to be. In Joey's case, the problem was not Joey, or the family. The problem was maintained by the behaviors of the family. In schools, the *system* a student experiences maintains school problems. The school program discussed in Chapter 4 will describe the importance of collaborations between teacher and student, teacher, parent, and administrator. It is because of interactions that problems are perceived as such. The use of the same interactions therefore can encourage solutions, by noticing how success has occurred before, when the problem was absent. This change in behaviors and perception does not allow the problem to remain.

Goals

The goals of Joey's family were discussed and again defined by using the *language of the family*. If I had questioned the family and hinted at any dysfunction on the part of Joey, his family or teachers, I would have run the risk of hearing blame for the problem. Instead, I asked for specific goals so I would be listening to what the family thought the problem was. Research has suggested that when clients describe their reason for coming to counseling, and are given an opportunity to work on exactly what they came for, and not what the *counselor* thinks they should work on, they leave satisfied (Metcalf &  Thomas, 1994). It is vital that this type of goal setting be considered when working with the school client. The questions used in Joey's case were constructed to cooperate with the family and defeat the tension that the family described.

Problem Maintenance

The family's discovery of their problem maintenance seemed helpful since it revealed how each family member encouraged the tension in their family life. This way of working lessens the chance of blame on one person in the family and encourages responsibility from everyone in solving the problem. Using White's ideas of problem maintenance within families or school settings with several people working on a concern is helpful for lessening blame. For students and parents who insist on digging deeper into a problem, identifying problem maintenance behaviors briefly exposes responsibilities and helps people to move on, away from problem-saturated discussions. Once everyone knows their role in maintaining a problem and realizes that blaming is not productive, discussing "what's wrong" seems to be of little interest.

Exceptions

The exceptions to the problem offered clues for solutions. The exceptions empowered the family members and offered them a different focus. Exceptions exist in all of our lives, we just don't tend to notice them as much as the problems or interruptions that occur each day. For example, think of the intrusions you may have experienced last week which kept your stress level high. Probably, they come to mind rather rapidly. Now consider *exceptions* to the stress you felt. How did you encourage or help this happen? Think about how you did that and consider doing it again the next time you feel stressed! "Do what works!"

Task

Task development was collaboratively constructed by the family through their examination of the exceptions they themselves described. The family was encouraged to do what worked previously. I make it a point never to ask people to do anything they have not already been doing. This lessens the possibility of failure. It has been my experience that when people do not feel comfortable with a suggestion, they simply do not do it. However, saying to a client "since you've done this before, I feel certain you may be able to do it again," encourages confidence and lessens the feeling of risk.

CONCLUDING THOUGHTS ON HOW WE THINK

Considering and questioning how we think about school, students, teachers, parents and administrators is as important as assessing a school "issue," because our reactions will differ if we think about *problem focus* rather than *solution focus.* Our beliefs and theories about people and their competencies are evident from the moment we shake hands with someone in distress until we help them reach resolution. Consider then:

How do you think about people and their abilities to change when they are given the opportunity? How have you created that opportunity before?

Do you believe that your students have competencies or, that they need you to solve all their problems?

The SFBT educator is more concerned with discovering competencies than labeling or solving problems for students, staff, or parents. The educator listens attentively to the description of the problems brought to him/her, makes sure the definition of the problem is agreed upon by the school client and himself/herself, and then *refocuses towards solutions*. This new *solution focus* changes the context from one of blame and failure to hopefulness. It allows relief to settle within the context of the discussion at hand, opening the door to listening and communication between the school client and the educator. When this open door policy is in effect, solutions can develop because defensiveness diminishes.

Joey's case illustrates how closing the book on the problem and looking at him differently, as a competent student, can assist his family in lessening tension. A summary of the case notes taken during the first session is offered on the following page. On the next page, a *Case Notes* worksheet is provided as an example. This worksheet is included for duplication in the Appendix. Consider photocopying the notes you take for students and parents. Tell them you have been impressed by their good ideas and would like them to keep the notes with them should the "problem" try to take over during the week. This collaborative written solution-focus of the issue at hand becomes a practical, contractual agreement to defeat the problem.

Learning to think differently about people often leads us to noticing many avenues in which others have discovered the same secret holds on to the magic. In an episode of "Northern Exposure," (CBS, 1992) a popular television show, a scene involving the carving of a flute sends us a metaphorical message about students. In the episode, a native American woodcarver carves a flute as a younger, native American man watches him. The woodcarver is focused and quite careful. He says politely and respectfully in reference to the wood that he holds in his hands:

"Inside every alder branch, there is a flute—your job is to find it."

The ideas presented in this manual can be utilized by any school staff member, for they do not require any counseling experience! The competencies of the educators and students suggest the best solutions and strategies. Competencies are not always visible upon first observation. Searching for the perfect pearl, sculpting a figure from a lump of clay, or finding just the right words to say to someone important to us...takes time.

CASE NOTES

Name:

Joey Smith and Family

Presenting Problem:

Joey's angry outbursts, failing grades, isolation from family and reluctance to follow curfew.

Externalized problem:

Tension

Goal:

The family wants less tension in the household: Joey will have fewer angry outbursts and he will do better in school. Mom will notice when Joey improves and will not hear from the school as often with complaints about Joey. Step-dad and Joey will get along once again and do homework together. Tommy will not report Joey to his parents as often and will have more friends over. The tension will be replaced with better interactions among the family members.

Problem Maintenance:

Mom badgers Joey

Step-dad yells at Joey

Tommy tells on Joey and complains about him

Joey gets angry, doesn't come home or do schoolwork on time

Exceptions:

Joey is age-appropriate for his grade in school.

Joey is passing four of six subjects and does so by Academic Opportunity course training and by turning in all work.

Joey has been in difficult situations and has not had an angry outburst by responding politely before losing his temper.

When mom was supportive and complimentary of Joey in the past, he did better in school.

When step-dad checked Joey's schoolwork, he was more patient with him and Joey did well.

When Tommy did not "report" Joey to his parents, there was less conflict between him and Joey.

Joey loves his mother very much, and does not want to hurt her.

Joey came willingly to counseling and seems to want his life to change.

Task:

Ask the family to fight off tension and notice how they do so for a week. Ask Joey to pay more attention in school regarding how he passes other classes.

GUIDELINES FOR USING SOLUTION-FOCUSED BRIEF THERAPY IN THE SCHOOL SETTING

As with any new concept, it is helpful to understand the basic assumptions behind the ideas in solution-focused brief therapy. The work presented in this manual is based on a cooperative relationship between the educator, student, parent, and counselor. The following guidelines were developed from the work of Michele Weiner-Davis and William Hudson O'Hanlon, authors of *In Search of Solutions* and are applied to the school setting:

1. Use a a nonpathological approach to open up possibilities.

When the educator or counselor "redescribes" the problem in a "normalizing" manner, hope and possibilities emerge as problems seem to become more solvable. The counselor/educator then looks for exceptions to when the problem occurs, again inferring that solutions exist. For example, a student who is sent to the counselor for being hyperactive may experience the counselor reframing the complaint as "very energetic," a nonpathological term. This nonproblem approach lessens resistance by replacing it with a notion of normalcy. When the counselor talks to the student about the times when he/she is controlling the energy instead of it controlling him/her, he/she is challenged to gain control over the problem which is interfering.

A high school junior might be referred to the vice principal for an anger problem that often causes disruptions in the classroom. An administrator might notice (as the student sits quietly) in the lunchroom one day, that the student could have been tempted to explode in anger, but did not. The next time the vice principal sees the student, he might comment on his amazement that the student could have gotten angry but instead, refused to explode. He might ask the student "how did you manage to be in control?" The student might then experience the vice principal differently, perhaps not as an enemy, and become aware of some positive behaviors that he himself did not know existed.

2. It is not necessary to promote insight in order to be helpful.

Insight is interesting but does not tell us how to change. As mentioned previously, knowing why we are the way we are doesn't offer solutions. In fact, as students discover why they're sad, angry, or shy, they often use the information as a symptom and reason for not succeeding. Even in severe cases of past sexual or physical abuse, students who are complimented on their strength to survive often blossom into competent, confident human beings who can deal with problems and events more efficiently. It is our job to assist them with noticing their competencies. One of the easiest ways of noticing a student's competencies is to *notice if the problem is occurring at the time of intervention or initial interview*. For example, a child who is sent to the counselor's office for not talking in class, may be observed as opening up to the counselor and talking nonstop for twenty minutes. If the counselor asks the student "how have you managed to talk to me for twenty minutes?" both he/she and the student may realize some exceptions to the teacher's concern. The task can be developed according to the student's answers and counselor's observations.

3. It is not necessary to know a great deal about the complaint.

School counselors, administrators, and teachers have appropriately set boundaries by certification boards and school boards as to confidences offered to them by students. In addition, gathering past histories is often difficult for school staff to handle because of the school counselor's time limitations. Also, many school districts discourage "therapy." Using SFBT does not necessitate that the counselor know everything about the problem in order to be helpful. The counselor can refer to the problem as either "it" or "the problem" utilizing the student's language. This is protective and often less threatening for the student as well as for the counselor. Helping a student become more stable in a crisis situation merely by talking about the "situation," will create confidence in the educator and will create an atmosphere of trust between student and educator.

A kind and understanding teacher once related a story to me about a seventh grade student from a neglectful home (under investigation by authorities) who repeatedly came to her for nurturing when tearful. The teacher attempted to talk to her about the sadness and the student refused. The teacher wisely and respectfully recalled times when her own daughters were young and felt a need for attention when they were saddened. She told the student it was fine with her if she needed attention at times, even if she did not want to relay the "problem" at hand. The student continued to approach the teacher for attention at times, and eventually developed more trust with her. The teacher never knew what the exact problem was and did not find that information necessary in order to be helpful with the solution. In many situations, respecting a student or teacher's need for privacy will lessen the resistance to communication and open up possibilities for solution talk.

4. Students, Teachers, Administrators, and Parents have *complaints,* not *symptoms.*

Anyone who has ever been labeled knows how it can change self-perception. I recall a young woman who came to counseling and declared that she was manic-depressive, suicidal, bipolar, and had post traumatic stress disorder. After this resume of pathology, I looked at her and said, "You know, you seem like a really neat person. Can we leave the labels out of this for a few minutes and just talk about what it  is that you want to be different?" When the session was over I asked: "What did we do here that might have made a difference?" She said: "It was nice to talk about something besides 'the problems,' because now I don't feel as sick.... I don't feel as hopeless as I did before." Students have complaints, not symptoms, and when responded to in that manner, possibilities unfold for the development of solutions.

Principals and vice principals are often asked to mediate and fix countless complaints by teachers and students every day. For example, an administrator who is listening to a frustrated art teacher describe a class as ruthless and impossible to control and then redescribes the class to the teacher as "a tough group to handle sometimes," offers the teacher a new way of looking at the class. The administrator may then remark: "This is the first time this year I have heard you complain about your class. What's been working this year so far, for the past four months, until today?" This new view of past success given by the administrator to the teacher, focuses on what the teacher had done successfully before the class began acting up. The rest of the consultation can focus on assisting the teacher to recall his/her strategies that perhaps he/she had forgotten worked before.

5. Students and teachers are more motivated when they define their goals.

Consider these bizarre statements: "All students who come from single-parent homes are not functional. All students who wear an earring are in gangs. All students try drugs and alcohol by the age of 12. His brother was a troublemaker so he must be one as well. She certainly must be promiscuous, look how short her skirt is. There is no way he can pass fourth grade with that attitude."

Do you see how globally ridiculous and unfair these statements are? Yet for years we have decided what students needed to do because they exhibited certain behaviors. There have been tasks designed by counselors, educators, and other experts who saw commonalties in behaviors and subsequently assigned solutions. Many times the suggestions worked, after much labor by the "experts." However, the expertise of the educators became depended upon by the students, placing more burden on the educator who eventually felt anxious and resentful for having to do it all! Even worse, the student got little credit except for a pat on the back for following the directions given by the educator.

Some of the most outstanding strategies for solving the problems of students, teachers, and parents have come from these very populations and are mentioned extensively throughout this manual. Many of the solutions are extremely simple and always are specifically behavioral. The solutions develop from exceptions defined by the person(s) involved. As I offered feedback about the exceptions I heard directly from students, teachers, and parents, tasks developed that were achievable and the responses from these populations were that of confidence and pride. The key to assisting students, teachers, and parents in solving their own problems lies in listening to their definition of "what needs to be different" and asking when it has been different.

6. A snowball effect can occur when one person makes a change.

Let's face it, to even imagine that educators will enlist the assistance of every parent, teacher, or administrator is unrealistic—they all have their own priorities and are sometimes difficult to contact and inform as to what is going on with students. Virginia Satir, an experiential therapist who believed in "the ripple effect" often remarked that when she wrapped a rope around a family, if only one person moved the rest would move as well. Students often come for help while feeling alone and hopeless. They perceive that they must deal with a difficult parent or teacher without cooperation. Students can often learn through SFBT that what they tried before may not have worked in one situation but did in others, perhaps with different teachers. Simply encouraging a student or parent to "do something different the next time something doesn't work" can produce changes in interactions with others.

7. Complex problems do not have to necessitate complex solutions.

An adolescent girl and her mother had difficulties with "telephone time" since it often interfered with the girl's completion of homework. The girl was failing several classes at school and was becoming disrespectful to her mom and dad. The girl was restricted to a 10 P.M. curfew, yet on several nights the mother would get out of bed at midnight to find her daughter on the phone. When I asked the parents how they had maintained rules in the past, the mother said she often set limits. For example, she would withhold her daughter's car keys, allowances, or rewards. In viewing these past successes, the mother told the daughter that at 10:00 she was to bring her the phone, which the mother then took to her bedroom before going to bed. The girl agreed and the two developed trust again. When the daughter began completing her homework earlier in the evening and passing classes, the phone time was extended again. While this may not be a terribly complex problem, it is an illustration of how focusing on "what worked before" can have an effect on related behaviors. Complex problems do not mean that solutions are necessarily complex— notice successes in similar circumstances and assist people in applying them to similar situations.

8. Fitting into the student's world view lessens resistance and encourages cooperation.

Many counselors have encountered students who felt persecuted by a teacher or parent. The adolescent often exaggerates his/her dilemma and appears to dramatize the seriousness of the situation. Suggesting to an adolescent that *they* must change is sometimes a guarantee that he/she will not—it is the nature of adolescence! However, *aligning* with a student, stepping into his/her world view to get the teacher/parent/administrator off his/her back is the quickest way to resolution. Resolved that the teacher/parent/administrator will not change, the student has no recourse but to come up with ways to just get him/her off his/her back. The results are the same: the student behaves differently and others respond in kind.

A high school student who feels the coach just won't get off his back and is full of complaints to the vice principal can be asked:

VP: How will you know when things are just slightly better for you, in regard to the coach?

Student: He won't hound me as much...he'll get off my back.

VP: When, this year, has he been off your back? I agree, getting him off your back is a good idea.

The vice principal can then explore times when the student felt less taunted by the coach; the student will then feel heard by the administrator, and the goal to "get the coach off my back" will probably develop into the student behaving differently, as he recalls days when the coach picked on him less. The student will solve his own problem by changing *his* behavior. While educators should support each other, it is often helpful to use this approach with students who complain about other teachers, coaches, nurses, and so on. The goal is the same: to assist the student in creating better relationships. Another approach to this same situation would be to invite the coach and the student for a joint conference. The conference might begin with:

VP: Coach, Todd's concerned about the way you and he have been dealing with each other lately. I want you to know that I called you both here because I want you both to get what you want in this situation. Can you tell me a time this year when you didn't find it necessary to keep after Todd? What did he do to help prevent this?

VP: Todd, do you recall what Coach Smith is saying? He said that when you showed up for practice on time in the fall, he had no reason to give you a hard time. How did you do that in the fall? (Response.) Sounds like it worked for you—how might you do that again?

9. Motivation is a key and can be encouraged by aligning with students against the problem.

In keeping with the ideas of this model of counseling, nothing is 100% effective, even the SFBT model. Many times, motivation is not present because people do not know what they want to occur differently; they do not have a specific goal in mind. Another reason motivation can be absent is if the student feels the problem is not his/her fault, but instead, someone else's. It is important that students, teachers, and parents want things to be better for SFBT to be helpful. The way to find out about motivation is to ask directly: "Are you willing to do whatever it takes to make things better for you?" If the answer is "yes," you have a customer. If not, let the student know you are there and that he/she needs to come back soon when he/she is ready to tell you specifically what it is that he/she wants changed. The following dialogue may be helpful:

Counselor: Sandy, it's obvious to me that you have some true concerns about Mr. Smith, your algebra teacher. One thing I've learned is that unless you know how you want things to be, it's hard to accomplish anything different. Let's take a break. For the next few days, I'd like you to think about what you want changed with Mr. Smith. You might try paying attention to times in his class that are slightly better for you, as well as in other classes. In a few days, I'd like you to stop by and tell me what you liked about those times and what you would like to happen more often.

If a student, teacher, or parent desires a change but is not quite sure what it is that he or she wants changed, or is wanting to change someone else, caution that he/she cannot change anyone but him- or herself. Then ask the following question to assist in identifying a goal:

Counselor: Notice this week the times when you feel slightly better. Notice where you are, who is there, and what you are doing. Come back next week and tell me what part of the week you would like to experience again.

10. There is no such thing as resistance when we cooperate.

de Shazer mentions that when we find ways to cooperate with people, there is no such thing as resistance. This does not mean we give in to a student's every whim about change, but it does mean that we align, sympathize, empathize and simply use language to connect with him/her. Children and adolescents are quite vulnerable to acceptance and validation. A student who fights constantly may be perceived as wanting some control in his/her life; a parent who overprotects can be perceived as protecting slightly more than necessary. These connecting statements and messages align with whatever the students are needing yet the reframing opens up possibilities instead of perpetuating the problem. For example, students who fight and like being in control can be discouraged from fighting:

Principal: Now that you are in the principal's office it looks like the problem is controlling you! I realize that fighting gives you some control, but gee, now I've got control over you. I'd like to give it back to you. I wonder what you might do to stay out of my office and under your own control?

A parent who is overprotective may be asked:

Teacher: You obviously love your child very much. I wonder, though, if it is working for him/her that you are at school constantly—now that he/she is interested in becoming much more independent.

Teacher: What have you done in other situations to help your child become more independent?

Teacher: I wonder what it is that you will be able to do when your child becomes more independent?

Both these situations *cooperate* with the student's view and *lessen resistance*.

11. If it works, don't fix it—if not, do something different.

One of the most helpful questions to ask students who keep trying the same ineffective strategy over and over is "is this working for you?' At times, it sounds absurd as they describe their previous strategies of smarting off, stomping out, or fighting in the bathroom. Often, both educator and student (or parent) end up smiling, realizing that everyone's strategy can be improved upon. The session can become more productive then by asking the same student "What *has* worked for you?" This allows him/her to recall successful interventions that have worked. The tasks for the days and weeks ahead develop from past successes, no matter how small and insignificant they may appear during the process.

12. Focusing on the possible and changeable lessens frustration.

Many children would like to be Teenage Mutant Ninja Turtles and many adolescents would like to stay out all night. Realistic thinking is the key in SFBT, and it must focus on the visible and specific. For example, a child who wants Tommy to stop teasing him can't change Tommy, but can change where he encounters Tommy on the playground. An adolescent who complains about his mom's yelling can't stop mom from yelling (although she would probably disagree) but can change his responses to those that work at other times with other people (or even mom).

Scaling questions (de Shazer, 1985) utilize a scale and are helpful in focusing on small changes. For example, if an adolescent is referred for a problem with anger, a counselor could ask:

Counselor: On a scale of 1–10, where 10 means that anger is in control of you totally and 1 means that anger is being controlled by you, where are you now?

```
_____X_____
  1    2    3    4    5    6    7    8    9    10
```
I am in control　　　　　　　　　　**Anger is in control**

Counselor: Since you are at a 9, where would you like to be by the time I see you again tomorrow?

These questions set up a goal for the student. To be in control of anger has a different meaning from a demand that the anger stop totally. The daily scaling questions also encourage short- and longer-term success. In elementary schools, a task should not be attempted for longer than an afternoon for a kindergartner, to two days for a sixth grader. In secondary schools, two days to one week should be the maximum time a task is to be carried out. Performing a task within this short time period is more achievable than attempting to change for an entire term. Besides, children and adolescents conceptualize the future in weekly terms. A sixteen-year-old can't always think (as her parents wish she did) of the job she hopes to get when she graduates from college—she is more interested in the dance on Friday night.

13. Go slowly and focus on tasks that lead to success.

Caution students to not go too fast. Typically, when we discourage adolescents from changing, he/she makes changes independently. Cautioning students to go slowly prevents slow success from being perceived as failing or not happening fast enough. In actuality, when defeating a problem is the focus, not going backwards into the grip of the problem should be grounds for success.

Another reason for encouraging students and teachers to go slowly is that lasting change takes time. A musician, practicing her flute, may find that improvement fluctuates with different musical scores. Change occurs similarly: There will be highs and lows, but the gradual climb to success will be more efficient if practiced and expectations are not as high. It is helpful to mention this fact to students as a measure of reassurance that change which occurs slowly but consistently is the most lasting.

14. Rapid change is possible when we identify exceptions.

Teachers who use SFBT in classrooms directly are often surprised at how quickly children change behaviors. An elementary counselor told the story of a kindergarten student who had temper tantrums at least three times a week, usually before 10:00 A.M. Tiring from the frequent referral, one morning she went to Scott and asked:

Counselor: Would you like to fight off the "temper tantrums" (his description) just for today?

Scott looked puzzled at first but then replied that he wasn't sure if he could. The counselor then replied:

Counselor: It's 9:45 and I've just realized that you have not had a tantrum yet this morning. How have you done that?

Scott: I just did it!

The counselor then briefly talked with the teacher, asking her to remind Scott *when* he continued to fight off the tantrums during the morning and to ask him "How are you doing this?" Scott did not have a tantrum that day and decreased his tantrums to once every two or three weeks. His teacher rewarded him with being line leader more often and his counselor presented him with a certificate stating that he defeated the temper tantrum monster.

15. Change is a constant.

New experiences cause a change of context. When you read a new book, experience a new workshop or develop a new habit, change occurs. The systems we live in change constantly. Change is not always easy, but inevitable. When students and parents express the sad notion that "he/she will never change" it is more helpful to acknowledge this perception and then cooperate with such a statement by saying:

Counselor: When have you noticed (name) making very small changes in other situations?

Counselor: Did you have a part in that? How did you do that? How did you see him/her do that?

16. Every complaint pattern contains some sort of exception—keep looking.

"I'm angry all the time." "He's hyperactive constantly." "She never stays in her seat." "I'm totally stressed out with all my classes." These global statements of complaints are typical from people who feel hopeless and out of control. Yet, no one stays angry 100% of the time, for they would surely be exhausted and have many premature wrinkles! When students talk about school being awful, ask "when is it not as awful?" Opening up the possibility that to each problem there is an exception gives opportunities for people to see that they are in control more than they think. Many times, counting the minutes, hours, or days, when a problem is not interfering with schoolwork or home, makes it seem more solvable and less intrusive in one's life. For example, of a seven-day week, three days might seem to be slightly depressing and only for three hours of each day. Thinking that nine hours out of 168 hours are "down time," minimizes the effects of the problem, lessens the burden, and helps the student or educator feel more in control.

17. Changing the time and place will change interactions and behaviors.

Students often complain about the teacher who never calls on them or doesn't pay attention to them. However upon examination, a student may realize that it's not the teacher but the *timing* that's crucial. Sending a student back to class to notice when the timing is better to approach the teacher may give him/her a whole new perspective on how to achieve the goal of getting called on or getting necessary attention. If available, encourage a teacher to visit with you and the student and ask the same questions. Together, changing the time and place according to what works best will benefit both.

18. Looking at problems differently can encourage their resolutions.

Normalizing problems through empathy and compassion goes a long way towards lessening hopelessness. When labels are placed on children, adolescents, and adults, self-perceptions change to that of pathology. However, redescribing problems of *hyperactivity* as *energetic*, or *depression* as *anger/sadness*, or *isolated* as *private* changes perceptions and encourages hope.

I once remarked to an adolescent who had been placed in a psychiatric hospital-based school how well he did on a weekend visit with his parents. In the past, he had talked to me about his violent outbursts and angry words that truly were interfering in his reconciliation with his parents. He described himself as doing "okay" but "stuffing my feelings" and feeling negative about his actions. I remarked that I saw it a little differently—I saw him as successfully disciplining himself around his parents. He stopped for a moment and then agreed that he had disciplined himself and kept control. From that point on when another peer talked of "stuffing" feelings, he retorted that the peer was good at self-disciplining!

19. What will be different when the problem is solved?

This question gathers the strength of the SFBT model in that it assists students, teachers, and parents to use their imaginations and desires to set specific behavioral goals. It also gives people chances to imagine life *without* the problem. This removal of the problem for a moment presents a clearer picture of life without the problem and allows specific behaviors of oneself and others to be imagined. The ideas of SFBT are centered around opening up possibilities to solutions. When people cannot see past their problems, they fail to see themselves as competent. The SFBT educator is encouraged to search extensively for competencies in students and as the competencies are mentioned and discovered, the problems become solvable.

BECOMING CODISCOVERERS WITH STUDENTS

Educators who try to see students as competent usually find such competencies because they relate differently when searching for them. Students, in response to such relationships, respond nondefensively. This makes for a more cooperative atmosphere within the school setting. Students are often taken by surprise when a teacher begins to compliment them when they do well, and respond with curiosity themselves. Becoming codiscoverers together, the student and teacher can develop a more collaborative relationship. The attitude of the teacher becomes contagious to his/her students, and the results lead to calmer classrooms and more motivated students.

How Often Does the Problem Bother You?

In developing a new way of thinking differently towards students, it is important to think about how often problems *do* occur in different contexts. People who are saturated in the negative events of problems tend to feel that problems exist 100% of the time. After all, negative behaviors are often more keenly visible. However, if it were true that problems occured 100% of the time, many people who have experienced traumatic events would never have been able to recover sufficiently (because they would not have had any relief from the problem) to get out of bed in the morning, much less have careers, families, or feel happiness at least *some* of the time. Yet they do! As students, parents, or teachers remember and identify the times when they have not been taken over by the problem, they allow themselves to think differently about their success in dealing with the problem. By identifying these successes, they are more likely to repeat what worked in the past.

SEEING PROBLEMS AND SOLUTIONS DIFFERENTLY: BUILDING SELF-ESTEEM

Behavior Modification vs. Solution-Focused Brief Therapy: What's the Difference?

The guidelines mentioned in this chapter are quite different from other models of working with students, teachers, parents, and administrators. Past problem-focused assumptions focused on *understanding the root of the problem, or why the problem was occurring.* While the attempt to understand is a viable strategy, often the answers lead to little change and minimal understanding. For years, educators have often successfully subscribed to behavior modification plans. However, there are some students who do not conform to behavior modification approaches, and this presents frustrating dilemmas for school staff. I once asked an audience of teachers and administrators how the SFBT ideas seem different from the behavior modification approach:

"This is a positive approach..."

"This is an optimistic way of seeing students..."

"It's a new way of rewarding good behavior..."

While these perceptions are correct, the SFBT approach to school settings is different from behavior modification because it does not *talk* about positives and instead, develops a different relationship between problems and solutions. For example, observe the following dialogue from various educators with a behavior modification approach:

BEHAVIOR MODIFICATION APPROACH

Elementary: Students, thank you for your straight line....

High School: Students, the art room looks great today. Because of your help, we can use the watercolors this afternoon.

Athletics: Guys, good practice at football today. You did much better than yesterday.

Special Education Class: Charlie, you stayed in your seat nicely this morning—there have been no conflicts with Jonathan this morning like yesterday. Good for you! You are on your way to getting a reward this afternoon when school is over.

This first group of questions make the *educator* the expert on what works, as he/she acknowledges, judges and affirms the student's actions and deems them as important accomplishments.

SOLUTION-FOCUSED APPROACH

Elementary: Students, this line is so straight...how have you managed to be so cooperative with each other?

High School: Students, this room was a mess earlier! How have you transformed it into such a great looking place

Athletics: Guys, I can't believe your performance! How have you turned this team around this afternoon?

Special Education Class: Charlie, I am amazed at you today! I've noticed how you sat in your chair and did not allow Jonathan to distract you! Wow! How have you done this?

The second group of questions made the *students* experts of their behaviors. They were viewed by the educator as totally responsible for the success. Students and parents are aware of an educator's training, and a look of puzzlement or amazement by an authority towards students or parents is a compliment! When students think they have done something that the teacher cannot explain or understand, it becomes very motivating. It seems to be an age-old tradition that students challenge their teachers—why not cooperate with this tradition?

SELF-ESTEEM: WAYS TO HELP IT HAPPEN

Whether they find themselves challenging students or offering empowering affirmations with curiosity, many SFBT educators discover through using this approach that self-esteem grows enormously for their students. There have always been programs developed to motivate students and reward them for good behavior. We have given and encouraged self-affirmations for students to say to themselves and to one another. While these ideas have been successful in many programs, they often missed the students whose negative behavior kept them from feeling good about themselves.

The individual approach of SFBT makes the ideas even more exciting for teachers and counselors. Many who try out the various questions and the approach report that hyperactive children calm themselves, complaining children stop to think before blaming others, and angry, rebellious adolescents lose their defensiveness. One counselor told me the story of a "whining fifth grader" who was sent to her by his teacher for being upset in class after someone had stolen his lock from his locker. Standing with lock in hand, whining over the experience, the student was surprised when the counselor *bypassed the problem* and asked: *"Wow, how did you get it back?"*

The student stopped his crying so suddenly, the counselor was mesmerized. He had undoubtedly thought he was going to discuss *why* he was crying so he could enlist her help in fighting off the bullies. Instead, he told her how he rescued his lock. The teacher was stunned as she listened to the discussion and later inquired to the counselor "how she knew to approach him so effectively."

Providing a New Context for Students to See Themselves Differently

The SFBT educator knows that looking for exceptions in students who let negative behaviors bother them is sometimes difficult but essential in helping those students see themselves differently and feel good about themselves. Self-esteem happens when we feel successful about ourselves. I often tell parents the following metaphorical story of teaching a child to ride a bicycle, and let them think about how giving their kids a context to feel competent in can make a difference.

The day often comes when a young child asks his/her parents to take off the training wheels of his/her bike. The parent can respond in many ways. The parent might respond with worried apprehension and reluctantly take off the wheels, stand by as the child falls, pick him/her up and say "see, it's not time to do this yet, let me help you up. I'll hold the bike while you pedal to the corner." The child eventually gets to the corner, looks up at mom or dad and says, "Thanks for helping me get here. Can you help me do it again?"

Another way a parent might respond is by saying: "Okay, let's see what happens." The child gets on the bike, falls a few times, looks back at mom/dad and asks for help. The parent helps the child up and supporting his/her efforts says, "Try again, you made it a whole two feet!" The child falls again and again, but the parent waits patiently and encourages each small success. When the child eventually makes it to the corner, he/she looks back at his/her parent and exclaims, "Look what *I* did."

Building self-esteem is indeed a by-product and a building block of SFBT. A child or adolescent (even a parent) who experiences himself/herself as being competent, is less likely to be dependent on others and instead, begins to depend on himself/herself. The educator need only say to a student asking for assistance, "What did you do last time that worked for you?"; "How did you make that happen specifically?" If schools can teach students to solve their own problems by encouraging them to think of times they were successful, they are giving them a life skill, and lessening school conflicts.

CONCLUDING COMMENTS: CHAPTER 1

Today's school counselor and administrator have little time, and in some cases are not allowed to probe into the lives of their students. Today's teacher has a classroom of students full of needs, learning differences, and expectations/abilities. Solution-focused brief therapy does not necessitate probing or extensive examination for the ideas to work. The model simply invites investigation of past success and encourages the success to continue. The magic of SFBT lies in the educator's ability and the student's ability to notice the exceptions to problems and act on their discoveries.

Teacher-Parent-Student Conference
A collaborative effort

Problem Definition:

To Student:

What reason do you think your teachers will give for meeting with us today?

To Teachers and Parents:

What do you hope happens in our time today?

Goal:

To all present:

How will all of you know when things are better for _____ (student)?
What will you see him/her doing soon that will tell you things are better?

Exception Identification:

To all:

In what class(es) does this goal already exist?

To Teachers:

How have you seen (student) do this? What have you done that helps this happen?

To Student:

How did you manage that? What does the teacher do that helps this happen? (Continue asking: "When else does this occur?")

Task:

To all:

For the next week, if you were to do more of what you have all said works slightly better, what would I see you doing more?

Name: _____ Date: _____

CASE NOTES FOR STUDENTS

Presenting Problem:

Goal:

Exceptions:

   1.

   2.

   3.

   4.

   5.

Task:

   1.

   2.

   3.

_____
Educator's Signature

SFBT Educator Training Exercise: Chapter 1
Thinking with a Solution Focus

The following questions have been designed as a personal exercise to assist in understanding SFBT ideas. The exercise can be duplicated for faculty meetings. For maximum benefits, discuss your findings in groups of two or three people.

The Problem-Focused Approach:

What has been the most frustrating problem for you this year at school? (A problem)

What did you do to solve your problem? (Your strategy)

Did it work?

If your answer was full of success, congratulations! If however you were not satisfied with your strategy, please read on. The problem with "problems" is that we only notice them when they're bothering us—when they are *present*. Our clues to solutions lie in the times when problems are *not present*. These are called "exceptions."

The Solution-Focused Approach:

How would you like things to be for you this year in school?

When was the last time you were just slightly successful in achieving your goal? (Searching for exceptions)

How did you do that? (Exceptions = Strategies)

Where else in your life, profession, job, or personal life are you successful at accomplishing something similar to the above goal?

What are your strategies to accomplish such a personal task?

How do you do this?

If you tried just one or two of these strategies in your work for just a week, what would you do? What would someone see you doing differently?

Task:

Today, notice what goes well for the rest of the day. Make notes of what "works" instead of focusing on what doesn't work in your job, with your kids, or family. Notice how you feel when these "exceptions" to life's stresses occur. Consider prescribing this for yourself the next time you need a solution!

CHAPTER 2 | CREATING POSSIBILITIES THROUGH LANGUAGE

If in our world language plays a very central part in those activities that define and construct persons, the redescription of persons is called for.

NARRATIVE MEANS TO THERAPEUTIC ENDS,
DAVID EPSTON, MICHAEL WHITE

TELLING THE STORY DIFFERENTLY

We describe our world and ourselves through language. Problems to one person are not always problems to others because of the *meanings* attached to them. Because language plays such a central role in how we perceive ourselves and our behavior, redescribing situations can often lead to different perceptions and to differing behaviors. It makes sense then, that assisting students, teachers, and parents to see themselves as competent may require redescribing their concerns with a more solvable description. Ours is a problem-focused world, and most of us go through our days noticing primarily the obstacles placed in our way. For example, consider for a moment the worst situation you dealt with yesterday. Remember the details? Now, consider another situation— the *best* situation you encountered yesterday, or the day before—one that you would like to repeat today or tomorrow. Slightly more difficult? Be assured that you are not alone in having difficulties remembering the times life *worked*. Consider however, living your life in this way, learning what worked and doing more of it.

CHAPTER 2 FOCUS

- Changing "problem talk" into "solution talk": New ways of viewing problems

- Case study: A short story about school refusal

- Guiding questions: Ideas for discovering "exceptions" and writing new life stories

- Externalizing problems: Finally, a way to avoid blaming

- Scaling questions: Strategies to help minimize the effects of problems

LIFE'S LITTLE ALTERNATIVES: NEW WAYS OF SEEING OLD PROBLEMS

Epston and White mention that people give meanings to their lives through the stories of their experiences. The description given in storytelling by an individual is his/her unique "reality," and that reality directs the way he/she lives life. Most of us seem to notice the tragedies in our stories and ignore the rich unique outcomes or alternative stories in our lives that might make the story less dreary if we added them. White encourages us to notice the "unique outcomes" and insert them into our life stories in *place* of the problems, thereby creating new possibilities in which to live and perceive our experiences. The following explanation of this process by White and Epston is very interesting:

> *We believe that persons generally ascribe meaning to their lives by plotting their experience into stories, and that these stories shape their lives and relationships.*

As students, parents, and teachers describe their stories, they tell us about the experiences that directed their past behaviors and contributed to their current problems. It is important to listen to what de Shazer calls "the world view of the client" as it helps the SFBT educator to know how to assist in coauthoring the story. Listening and suggesting different descriptions of the story is a way of assisting students, teachers, and parents in new ways of seeing their problems. This reauthorship may then encourage new behaviors and relieve the person of feeling hopeless, motivating him/her to engage in new behaviors that do not support "the problem."

A way to change the focus from doom to dream is by redescribing the presented problem into "solution talk." The two lists below were composed by school counselors and educators who received training in SFBT. They listed the common complaints they experienced in their schools as *problem talk*, then developed a more solvable *solution talk* list:

PROBLEM TALK	SOLUTION TALK
hyperactivity	very energetic at times
attention deficit disorder	short attention span sometimes
anger problem	gets upset sometimes
depressed	sad
oppositional	argues a point often
rebellious	developing his/her own way
codependent	people are important to him/her
disruptive	often forgets the rules in class
family problems	worries about his/her home life
shy	takes a little time to know people
negative peer pressure	people try to influence him/her
feelings of rejection	people forget to notice him/her
isolating	likes being by himself/herself

The lists do not in any way minimize the severity of the problems listed under problem talk. Students, teachers, and parents often feel more *heard* when their problem is redescribed, and relax at the suggestion that things are not as bad as they thought. Describing a problem as terrible and difficult rarely motivates people to change. For example, if you have the choice to be described as having a major depressive disorder or as being "sad," which would you rather be *labeled* as having? Which one seems temporary or incapacitating? New descriptions assist students, teachers, and parents by helping them feel more normal. This approach acknowledges that the consequences have already been experienced as negative and opens the door to solutions by describing them more hopefully. The descriptions do not change the problem, they change the *meaning* ascribed to the problem.

Getting Specific

An integral part of SFBT is in developing a goal that is realistic and specific. The following two lists show the difference between a vague goal and a specific goal. The

SFBT educator can assist in the process of writing and developing new stories with students, teachers, and parents by helping them define the desired future behavior specifically. It is better to work toward a specific goal such as "talking to a new friend" rather than "being happier at school," a vague goal. One way is to ask a student, parent, or teacher: "What will I see you do when you are (happier, less angry, less sad)?"

Adolescents have different perceptions of things such as cleaning their room, being home on time, completing assignments to the best of their ability, and effective study habits. It is helpful to be so specific that any wavering from the expectations cannot be blamed on the educator or parent. SFBT encourages people to be responsible for achieving their own goal. The language must be specific and competency-based if it is to create an atmosphere conducive to responsibility and cooperation. In Chapter 4, more ways of having *competency-based conversations* will be discussed as ways of helping students and teachers to collaborate in developing new behaviors. The message is the same: When new, specific descriptions are given, new behaviors can then emerge and possibilities for solution exist.

The following two lists show how goals can be redescribed so that they are observable and realistic:

VAGUE	OBSERVABLE
I want my father to listen to me more often.	I will talk to my father in a quiet, calm voice so he will listen.
I want to stop being sent to the office every day.	I will follow directions in class and do my assignments on time.
I will stay out of fights.	I will walk away from trouble in the cafeteria and go to the gym."
I want to get out of this alternative program.	I need to stay in my seat and let the teacher see me raise my hand so she knows I won't need the alternative program.
I want Ms. Jones to get off my back.	I'll do what Ms. Jones thinks I should do in class to stay out of trouble: do my homework and sit far away from my friends.
I just want to be happier.	When I make new friends and do fun things with them I will feel happier.

ASSUME CHANGE WILL HAPPEN: SUGGESTIONS FOR HELPING TO CHANGE NEGATIVE ASSUMPTIONS

The attitude and perspective of the SFBT educator when working with students, parents, and teachers is as vital to the process of assisting people as are the questions that are asked. The following suggestions are ideas for presenting an "assumption" and confidence that change is imminent:

1. Talk about the experiences as if they were in the past, available for reference, but also workable enough for redesigning in the future. For example:

   Sue, I certainly understand how moving four times in the past two years has made it difficult for you to feel as if you are a part of the social life at high school. Since I have learned from you today how important it is to feel part of your school, I wonder how you might like things to be different now that you know you will be at this school for the next full year at least.

2. Encourage and invite very young children to imagine describing their story to a child in need of a solution. Help change their negative experience into a successful triumph over their problem. (Suggested by Keeney, 1994).

   Alex, I often work with children such as yourself who are very angry at their parents for one reason or another. You and I have talked about how you want things to be today, and described to me what you are going to do the next time anger gets in your way. I'd like you to tell me in your own words what I might tell the next child I see who is dealing with anger, based on what you now know.

3. Redescribe behaviors that sound "pathological" into behaviors that seem "solvable" and "normal":

   So you get upset sometimes when people tell you what to do. Gee, it sounds like you've got your own ideas, and people aren't listening to you right now. That seems to happen to many students. How would you like your teachers to see you, as an angry student who closes his/her mind, or as a creative student who has questions and suggestions about assignments?

4. Normalize behaviors for the school student, teacher, or parent. Help them feel as if their situation occurs commonly and that they do not have a severe problem.

   Ann, I am really impressed that you have stayed in the Geometry class this year. Many students wouldn't have forced themselves to get tutoring, or persevere like you have. Even though your grade is low, you keep on going. How do you manage such drive to finish this class?

5. Pretend that the student's life is considered to be "Act 1" in the Play of Life. Now, construct "Act 2" with the student. Change the characters, the interactions, and

behaviors into a new scene in which the student does things differently. Ask the student how his peers, teachers, or parents would like to see the "play" change.

John, until now, things have been tough as your parents divorced. Now that you have moved here and you say your mom is happier, let's consider all this "Act 1" in your life of sixteen years. Now let's talk about how you want "Act 2" to go. If we used your friends, mom, and other close relatives in your life as the audience, how do you think you and they might write "Act 2?

6. Assume change will occur or has already occurred.

Lauren, someday soon when the sadness about your grandfather's death is not bothering you as often as now, what will you be doing more of?

Jonathan, when you bring your grades back up to passing in the next few weeks or so, what will be different here at school and at home?

Ms. Smith, when Lee begins to comply with your rules at home, using the ideas we have discussed here today, what do you see as happening more often at home, or in your relationship with her?

A CASE STUDY: A SHORT STORY ABOUT SCHOOL REFUSING —BY DAVID EPSTON

The following case contributed by David Epston, shows how a new focus on an old problem motivated the student to change his behavior. The case illustrates the use of various narrative ideas so that the adolescent concerned begins to see himself differently, and gives up negative behaviors for new ones. Because Epston wrote the case study, the "I" mentioned throughout refer to Epston.

Fifteen-year-old Ronald was the very intelligent only son of a frail 70-year-old father and 54-year-old mother. This family had been known to our agency for some time. His father had retired recently and ever since that day, Ronald started refusing school. My colleagues asked me to see this family, as they had grave fears that Mr. Peterson, who had had open heart surgery recently, would not survive Ronald's temper tantrumming which involved breaking windows and smashing furniture. Mrs. Peterson also suffered from angina and there was concern for her health too. Several things impressed me upon reading the file. Ronald, despite his infrequent attendance at school, was maintaining an A average. Secondly, he had suffered from a neurological disorder as a three-year-old, and, despite reassurances from a neurologist, pediatrician, and child psychiatrist, that this had resolved itself without incident, Mr. Peterson remained unconvinced.

The family entered my room with Ronald at its head followed by his mother and then some time later by his father. I asked Ronald why he wasn't attending school. He said: "Because of the headaches!" Before the word was hardly uttered, Mr. Peterson offered me the medical history of Ronald's neurological disorder. When he was finished, I said: "Ronald, what did you get in history?" He said: "A." I turned to his father: "Mr. Peterson, do you think some of your son's brain is missing?" "No!" he said with increasing gusto. "Ronald, what did you get in biology?" "A." "Mr. Peterson, do you think your son's brain is moulded?" "No!" I then turned my attention to Ronald: "Ronald, how long did your last headache last?" He told me proudly: "Half an hour." "That's nothing! Why last week I met a boy your age who had a headache for three days. Matter of fact, he sat in the chair you are sitting in now. Guess how long it took for his self-hypnosis to work?" Ronald said "I don't know." "Twenty minutes. That's all. Do you want to ring him up? I know he'd be glad to tell you all about it. He's a smart kid like you." As usual, he declined my offer, but showed a keen interest in "self-hypnosis." "I suppose you want to learn about hypnosis?" He agreed. I outlined what practice was required of him and ushered the Peterson family out of my room. They were surprised that their consultation had lasted over twenty minutes. I sent them the following letter:

Dear Friends,

Ronald has agreed to return to school in return for hypnotic anaesthesia training. I will expect 95% attendance and that sickness be defined as at least 101 degrees Fahrenheit. Ronald will practice having headaches at home for one hour per day. His parents have agreed to leave him alone for this period of time. Ronald has agreed to keep a daily record of the time he induced his headache, the time he stopped his headache, what was going on, etc. In general, Ronald will take over responsibility for his headaches.

I will contact you on the first day of the next school term to see if you have proven yourself.

Good luck!

Yours sincerely, David Epston

I contacted the family on the arranged date. Ronald's attendance had been 100% since I saw him and he had gone happily off to school for the first day of this term. There had been no headaches or "temper outbursts." Mrs. Peterson also noticed that he had even shown restraint on a number of occasions.

I wrote Ronald the following letter:

Dear Ron,

I know you have lived up to your side of the bargain and that your headaches have disappeared. If you wish to commence your self-hypnosis training, fine. Ring me. If you feel it is no longer necessary, get in touch with me when you stop attending school the next time.

I know I can depend on you.

Yours sincerely, David Epston

*Reprinted with permission: *Collected Papers*, David Epston, 1989

David Epston makes it a habit to write notes to his patients. This is another way of reinforcing a student's new discovery and changing his/her thinking with language. Remember when someone in your life put a note in your lunch box, or when your husband remembered to write down just the right message on your anniversary card? How about your relative who searched for just the right Christmas present? The teacher who takes the time to write a special note or compliment on the back of a report card is remembered for *years*. Michael White says that a note sent to someone in counseling is worth six visits of counseling in terms of influencing the student to see himself/herself differently! Observe the following note sent to a child who was working on controlling his energy:

Dear Joey,

I wanted to write you this note to tell you how impressed I was at your plan this week to control "energy." As you mentioned in my office, "energy" ruins your days sometimes when it makes you get up and run around the class when you are not supposed to. I liked your idea of "telling energy to take a hike." I look forward to seeing you again soon. Good luck with fighting the energy—you're winning so far.

Sincerely,

School Counselor

Take Time to Notice—and Write It Down!

Notes can be sent after sessions and given to the child or adolescent during class or at the end of the day. Terry Walkup, school counselor in Plano, Texas, learned last fall that an adolescent he had been working with had walked away from a gang fight for the first time that year. He wrote a note to the student, commending her on the courage it took to walk away. The student, upon their next meeting, acknowledged how nice it was to get the letter and for him to notice. The note took about *two minutes* to write. The effects lasted the rest of the term. She might not have acknowledged that it was her "courage" that helped her back down until the counselor took the time to describe it as such. The student, having thought of herself as stuck in the gang, changed her thinking after reading the note. Take the time to notice when life works for your students...and write it down.

GUIDING QUESTIONS FOR WRITING NEW STORIES

The following questions are examples of ways to gather information about how a person perceives his/her story and assist in reauthoring the experiences through new descriptions:

FOR SCHOOL PROBLEMS:

1. If I were a fly on the wall, what would I see you doing this afternoon in your first grade classroom that would tell me things had changed for you?

2. If I asked Ms. Jones, your History teacher, how she saw you behaving differently during the next week so that you could end your time in D-Hall, what do you think she would say?

3. When your classes run more smoothly, and you are able to be the teacher you have always wanted to be, what will you be doing during class time?

FOR FAMILY PROBLEMS:

1. What new behaviors will tell you when your daughter is capable of being responsible for her curfew? When have you helped her achieve this behavior in the past?

2. When this problem is no longer intruding in your life at home, what do you think you will be able to do that you haven't done in a while, with your mom?

3. If I followed you around tomorrow (or next week) when things are different, what behaviors would you point out and describe to me as different?

4. Someday, when this problem is not bothering you as much, how will you know? What will you be doing, exactly, that will tell you things are much better?

Key words such as *sometimes, part of the time, not yet, instead, for a while,* and *until then,* are helpful in assisting students, teachers, and parents to see their problem as temporary. For example, if a teacher should respond to a SFBT educator that she simply wants a student to "stop behaving so badly in my class," asking the teacher "What will he/she be doing instead?" will probably yield more concrete behaviors that she expects from the student. Students need to know exactly what teachers expect of them, as do teachers need to know what students need.

THOSE TIMES, THEY ARE "EXCEPTIONAL"

Many educators have been taught to work with students by trying to identify an underlying problem, discover why it is a problem, and what occurred to cause it. For decades, these strategies have given us hope to discover and become insightful, so we might understand and then find ways to solve problems. Unfortunately, understanding is often not enough to produce change. The SFBT educator has little time for insightful sessions. The guiding ideas of SFBT suggest that insight is not necessary for change. Knowing what is wrong does not provide suggestions for doing things better. However, gazing into past successful behaviors or "exceptions" gives us clues to doing things successfully once again. These become solutions for change.

For example, if a nine-year-old soccer player understands why he does not kick the soccer ball into the net (he's not fast enough for the goalie) it does not tell him how to kick the ball into the net. However, if he and his brother practice one evening and he scores somehow catching his brother off guard, he learns that there may be a way he can do it again. A football quarterback may take the time to watch films of his performance at Friday night's game. As he sees his mistakes, he becomes familiar with *plays that did not work.* However, watching plays *that did work* will give him clues to being more successful. If I want to learn how to play the piano, I might not learn well if I hear someone playing the wrong notes. However, hearing the correct notes and practicing until I can play them, may help me learn how to play. Checking out with students the times when they have experienced some of the newly described goals becomes what de Shazer refers to as "exceptions" to the problem.

Bill O'Hanlon and Michelle Weiner-Davis talk of searching for exceptions as ways to direct students, teachers, and parents to search in the present and past for times when they did not have their problems. It has been my experience that many counseling tasks fail when people are asked to do tasks so foreign to them that they simply do not have the skills to carry them out! By focusing on present or past exceptions to the problems, and assigning tasks familiar to the persons in counseling, the chances of success increase. As I mentioned earlier, I make it a habit to *never* ask people to do something they have never done before unless they suggest it. Instead, I try to connect familiar behaviors which work for them in other areas of their life.

Using Exceptions in a New Context

A certain teacher came to counseling to learn to deal with stress. She was recently divorced and experiencing lots of difficulties with her two children. According to her, the children refused to do chores, listen to her expectations, or come home on time. She was sure that her parenting skills would end up costing her custody of the children. Her goal was to "learn how to get my children's attention, so they know I am serious about my expectations." After asking about her occupation, I learned that she had taught fifth grade for almost ten years. During that time, she told me she had received excellent reviews and was team leader in her grade level. I asked how she managed to run such an effective classroom. She then told me her solution:

"I have rules to go by; the first day of school I go over them until they are crystal clear."

"I stick to my guns about the rules. I'm fair but I always follow through. With fifth graders you have to, so they don't run over you."

"I give assignments that are fair. If the students want to question my assignment, I go over it with them and compromise."

"I'm really consistent. When I say I'm going to do something, I do it—that goes for rewards and punishments."

After she described the effective way that she managed her classroom, I commended her on her ability to run things so smoothly and then *wondered out loud* how she might begin to apply the same excellent methods at home. She became very quiet. She then said that home was different, with different types of relationships. I agreed with her yet wondered out loud if the skills might just be as effective with her children (ages 10 and 12) as they were for the approximate same-aged child in fifth grade. She said she would try. In two weeks she returned, saying that her children were behaving better and she was less stressed. I complimented her on her ability to transfer what worked from school to home.

QUESTIONS FOR FOCUSING ON PAST "EXCEPTIONS"

Have there been times when you *were able* to speak to your mother in a calm way? How did you *do* that? What would she say you did?

When was the last time you *were successful* in school? What did you do *then* that worked? How did you do that?

When was the last time you *did notice* John sitting still in his seat? What was going on in class at the time? Where was he sitting? Who was there?

How have *you controlled* this problem with anger before? How did you do that so you were in control?

I see that you passed 6 out of 8 classes. How did you manage to pass them? What would the teachers in those classes say you *did* that worked for you? What did the teachers *do* that worked for you?

You have been straight for almost two months now. I am so proud that you've stayed away from marijuana that long. Today you are telling me how hard it is to be around it at times. How *did you make it* for two months? What was your strategy?

Your concern about alcohol at the next party is admirable. Not many kids can tell me about their fear of alcohol. You seem like the kind of person who really takes care of yourself. *How have you avoided* similar situations in the past?

The idea of sex with your boyfriend is a real worry to you. I'm proud that you took the time to talk to me about this. I've noticed over the past months that you are a very careful young lady. You choose your friends carefully, and you take the right classes for college bound students. How *have you made such effective decisions* in the past? I wonder how that might help now?

Mr. and Mrs. Jones, you must be extremely proud of your son chosen by four top colleges for admission. Henry, I am very excited that you have been chosen for admission to Harvard, Stanford, Rice, and Baylor. What a tough decision! *How have the three of you made decisions* in your family before? What do you know about your son, Mr. and Mrs. Jones, that could guide your decisions further?

QUESTIONS FOR FOCUSING ON PRESENT "EXCEPTIONS"

Tim, I've noticed that you haven't let "energy" take over this morning, and keep you out of your seat in class. *How have you done that?*

Todd, I can't believe your performance on the court today. I haven't seen you as quick and sharp in a while. *How did you pull it all together out there?*

Sally, your teacher sent you to talk to me because she was worried about your being so quiet in class. *How have you managed to talk to me* so freely for the past twenty minutes?

Mark, your vice principal sent you here and said you were very unruly and angry in the lunch line about twenty minutes ago. I'm wondering *how you calmed yourself* so quickly? Does this happen often, that you calm yourself so well? How long does it take and how do you do that for yourself?

Jeremy, your mom said you forget papers in your eighth grade math class very often. Today, I sent for you early in the morning and it's 2:30 now. You brought me the pass I sent you at 8:30 this morning. *How did you keep from losing it?*

Ann, your grandmother died so suddenly last week. I am amazed at the peace in your eyes as your talk of your special times with her. *How have you managed* to deal with her death so peacefully?

DEVELOPING TASKS FOR SUCCESS

The language used in the above questions *assumed change would occur or was occurring*. The student was addressed by *name*, the presenting *problem* mentioned clearly, and then an *exception-searching question* was given. The intervention ended with a *curiosity-based question* similar to "How did you do that?" As the exceptions develop, *tasks* are assigned and presented with an attitude of "since you've successfully done this before, let's do more of it...it works!" On the following page are principles for task development by William Hudson O'Hanlon. The SFBT educator and student might discuss the tasks, write them down and set a time to meet again. Upon the next meeting, beginning with "What's better?" the educator and student can discuss the events occurring between the previous and present session. The session might end with a reinforcing question such as: "what do you want to keep on doing that's working for you now?"

SUGGESTING AND REINFORCING FAVORABLE BEHAVIORS

It has long been a motto among many educators that "you will get more with sugar than with vinegar," when it comes to responses in the classroom. My daughter attends a gifted program in a nearby public school. The first day of school several years ago, I went to meet her after school as the bell rang, only to find her teacher speaking softly to the children in her class:

"Students, in all my years of teaching, I have never experienced such a wonderful first day of school with such wonderful children. We are going to have a great year."

As I approached her and watched inquisitively, she turned to me and said, "Linda, I can't believe it, they are all angels." The children glowed, lined up for their bus trip home and *did indeed act like angels.* Across the hall, I could hear another second

COLLABORATIVE TASK ASSIGNMENTS: BASIC PRINCIPLES*

William Hudson O'Hanlon, M.S.
The Hudson Center for Brief Therapy, 11926 Arbor, Omaha, NE 68144 U.S.A.
(402) 391-4223 or (402) 330-1144/Fax# 402/397-4913

Task assignments are to help bring about changes in *doing* (action/interaction) and/or changes in *viewing* (perceptions/attention/frame of reference) in the situation involving the complaint or negotiated problem in therapy. They are directed toward having people make changes outside the therapy session.

The assignment should emerge from the conversation and be cocreated and negotiated between students, parents, teachers, and therapist. Be sure to include or preempt any objections or barriers to carrying out the task assignment before finalizing it. This is a collaborative intervention, not one that the therapist imposes on the person in counseling.

Frame the task assignment as an experiment. The clients are to make no conclusions before doing the experiment. Make it time limited and adjust the assignment as needed.

Use presuppositional language when giving the assignment, e.g., "*After* you do this, I will want you to tell me exactly what happened, as if you could have seen it on a videotape."

Direct the assignment to breaking up patterns of doing and viewing. Find the places where the pattern seems especially repetitive and predictable and direct the assignment to making the smallest noticeable difference.

Include multiple levels of meaning (symbols and metaphors) that may speak to the multiple levels of meaning of the situation, if possible.

Write down the assignment and keep a copy for your files to increase the likelihood of follow-through and continuity.

If the assignment isn't done between sessions, don't immediately assume resistance. Discuss the matter with the person and, if necessary, make adjustments in the assignment until one is found that works for all parties. If the assignments are not completed, confront them about motivation or find another direction for intervention.

---

*Reprinted with permission.

grade teacher, who apparently, did not have such a favorable day. She wasn't speaking softly, she was screaming:

"This is the first day of school and already you are not following the rules. Move here, stay in line, no talking...stop that...."

I again watched inquisitively as the children followed suit to her description and reacted accordingly—disrupting the hallway and giving the teacher a really hard time. Her attempts were too direct; her affect conveyed her frustration and the children responded in kind. While this is also an example of "the snowball effect," it proves that reinforcing with curiosity and compliments is much more effective. The following dialogue shows another form of "redescription" used with a sixteen-year-old mentioned earlier, who had complained about a poor relationship with his parents. He and his parents had fought consistently over the past three months, and they had grounded him until his attitude changed. I was impressed by his new behavior, and reinforced it through redescription:

Counselor: What went a little better over the weekend, with your parents?

Student: Things were quiet, but only because I stuffed my feelings down when I got angry. I know that was wrong.

Counselor: Really...how have you decided that your strategy was wrong?

Student: I used to go to another counselor who told me never to stuff feelings.

Counselor: How was the weekend?

Student: Pretty good, because we didn't fight.

Counselor: What did you do to help that happen?

Student: Like I said, I stuffed my feelings down and tried to be decent with them.

Counselor: Wow, you know, it sounds like you "disciplined" yourself.

Student: Yeah, I guess so.

Counselor: Did it work for you, disciplining your negative feelings, so that you could enjoy your family and they could enjoy you?

Student: Yeah, come to think of it, it did.

Counselor: Sounds like you had a pretty good idea. I wonder, since it worked to discipline yourself, would there be an opportunity for you to express how you feel next time, in a calm way, because that sounds important to you?

Student: Probably, if I watch for it.

Counselor: Okay! How about watching for a calm time the next time you are with your parents, and notice when you think the best time to express yourself might be.

The "Columbo" Strategy

Reinforcing behaviors using SFBT is different than strict behavior modification approaches because of the different relationship between the problem and solution. One way to approach and reinforce an educator or student is to act honestly perplexed and ask them: "How did you know to do that?" This can work for a teacher who is concerned about an unruly student and chooses to complain more than work out a solution. The SFBT educator can compliment a student very effectively by acting puzzled—the "Columbo" strategy. Another possibility is to ask students how they learn well, or, how they could complete an assignment efficiently:

Teacher: "Bobby, I noticed you need to work on your spelling words. How would you suggest you study them for the next test?"

Bob: "I don't know...maybe Tom and I could study together."

Teacher: "Where might you do this in the classroom? How many minutes do you think you could study and stay calm and quiet?"

Bob: "Probably about 10 minutes."

Teacher: "Okay, I can try that for 10 minutes. When you two study enough, let me know and I will give you a pretest. When this works, we can do it again when you need extra time, okay?"

The teacher encouraged the student to set his own strategy for learning by questioning his expertise. In a research project that explored the dynamics of "change," Metcalf and Thomas found that teachers rarely ask their students what helps them learn. As with many professions involving *provider-receiver* relationships, theories or philosophies based on previous successes are reasons for delivery of certain strategies to the receiver. However, using the idea of a *competency-based program* such as this one, it makes sense to ask the very population we are serving: *"What do I need to know about how you learn best?"* Many responses may seem a little unrealistic, but the educator can assist the student in identifying a strategy that fits for both of them. The research concluded that when people feel heard and have the opportunity to give clear reasons for seeking help, their needs for help are satisfied more often. Again, giving responsibility for their own success often diminishes resistance and allows self-esteem to blossom in students, parents, and teachers.

EXTERNALIZING PROBLEMS: FINALLY, THE DEFEAT OF "BLAMING"

Michael White talks of "externalizing" problems as a way to objectify or personify problems that intrude in our lives. As people begin to see themselves as "intruded upon" by problems, they begin to "look around" the problem to get back on track. The road may have two routes: One route may be scenic, taking in all kinds of issues, looking at the back roads of history, and the other route may be the freeway, getting to the destination faster, without all the intrusions and scenery. Solution-focused brief therapy is the express route. Knowing how to get to the desired destination means looking for the "unique outcomes," or times when the road is clear.

As Michael White began working in this approach with families in 1980, he found that the families often felt like failures, since systematically everyone had tried various ways of solving the problem. Working with ill children primarily, he began to *externalize the problem as an entity in itself which could either be maintained or dissolved.* As he offered this suggestion for families, the families felt empowered and decided to eliminate the power of the problem over their lives by externalizing the problem and not maintaining its influences.

Externalizing problems with adolescents and children helps them see the problems as separate from themselves and see themselves not as failures, but intruded upon. The *Introductory Case Study* in Chapter 1 utilized the idea of externalizing problems. White mentions what externalizing the problem accomplishes:

It decreases unproductive conflict between persons, including disputes over who is responsible for the problem.

It undermines the sense of failure that has developed for many persons in response to the continuing existence of the problem despite attempts to resolve it.

It paves the way for persons to cooperate with each other, to unite in a struggle against the problem, and to escape its influence in their lives and relationships.

It opens up new possibilities for persons to take action to retrieve their lives and relationships from the problem and its influence.

It frees persons to take a lighter, more effective, and less stressed approach to "deadly serious" problems.

White also asks people about their influence on maintaining the problem that bothers them. I like to compare the idea of problem maintenance with firefighters who hold up nets for victims of burning buildings. As long as each firefighter holds up his part of the net, the net remains taut and safe. However, if one should begin to leave the scene, and then another, the net would not be maintained as well. In externalizing problems, the idea is not to maintain the problem, and instead, escape from its influence by doing things differently. Consider the following dialogue about *depression*: (client's description)

Counselor: How has this depression interfered with your ability to teach effectively?

Teacher: It keeps me from enjoying my students, being creative in the holiday activities I used to love, and from looking forward to the next day.

Counselor: How have you let the depression take over and intrude in your life, keeping you from these things that you just described to me?

Teacher: Well, I go home and just sit, or I go to school and think about how bad things are since Bob left me, or I think that things will never get better.

Counselor: How many hours a day would you say you let depression interfere like that?

Teacher: It's worse in the morning for about an hour and then at night for about 3 hours.

Counselor: Really, so about four hours a day?

Teacher: Yes.

Counselor: What about the other waking hours of the day...how many would that leave?

Teacher: About eight, I guess.

Counselor: Does the depression bother you as much during those hours?

Teacher: No, because I'm here at school or doing things for my kids at home.

Counselor: How do you keep the depression from bothering you so that you are able to do things for your children or at school?

Teacher: I have to...I have to do certain things to survive....

Counselor: That's great—wow—with all of this going on, you still think ahead, about surviving...and do it because you have to.

Teacher: Yes, my kids depend on me.

Counselor: You certainly are tuned in to what others need from you. Based on what you've told me this morning about how you keep the depression from interfering as much for 8 hours a day, what do you think you might try to keep it away, say for nine hours?

The dialogue suggests how externalizing the problem of depression as being maintained or not allowed to intrude in one's life can convey a person's strength and create an environment in which they feel competent to solve their own problems. The reference to the depression as external helps it to become a target to defeat. Since the depression did not paralyze the teacher's life completely, by diminishing her ability to go to school, care for her children and herself, the counselor assumed that she was winning the battle with the depression *at least part of the time*. The SFBT educator simply pointed out her competency. This normalizing of how she handled the depression encouraged her since it meant she was not paralyzed by its influence. A note sent by the educator to the teacher shortly after the meeting might be constructed as follows:

Dear Peggy,

I was glad to meet with you today. I have always been impressed with your dedication to teaching and after meeting with you today, that impression proved correct. You truly have your priorities straight. You want things better in your life and even though you are dealing with some "depression," you gallantly keep going, saying "I just have to." I was touched by your determination to do something different; I still am amazed that you fight off the depression so well, allowing it to bother you for short periods of time in a very long day. My hope is that you will continue this, as it places you in control. This next week, I hope you will continue to notice your ability to keep the depression from bothering your enjoyment of school and your children. My feeling is that you may be surprised at how the "depression" won't stand much of a chance when your "strength" takes over.

Sincerely,

Counselor

Externalizing problems and assisting people to move away from problem maintenance and the influence of the problem *frees them* to imagine how life will be without the problem. Most students, teachers, and parents do well with hope and encouragement. The following case is an example of utilizing the idea of externalizing with an adolescent involved in destructive behavior:

DR. JEKYLL VS. MR. HYDE

Michael, 16, was referred to me for counseling after he had been in a psychiatric hospital for 6 months. He had been placed in treatment after he was found to be taking and selling drugs, drinking routinely, and bashing in neighbors' mailboxes at night. His dad, a firefighter, was embarrassed and angry. His stepmom, a junior high principal, was confused and resentful of the chaos Michael had brought into her life.

Michael's biological mom, a member of AA, had remarried a man who liked Michael, but criticized Michael's biological dad for not spending enough time with him. Michael would then visit mom and stepdad, complain about dad and stepmom, then go home to dad and stepmom to complain about mom and stepdad. The sequence of interactions seemed to be maintaining the "problem" of Michael being irresponsible with drugs, drinking, and violence since everyone seemed more concerned with blaming someone else instead of helping the adolescent become more responsible.

As I thought about the family therapy session, I asked if all the parental figures could accompany Michael to the first session. As a conjoint session, I asked them to describe for me the "problem " which was bothering their son and stepson. Michael's biological mom said he acted like "Dr. Jekyll and Mr. Hyde." His personality would switch from location to location, and she realized after the session that Michael was playing all four parental figures against each other and was encouraging hostility in all of them, thereby lessening the focus on himself. I asked each of the parents when they might have helped to maintain Michael's Dr. Jekyll and Mr. Hyde personality. They each told me the following:

Dad: When I get disgusted, I stay away from Michael and refuse to work on his car with him. I ignore his negative language and behavior and let her (stepmom) deal with it.

Stepmom: I try to deal with him myself because I know it upsets his dad. I try to be firm, but he is so verbally abusive, I find myself less consistent.

Mom: I don't spend enough time with him. When he complains about her (stepmom), I tend to take sides instead of checking it out with her.

Stepdad: I guess I criticize his dad too much because after hearing him today, I realize he's just fed up...I guess I would be too.

Michael: I do drugs, get in trouble, and gripe at her (stepmom).

I then asked each of them what they could do to "not maintain" the problem until I saw them again in two weeks:

Dad: I need to keep a better watch on him—work on his car with him so he can get a job and get busy.

Stepmom: I'm tired of taking the responsibility for his dad...I'm going to tell him when Michael acts up.

Mom: I need to see him more. I need to have him over once a week on Sunday and then take him to AA with me. I think I need to check out his house too. (She then asked the stepmom if she could visit later that day and check on Michael's clothes, and so on, which he was complaining about.)

Stepdad: I need to butt out...and support his dad.

Michael: I need to stop drinking...I've already stopped the drugs...I guess stay out of trouble.

I complimented the parents on a great attempt to lessen the influence of Dr. Jekyll and Mr. Hyde on Michael's life. Michael's problem could no longer be maintained.

I saw the family two weeks later. Michael looked sheepishly better, for he now had four adults on his case who were determined not to maintain his problem behavior. Dad had taken more of an interest in him, and was more consistent freeing up the stepmom. Dad and mom had begun to "talk more than they had in seven years," according to dad. Stepdad continued to stay away from criticizing dad and instead, took an interest in Michael's car as well.

The Problem is the Problem

As the above case illustrates, externalizing problems encourages a systemic responsibility, or lessens blame and makes everyone within one's system responsible for lessening the problem's influence. Key words that a person or family uses such as "it's tough," or, "the problem is...," or, "the tension is terrible," all are cues to externalizing a problem.

Children respond well to the idea of externalizing. A unique way of working with children who are sad, angry, or energetic is to use stuffed animals as the symbolic "problem." An educator or counselor might keep an array or stuffed animals in his/her room and ask the child/adolescent to choose an animal that represents what the problem "looks like." The counselor might then ask the child to choose a *different* animal...one that looks like the solution, or how he/she wants life to be. The child might then take the preferred "solution" animal home "on loan" as a guardian against the problem. From that point on, the problem is truly externalized in a playful manner. This idea was first developed by Michael White.

Once students see their influence in keeping problems around or escaping or controlling them, they often come up with their own individual ideas to avoid the influence of the problem on their lives. As indicated earlier, personifying problems onto inanimate objects is a nice way of helping children focus on the problem differently. The following case is an example of using stuffed animals to represent temper tantrums and help protect a six-year-old from her taunting ten-year-old brother and twelve-year-old sister:

THE TEMPER TANTRUM IS REALLY A SNAKE

Kathy, age six, her two siblings, and mother came to visit the counselor after Kathy was reported to have temper tantrums in school as well as home. Her mother reported that she had recently divorced the childrens' father due to his alcoholism, and that all the family members had been experiencing difficulty with Kathy's tantrums, which disrupted the household. The mother described her older children as "taunting" to Kathy, which encouraged the tantrums. Kathy had a difficult time sitting still in the meeting, trying to capture the attention of everyone. The family presented a goal of "getting along better." When asked how that would take form, the mother described a possible scenario of Kathy being calm and the older children being more cordial to her.

The counselor presented Kathy with several stuffed animals from which to choose "the temper tantrum animal" and "the calm animal." Kathy quickly chose a bright snake for "temper tantrum" and a soft white elephant for "calmness." The counselor mentioned to Kathy that the "calm animal" was magical (White, 1989), and as long as she clutched the animal close to her, it would keep her calm. The counselor also gathered the older siblings around Kathy and told them, with Kathy's agreement, that as long as Kathy held the "calm animal," it was a symbol that they could not taunt her. The older children seemed quite intrigued by the idea and upon hearing their role, left the immediate area to play quietly by themselves. The mother liked the idea and promised to remind Kathy of the "calm animal" and its powers, should Kathy forget.

Get Rid of That Anger!

The following sequence of questions is an example of externalizing *anger*.

1. Tell me about the anger that caused you to be here. When do you notice "it" (emphasize) being around? What do you think you do that keeps "it" (or anger) around?

2. When does the anger not affect you as much?

3. What needs to happen with the anger so that you can stay in school, pass your class, and so on?

4. Who will notice when the anger is no longer bothering you?

5. How many days out of a week are you angry? How many hours are you free from the influence of anger on your life?

6. What are you doing differently to be free of anger during those times?

7. Based on what you've just told me, what do you think you might try to make the anger less of a problem for you this week?

Jean Cadell, a school counselor in Fort Worth, Texas, used the idea of externalizing in small groups that dealt with anger. She held out her hands in a way that indicated *larger* or *smaller*, to a group of 6 eight-year-old boys and asked them:

1. How big was your anger the last time it really bothered you?
2. How big is it now?
3. What have you done to shrink it?
4. How big do you want it to be today?
5. How will you do that?

At the end of a school day, one of her group members came up to her in the hall and said: Ms. Smith, help! I've got my anger back. Can I blow it into this paper bag and leave it in your office until tomorrow?" "Sure," she said, laughing "Why not leave it here permanently?" He blew the "anger" into the bag, and left her office merrily.

Cadell also began to ask the group members to *draw their problem*, a way of *visually externalizing* the problem. Her directions were to: "Use your imagination and pretend your problem is not you, but something that bugs you sometimes. Use the crayons and paper and draw what you think it might look like." She then asked them to think about how they would answer the following questions:

1. How the problem bothers me: (What it makes me do)
2. How I beat the problem: (What I do to win)

My problem:

What my problem makes me do:	How I win over the problem:
• I argue with my teacher	• I put a QUIET note on my desk
• I get out of my seat	• I sit by myself
• I forget to raise my hand	• I remember my reward

Cadell then drew a scale on her wall, using the numbers 1–10, with 1 being "the problem is in control" and 10, "I am in control." After some discussion of how the problem made the students do poorly and how they could win or defeat the problem, she asked them to cut out the pictures. Without putting names on the drawings for confidentiality reasons, she asked the students to tape the pictures on the scale where they currently saw themselves in relation to the problem. Then, each week, she asked:

1. Based on what you have noticed and your teacher has noticed about you this week, where would you put your picture on the scale?
2. What would your teacher (or parent) say you did this week that meant you were in control?

3. How have you managed to move up? Or, How have you managed to stay the same or not move backwards?

4. Where do you want to be when you come back to group next week?

5. Based on what you've told us today, how will you do this?

6. Do you all think your group members are where they should be on the scale?

7. Who do you think has done the best this week in defeating their problem?

8. What did you see him/her doing that tells you he/she is in control, and not the problem?

Language such as this helps children to visualize problems as external and controllable. When the counselor later saw the children separately or in the hallway, she would briefly ask them, "How big is the anger?" then, "How are you helping it to be so small?" If the anger reoccurred, as with any other normal human emotion, she would ask "What did you do before to shrink the anger when it was big like this?" This sequence of questions again placed the child in the expert role. The counselor simply guided him/her back on the route to control by asking competency-based questions.

ADDITIONAL WAYS TO ESCAPE THE INFLUENCE OF PROBLEMS

For children dealing with death or loss, sexual abuse or physical abuse, externalizing the *event* can be a gentle way of helping a child see the circumstances as something they can move away from at times and free themselves. Contextually, offering support to a child who survived abusive situations and *knew to talk to someone* is a therapeutic way of saying "You know how to take care of yourself." It offers a possibility that someday the problem will not be as big, influential, or intrusive in their lives—that things will get better.

Tricia Long, a school counselor related the story of a young student currently living with an abusive mother and her companion. The counselor had reported the verbal abuse to the proper authorities, but the child still was not removed from the home. In individualized counseling, the counselor began to brag to the child how brave she was, and asked her how she coped with things at home when it became difficult. The child described reading her book, calling a friend, listening to tapes, and holding her stuffed animals when she was sad that her mom yelled at her abusively. The counselor continued to affirm her methods to calm herself and remove herself from the tough situations. The counselor had encouraged her to tell her father, whom she visited every other weekend, about the abuse. The child refused in the past, for fear that her mother would become worse. After two weeks of working with the SFBT model, on her next weekend visit with dad, the child told him of the verbal abuse. He filed for custody and won.

As a counselor begins to externalize problems with students, parents, and teachers, he/she needs to look for language that conveys a message to be received and acknowledged. Questions that objectify or personify the problem as if it is separate from the student or parent are often helpful. For example, suppose a student is sent to the office for talking in class disruptively. A counselor might begin with the following questions or statements:

1. If I were to ask Mrs. Smith why she asked you to come to my office, what do you think she might say?

2. Do you usually know when your "talking" is disrupting the class?

3. Have you noticed times when your "talking" doesn't bother you and you keep from being noticed in a negative way?

4. When has it happened before that you managed your talking and kept it from getting you in trouble?

5. If I were to watch you during those times when your talking was not disrupting the class, what do you think I would see you doing?

6. What will be better when your talking is managed by you again? Who will notice? What will be in it for you?

Adolescents or children who have survived physical, sexual, or emotional abuse, chemically-dependent parents, or have observed violent acts often find great nurturing from a counselor who describes their survival skills as *the best she has ever seen!* As a counselor expresses to a child or adolescent that he is impressed how the child experienced awful events but has gone on to live his/her life, the child sees himself as victorious over the event. Placing the abuse in a context of being one small part of one's long, long life to come, changes the perception that a child or adolescent must be scarred for life. Talking to the child as if the *effects of the abuse are separate from his/her personhood allows him/her to escape, survive, and move away from the effects of the problem.*

Birth   Abuse   80 years

As the student returns to the next meeting, it is helpful to set the atmosphere with the question: "What's been better since I've seen you?" As the student searches for better times, again, it is helpful to write down the successes and compliment their abilities. As students complete their time with the counselor and termination of counseling is near, it is often nice to review what has worked. A counselor might end such a session with:

1. What do you want to keep on doing after our meeting today that is obviously working for you?

2. Like many problems, the problem we have talked about here may resurface someday. What will you do then to control it, as you have before?

Another nice way of reminding a student of what you noticed that worked is to offer him/her a certificate. A reproducible one is included at the end of this chapter. David Epston and Michael White routinely give certificates to their students and families. The certificate can be a surprise or a promise, whatever is most appropriate.

THIS CERTIFIES

that

Susie Smith

has successfully

defeated the "Worry Monster"

by requesting 10 hugs per day from her mother

and checking the doors only once each evening

Signed,

School Counselor

The certificate might include the "problem" description, the exceptions that helped solve the problem, and the signature of the educator. This *rite of passage* can be presented in several ways: in a group setting, teacher-student conference, parent conference, or individual session. Small groups or classes can vote each week and choose who has been the most successful at managing their behavior and contributing to the class/group, and so on. The nominations must be accompanied by specific exceptions in order to be considered for election. Hearing about what others think you've done well is usually a morale booster.

SCALING PROBLEMS DOWN TO SIZE

Lipchick says that "scaling questions" are therapeutic tools used to measure the effects of a problem on a person's life. The student, teacher, or parent can rate the following on a scale of 1-10: "At 1, the problem is in total control of your life and at 10, you are in complete control of the problem." The student is asked to tell where he/she is as the meeting begins. As the meeting progresses, he/she is then asked to tell where he/she would like to be by the next time he/she meets with the educator. The student then describes how he/she will do that. The following is an example of such a dialogue:

Administrator: Mom, you say that you are having a hard time trusting your daughter Sarah since she has failed three classes and skipped school four times this term, is that correct?

Mom: Yes, it's hard to trust her at all (scowling at Sarah). I would like to trust her again, but it will take a long time.

Administrator: Sarah, where would you say you are right now, on a scale of 1–10, where 1 means you are not trusted at all by mom and 10 means you are totally trusted?

Sarah: About a 2.

Mom: That's even lower than I would have said!

Administrator: Sarah, where would you like to be by the time I meet with you again?

Sarah: At least a five, but I don't know if that will make a difference to her.

Administrator: Mom, would that make a difference?

Mom: Anything will make a difference.

Administrator: Sarah, you say you are at a 2 now, and want to move to a 5 by next week. What would you suggest you do to move up 3 points?

Sarah: Probably come home and do homework so she sees me trying, at least. Not skipping would help as well.

Administrator: Mom, would that make a difference?

Mom: Maybe.

Sarah: See, she's so negative!

Administrator: I guess that happens sometimes, when the trust level goes down. What I'm interested in though, are your ideas. They are really good ideas. Have ideas like these worked before to gain trust?

Sarah: Sort of. I think she trusted me last year when I studied at home and didn't skip.

Administrator: Is this true?

Mom: Yes, I remember; last year was a good year.

Administrator: Looking back, where would you have placed Sarah on the same scale we've been talking about last year?

Mom: Probably about an 8.

Administrator: That's great. What did she do then to be that high on your trust level?

Mom: She did study, and her grades were good. She came home when I asked her, her friends came over, and I got to meet them instead of wondering who they were.

Administrator: So Sarah, you already know how to do this.

Sarah: I guess.

Administrator: Go for it. Sounds like a 5 is very reasonable for this week. I want you to keep thinking too, where you want to end up on that scale eventually, okay?

Sarah: Okay.

Administrator: Mom, I'd like you to notice specific things Sarah does this week that make your trust level rise, okay?

Mom: Okay.

Scaling questions assist school students and parents in defining their goals *specifically*, thereby making them easier to achieve. When they become "stuck," and have difficulty identifying exceptions to their concern or imagining a time when things were better, the scaling questions offer small steps to take to slowly move away from the problem's influence.

The way we describe our world through language and how we set our goals within our world has much to do with how we live. As educators and counselors, if we can assist students, teachers, and parents in perceiving their worlds differently and encourage hope and success, we give them a way of "reauthoring" their lives positively.

Certificate of Success

This certifies that

_____

Has successfully

_____

This success was achieved by the following:

_____

Signed, this_____ day of _____, _____

_____

Name_____ Date _____

GUIDING CASE NOTES

Referred by teacher:_____

Self-referred:_____

1. The reason for coming to talk today (According to the student)
2. The reason for referral according to the teacher (If applicable)
3. How will the student know when things are better? (Goal)
4. When was the last time that occurred? (Even in other situations)
5. How did the student do that? (Exceptions)

_____

_____

_____

_____

_____

On a scale of 1-10, 1 being the problem in control and 10, the student in control, where was the student when he/she came in today? (Circle and label "today")

| 1 | 2 | 3 | 4 | 5 | 6 | 7 | 8 | 9 | 10 |

Where would the student *like* to be on the scale, the next time you meet? (Circle and label "goal")

Task: Using the exceptions above, what does the student suggest doing to move up the scale:

_____

_____

_____

_____

_____

1. Who will notice the changes the student makes? (Networking)

2. What went on in our time together today that made a difference?

Next meeting date:_____

SFBT Educator Training Exercise: Chapter 2

Today, consider writing someone you work with a note. Remember a note you might have received once and how it made you feel about yourself or something you had done? Noticing is detective work! Exceptions abound but are often difficult for people to notice. Today, notice what someone does well:

- a teacher who always seems to have her/his students' attention
- the principal who puts in long hours
- the janitor who smiles and jokes with students in the hallway
- the bus driver who waits for that one last student to board

Write a note using the form below, describing what you noticed him/her doing that seemed to make a difference. Watch the reactions!

- - - - - - - - - - - - - - detach here - - - - - - - - - - - - - - -

To:_____

From:_____

I am amazed at you!

_____

_____

_____

_____

_____

_____
Signature

CHAPTER 3 | # COMPETENCY-BASED CONVERSATIONS

THE EDUCATOR AS A CONSULTANT FOR PARENTS, STUDENTS, AND PEERS

A closer look at schools today reveals school counselors and administrators placed in the position of being asked to "fix problems." Those students and parents who seek help often feel as if they have failed or that someone else has a problem. Working within the SFBT framework, students, teachers, and parents come to the counselor or educator with little thought about how they can solve their problem and often leave looking to their own competencies to solve the problem. This is because SFBT educators rely on the competencies they codiscover in the students, teachers, and parents, not on themselves as problem solvers. An SFBT educator knows that students, parents, and teachers are competent, *but are often unaware of their competencies.* The SFBT educator sees his/her job as that of a consultant: a codiscoverer who simply points out and helps students, other teachers, and parents to see the exceptions to the problem.

As educators begin to *consult* with school populations, it is helpful to follow a few basic steps as skills develop. The suggestions presented here serve as strategies for conducting competency-based conversations. They are designed to assist the educator in identifying competent behavior in student and teacher behaviors which develop into solutions. The motive is to make the student and teacher part of a collaborative team.

CHAPTER 3 FOCUS:

- Suggestions for competency-based conversations: Steps that make a difference
- Case study: "Getting to Know You Again"
- Guidelines for competency-based conversations: Aligning against problems
- Resolving differences between students and teachers: Giving them responsibility
- When the problem is someone else's fault: Developing personal strategies

SUGGESTIONS FOR COMPETENCY-BASED CONVERSATIONS*

1. *Socializing:* Listen to the teacher and student's language, metaphors, and self-description so you can align yourself to their description. Ask about success-possible topics such as occupation, school, hobbies, and other areas of interest.
   - Where else, in your time here at school, home, or other activities, have you been able to prevent this problem from bothering you?
2. *Problem Definition:* If you talk about the problem, get each person's view of it. Pay attention to language:
   - What brings you in today?
   - What would it be helpful for us to talk about?
   - What is the most important thing I need to know about your situation?
3. *Setting Goals:* How does the student or teacher want things to be different? Use language that reflects an assumption of positive change. Start small, be concrete, and compliment often.
   - How will you know when things are getting better for you?
   - What will be different when school (life, home, your relationship with _____) is better?
   - What will your_____ (student, teacher, and so on) notice that will indicate to them that you're doing better?
4. Separating the person from the problem:
   - How have you allowed this problem to hold you back from where you want to be?
   - In what way(s) has this problem kept you from moving forward in a way you would like?
   - What kind of an effect would your (teacher, parent, vice principal, principal, nurse) say this problem has had on your time at school? Would you agree?

- What do you wish they were seeing now...that they haven't seen lately?

5. Identifying exceptions to problem-dominated perceptions and behaviors:

   - Are there ways you have been able to fight the problem and not allow it to bother you?

   - Were there ways that the problem tried to stop you before, but you defeated it?

   - How did you do that?

   - There are times, I am sure, when you would expect the problem to happen, but it doesn't. How do you get that to happen?

   - Who else has noticed? In what ways could you tell that s/he noticed?

   - When is it less frequent (severe, intense)?

   - When is it different in any way?

6. Task Development/Assignment:

   - On a scale of 1–10 (draw for the student/parent, teacher) where 10 means you are in control of the problem and 1 means the problem is in control of you, where do you think you were when you came in today? (Show the scale [de Shazer, 1989] and allow the person to identify his/her position. If there is more than one person present, ask each person for his/her position.):

Problem in control _____Student in control
                  1   2   3   4   5   6   7   8   9   10

   - Where would you like to be by (tomorrow, next week, two weeks)?

   - Based on what you have told me today has worked in the past (exceptions), what might you try doing today (tomorrow, next week, two weeks) to move closer to being in control of the problem?*

Case Study: Getting to Know You Again

Chris's mother Linda brought her seventh grade, fourteen-year-old daughter to counseling because she was concerned about her daughter's sudden drop in grades (from all As to some Bs) and her isolation from her family. Linda said that Chris preferred talking to friends on the phone to talking to her, and she was concerned that all Chris and she did when together was fight. Linda said that Chris's father agreed that life around the household was frustrating to him as well, espe-

---

*(The previous questions were influenced, constructed, and applied to school situations from various works and contributions of Durrant, de Shazer, O'Hanlon, Weiner-Davis, Epston, White, and Cade, all of which are listed in the reference section of this manual).

cially when he came home from work each night and was asked to referee disputes between his wife and daughter.

Linda mentioned that she had recently been in drug rehabilitation for her use of prescription drugs and she wondered if that situation had caused Chris to become angry with her. Chris complained instead of her mother, criticizing her friends, her school work, and her appearance. Sitting with her finger over a blemish on her face, Chris explained that she had an allergic reaction to some antibiotics and had forgotten to put cream on the night before. She angrily blamed her mother for her forgetfulness and Linda looked painfully guilty. Mother and daughter were physically distant as well as emotionally distant in the therapy room, both exchanging angry glances and responding with resentment and defensiveness.

As educators know, conflicts between parents and adolescents are part of the normal developmental process; however, they are often the reason for seeking help. Even though today's school counselor is not encouraged to be a clinical "therapist" by certification boards, skills for helping parents and adolescents though communication difficulties are important in order to deal with school issues. There are many influences within the systems in which people live. These influences, if not dealt with in the prioritization brought to the counselor, live on and continue to contribute to the problem. Parents and adolescents, with their conflicting desires for responsibility and protection on the one hand and freedom and independence on the other, easily become caught in interactional patterns of guilt and blame. Telling them what to do differently often doesn't work.

As parents and children begin to disagree during this developmental stage often labeled as "rebellion," many parents bring their children to counseling hoping to mend the conflict that has developed. These conflictual relationships also occur in the school setting between teacher and student, even teachers and administrators! The counselor may be presented with a very angry adolescent such as Chris (who blames the parent for the conflict, and fears that the counselor may simply be another adult who will take the parent's side), and with a parent who feels abandoned and helplessly frustrated.

The mutual blaming that occurs manifests itself as parents seek some recognition in their being older, wiser, and more responsible, and adolescents seek some confirmation that their parents are being unreasonable. This interaction can be a disaster for counselors who try to assist the parent and child to "work things out" without taking sides. Counselors and other school staff members often get caught between such conflicts in the school setting. Often, school staff deals with parents who expect the school to take over and solve the problem for them. This places schools in a role of a) being the expert, b) being responsible for the solution, c) encouraging dependency by the parent and student, and d) releasing parental compliance and cooperation. Simple negotiation is unlikely to be effective as both sides are assured that their positions are correct.

Attempts to uncover and understand the disputed issues thereby seeking "the facts" may lead to further arguments, angry accusation, and blame. Even *if* facts surface and everyone thinks they know *why* the conflict is occurring, the facts and explanations still do not assist anyone in knowing *what will solve the problem*. It is at this point many counselors, teachers, administrators, and parents become stuck. This often results in the school staff offering solutions that may have worked with other students in general. The recipient of the information will often reject the suggestions or give it a try. It has been my experience that the reason most counseling efforts fail is because people are asked to do things so differently, they simply do not know how.

Counselors and other educators can avoid the problem-focus, lessen dependency, relinquish expertise, and involve the parents more if they move into more of a solution-orientation for situations such as these. The process of listening for exceptions, and developing goals mutually acceptable and motivational for both mother and daughter will direct the time with the counselor or educator into a more productive direction.

THE PROCESS: LISTENING FOR GOALS AND EXCEPTIONS

According to Linda, the problem was the conflictual relationship between her and her daughter. Their goal was to resolve the conflict and develop a communicative and interactive relationship. Mother was also concerned about whether her drug rehabilitation had caused Chris to be distant.

In the following excerpt, I sought to assist Chris and Linda in identifying those aspects of their previously close relationship on which they might now be able to build:

Counselor: Chris, what would mom say she misses the most from your relationship?

Chris: I don't know: Ask her, she wanted me to come here.

Mother: This is what it's like at home...she won't look at me or talk to me. I don't know what's wrong.

Counselor: How often is it like this?

Mother: Every time we talk.

Counselor: How often—daily, weekly?

Mother: Daily.

Chris: When she criticizes my friends and tells me I should do good in school like she did—that's when it happens, and that happens every day.

Counselor: How long has this gone on?

Mother: It started six months ago. I was in rehab two months ago, so for a few months, things were tough when I was having problems.

Counselor: And how are you now?

Mother: I'm much better. I no longer take pain medications. My doctor is giving me muscle relaxers sparingly for my back pain.

Counselor: How would the two of you like things to be...if you both had your say?

Mother: I'd like us to talk more, and not fight.

Chris: I'd like her to get off my back about *everything*!

Counselor: Linda, Chris is saying that you criticize her. Can you tell me some of the things about Chris that you appreciate?

Mother: No. I can't think of anything that I really like about her now. She's cruel to me and her friends are not the kind I want her around.

Counselor: Chris, can you think of some positive things to say about your mom?

Chris: Not really. She thinks her hospital thing made me different. It didn't. I'm just tired of being criticized.

These goal statements were constructed initially in what Chris and her mother wanted less of: their complaints. In SFBT, it is important for the goals to develop into what the parent, teacher, or students *do* want. Often, this solution-focused goal develops as exceptions to the presenting complaint are identified. The continuing dialogue attempts to accomplish this:

Counselor: Chris, take me back to a time when you and your mom got along a little better than now and you didn't feel as criticized.

Chris: It's hard to remember...it's been a long time.

Mother: (interrupting) Two years ago it was perfect.

Chris: (brightening slightly) Yeah, when I was in the sixth grade things were pretty good between us.

Counselor: Tell me more, Linda, about what you liked about your daughter two years ago.

Mother: She and I did a lot together. We shopped, took walks, you know, she wasn't so worried about boys then, so she and I were really close. There was a lot I liked about her.

Counselor: Chris, what did you like about how things were two years ago, with your mom?

Chris: What she said is true...we spent time together and I didn't mind talking to her. She liked my friends too. That made it easy to bring them home. (*glancing*) She didn't put me down either. I felt like she was proud of me...she said nice things to me once in a while. (*crying*)

As Chris and mom reminisced about times when they got along better, exceptions began to emerge:

Chris: I enjoyed my relationship with my mom when I felt she was proud of me, when we spent time together, talked, and she liked my friends.

Mother: I enjoyed our time together; shopping, taking walks, feeling close.

The similarities in the above goal developments are obvious. Both mom and daughter had been close previously and had accomplished this through mutually enjoying time together, validation, providing acceptance, and offering compliments. With these goals in mind, the dialogue continued, focusing now only on the exceptions that encompassed their goals:

Counselor: Mom, tell me about some of those nice things you noticed about your daughter two years ago.

Mother: She was pretty, as she is now, and she talked to me a lot. She did okay in school and her friends were pleasant. It seemed like it meant something to her to do things with me. She smiled a lot and helped me around the house.

Counselor: What about those characteristics today? Are they still there?

Mother: You know, I haven't noticed in a while, because we fight so much, but I still think she's pretty, it's just that we can't cooperate much today like we did then.

Counselor: If you could come up with some of the things you and she did then, how would you describe the way you were able to get your daughter to be so close to you?

There were many issues that could have been seen as important in this case. Mother's drug abuse, Chris's isolating behavior, or father's "triangled" role might have been interesting to explore, but such exploration could have magnified the issues between mother and daughter, increased the feelings of blame, and lessened the hope of reconciliation.

The discovery and questioning of past success with current exceptions, however, quickly stopped the resentments from surfacing and allowed mother and daughter to reminisce about good times. In situations such as these, reminiscing about past enjoyable experiences in an hour meeting can be like an oasis. Mother's rediscovery of the daughter of two years ago brought back parental memories which obviously were dear to her. The daughter, with her current need for validation and acceptance as an emerging young woman, was able to recall the compliments given to her two years ago and place them in a present state, as if there was an imminent chance her mother would accept her once again.

As the positive events from their relationship began to emerge, each attributed the times when things were better to a difference in each other. However, within the more positive and hopeful focus that emerged, it was easier to ask questions that encouraged mom to identify what her part was in fostering the close relationship and Chris to consider how her behavior encouraged mother not to criticize her. This is very different from asking either of them to tell the other what they wanted changed. By asking each of them to identify past, successful behaviors that alleviated the problem, blame was dissolved and competency-based conversations emerged:

Mother: Probably in the time I spent with her.

Counselor: Chris, if you could think of some of the ways you kept mom from criticizing you two years ago, what would you say you did that helped?

Chris: I guess I didn't blame her as much and I talked to her more.

Counselor: So, two years ago when you and your mom talked more and you spent more time with her and she did not criticize you, things were much more pleasant between the two of you, would that be correct?

Mother: Yes.

Chris: Yeah.

Through the questioning, mother and daughter came to an agreement that talking together was something that worked in the past. In contrast to the very global, all-encompassing picture of their conflict, this was a very specific behavior that they were able to agree upon.

PREVIOUS SUCCESS = TASK

I suggested a small homework task that utilized the described behavior as suggested by de Shazer, by asking them to "do more of what works." Had I simply asked them to spend time together and refrain from criticism in a kind of "mediation" manner, it would have been unlikely to be successful, since each might still have felt that it was the other who needed to change. The importance of this task was that it flowed *directly* from the exploration of previous success and current exceptions. That is, asking them to do more of what they had already agreed worked in the past was much more likely to be successful than if I had simply designed something different for them to try. The following dialogue shows the task development and assignment:

Counselor: "You know, it's reassuring to me that you both have already experienced some really good times together. It's no wonder that you want those good times back. It sounds like those were good times for both of you.

What I'd like to ask you to do this week is what you've told me worked just two years ago. Linda, I'd like you to compliment your daughter once a day, based on what you notice that you like about her. It can be anything you notice. Chris, would you be willing to give maybe thirty extra minutes a day to your family time, especially to mom, if mom drops the criticism?"

Chris: I can try.

Counselor: Mom, can you agree not to criticize your daughter for just a week, until I see you again?

Mother: Okay.

One week later, mother, daughter, younger sister, and father were present in the session. Mother mentioned immediately that she and her daughter had experienced a wonderful week. Dad volunteered that he had enjoyed a week of freedom. He had not had to discipline or referee his wife and daughter all week. He said that the atmosphere of the home had improved drastically and that he and Chris had also enjoyed more fun times together.

Linda said that at first Chris only came out of her room for short periods of time each evening, but by the end of the week, she was spending most of her time with the family. Linda also commented that, to her surprise, she had noticed many, many things about her daughter that she liked but had not noticed before. She felt that the compliments had at first seemed artificial to Chris, but as she discovered more of her daughter's positive assets and the compliments continued, Chris accepted them readily.

Jenny, the younger sister, told me that she and  her sister played together during the last week and that she liked the fact that the house was quiet. Chris, while still concerned about her complexion, smiled more and began to discuss other issues with me and her parents regarding her friends. The second session continued with much more open communication between her and her parents regarding a friend with whom she was having difficulties. The family dynamics had switched from a focus of conflict between each other, to communication and concern for each other.

As a counselor, my position in this second session was that of "cheerleading," and asking questions with curiosity such as "How did you manage to do that so well?" The developing answers were then credited to the individual family members. This competency-based focus encouraged the family to continue their newly rediscovered abilities to interact positively with each other. The counseling ended after the third session.

This case represented an example of the use of competency-based questions that promoted a rekindling of relationships between parents and their adolescent. Their skills at making their relationship successful, discovered during the counseling sessions and then designed into tasks for mother and daughter, were able to be implemented successfully in the present day as they had been two years ago. The ability of mother and daughter to attempt to try these steps was found in their knowledge that they had performed them before. The fondness that existed between mother and daughter at that time in their lives was too attractive in their memories to pass up in the present. The reminiscing changed their strategy from a problem-focus to a solution-orientation. All they needed to do at that point was to see their successes as a possibility for the future.*

The following guidelines were utilized in working with Chris and her mother. The theoretical orientation that prevails within the guidelines is more important than simply using questions to solicit information. The theory that people are competent and our job is to consult with them and codiscover their competencies is the underlying strength of SFBT.

---

*(The above case, dialogue, and parts of the explanation first appeared in *Family Therapy Case Studies*, 1991, 6(2), pp. 25–29.) Printed with permission from the editor.

GUIDELINES FOR COMPETENCY-BASED CONVERSATIONS

1. By listening to the given language, assist the student and/or parent in identifying a goal that is relevant for him/her.

Goal setting is most effective for school students, teachers, and parents when the goal is stated in specific, behavioral terms. "I want to be happier" is a nice goal, but needs to be more specific. An educator can ask, "What would I see you doing when you become happier?" as a means to verbalizing a more specific goal.

2. Search for exceptions to the problem—times when the problem did not occur.

Problems do not occur 100% of the time. If they did, most people would not make it out of bed, go to work, or take care of their children. The exceptions to problems give clues to solutions. Focusing on the problem gives credence to the problem's existence and can become immobilizing to the person in counseling.

3. Assist the student/parent by creating possibilities for the problem to be solved through redescription (Epston & White, 1991) of complaints and exception identification.

Renaming a problem into a "solvable complaint" lessens hopelessness and encourages the student's, teacher's, or parent's hope that the problem is not impossible to solve. Changing a description of "hyperactivity" to "energetic" sounds more promising and workable.

4. Reminisce about past successes in the relationship.

Looking back over times when a parent and child were able to enjoy each other gives relief from the "problem" at hand. As children grow into adolescents, their parents often perceive them as "grown up" since their bodies have changed. However, the human they brought into the world is often the same...and the tactics used by the parents early in the child's life to communicate, express love, and acceptance may still work.

5. Develop a task collaboratively with the student and parent, based on the identified exceptions to the problem.

It is helpful to check with the person(s) in counseling upon task assignment, so the process continues to be collaborative. This team work against the problem lessens failure and continues to place the student, teacher, or parent in the role of the "expert."

As educators and students begin to look at problems with a different focus, they often notice the simple solutions which were there all along. The following excerpt from Jay Haley is illustrative of this point:

A young man wanted clear statements about (Milton) Erickson's method. Erickson interrupted the discussion and took the man outside. He pointed up the street and asked what he saw. Puzzled, he replied that he saw a street.

Erickson pointed to the trees that lined the street. "Do you notice anything about the trees?" The young man eventually noted that they were all leaning in an easterly direction. "That's right, all except one. That second one from the end is leaning in a westerly direction. There's always an exception.

ADVANCED TECHNIQUES OF HYPNOSIS AND THERAPY—JAY HALEY

BETWEEN TEACHERS AND STUDENTS: IDEAS FOR RESOLVING DIFFERENCES

Being in the business of discovering exceptions to student behavior can be exciting. This is different from constantly focusing on problems. This new approach stirs excitement within the student as well, and excitement often develops into motivation. When teachers see and hear motivation from their excited students, they often act differently. Many counselors/administrators do great work with students, only to send them back to class to an uninformed teacher, who may undermine the progress by again expressing his/her frustrations to the student. It is therefore very helpful for students to have a conference *with* their teacher. More information on developing different kinds of perceptions of students in the classroom will be presented in Chapter 4.

Often, relationships blossom when students see the teacher in a different context, a context in which he/she is not the enemy. As a student hears the teacher describe how he/she (teacher) will do what worked before, the student often becomes motivated as well. Again, the lack of blame encourages motivation on the part of the student. It will be important for the SFBT educator to explain briefly the approach about to be used. Such an explanation might be given in the following manner: "Susie and Mrs. Young, I've asked you both here today because I've become aware

 that you have some concerns. Mrs. Young, you've been by to talk to me about your concerns for Susie. I want you both to know that I'm not going to talk about what's been going wrong...I feel you both have probably discussed that sufficiently. I'm going to talk to you instead about the times when things *have* been working a little better."

Using the Student-Teacher Conference Worksheet

The next page shows a worksheet that can also be utilized in a teacher-student conference. The **Student-Teacher Conference Worksheet** can be used in all grade levels. Language may be changed/simplified for the very young student. The questions utilize basic ideas from SFBT and place them in a process easy to follow. Consider copying the worksheet and giving it to both teacher and student after the conference. Upon a parent conference in the future, the worksheet can serve as a valuable tool not only in informing parents of "what works" but in demonstrating a sincere effort by the school to resolve the student's concern.

STUDENT-TEACHER CONFERENCE WORKSHEET

To the student:

What behaviors would your teacher say are not happening as often in class lately that he/she would like to see?

_____

_____

How often, or how long has this been going on, in your point of view?

_____

_____

_____

To the teacher and student:

How would both of you (teacher and student) like things to be? (Goal setting)

Teacher:_____

_____

_____

Student: _____

_____

_____

To both teacher and student:

Take me back to a time when that occurred more often. What would I see that was different? (Discovering when the goal was occurring)

Teacher:_____

_____

_____

Student: _____

_____

_____

How did you make that happen?

Teacher:_____

_____

_____

Student: _____

_____

_____

What did you (student) notice/like about (teacher) when (goal) was occurring? What worked better for you in class? (Specific, concrete, observable behaviors)

_____

_____

_____

How did that make a difference for you?

_____

_____

_____

What did you (teacher) notice/like about (student) when (goal) was occurring? (Specific, concrete, observable behaviors)

_____

_____

_____

How did that make a difference for you in how you reacted to him/her?

_____

_____

_____

Task Development from Exceptions:

_____

_____

_____

_____

THE UNMOTIVATED STUDENT (OR TEACHER)

The questions from the worksheet work well with motivated teachers and students. However, counselors and other educators are not always as fortunate to have such motivated, cooperative students at school! In the case of a student who may repeat over and over "I don't know," or an educator who might do similarly, de Shazer suggests giving the "formula first session task:"

FORMULA FIRST SESSION TASK:

For the next few days, I'd like you (teacher) to notice times when (student) moves away from the behaviors that brought you both here today.

I'd also like you (student) to notice times in the classroom with (teacher) when you don't find yourself giving in to the behaviors that brought you here today.

I'd like you both to really watch for times when the behavior loses. I have to caution you though that different behaviors are sometimes hard to recognize when they are losing. It might be helpful to write them down. When you do, also write down what you were doing at the time that helped the behaviors lose.

I'd like you both to meet with me again for just a few minutes on _____ so we can talk about your discoveries.

The formula first session task can be described as an experiment, and given as a means to learn how to notice when school works. If a person is unable to name a specific problem, he/she can simply watch for any time over the next few days that he/she enjoys or feels successful. As the school student or teacher attends to this task, he/she may become so consumed with searching for preferred times, that he/she acts differently in class. This same assignment is effective for teachers and administrators who can't find time to attend to larger issues. Asking educators to notice when their job is less stressful, more effective, or consistent encourages them to begin to see their job differently. A reproducible page for the formula first session task is included at the end of this chapter.

USING COMPETENCY-BASED CONVERSATIONS TO ASSIST FRUSTRATED TEACHERS, STUDENTS, PARENTS, AND COLLEAGUES

Students are not the only population who come storming into a vice principal's office convinced that they are experiencing the "dilemma of the day." Often, teachers get frustrated with parents, students, or other teachers and run furiously to the administrator with a situation. Administrators can easily find themselves in the role of placator but often end up on someone's side if not careful, and in many instances, that side is the teacher's. While being loyal to a peer is extremely important, it often relieves the "complainant" of responsibilities to solve his/her own dilemma. This is especially true in the case of classroom teachers who have difficult class situations and would rather "fight than switch."

As mentioned before, perceiving oneself as a "consultant" lessens the dependency often put upon administrators and counselors. The following case was shared by a vice principal of a junior high school. The vice principal is often one of the busiest administrators in a school, as he or she is expected to perform administrative *and* disciplinarian roles at the same time. There is often little time for explanation or "digging to the root of the problem." However, most vice principals are concerned about making the right intervention, yet find their backs against the wall. In the case of "the flaming teacher" a vice principal describes a different way of thinking:

The Case of the "Flaming" Teacher

Ms. B came "flaming" into my office with her student, John W. Apparently, John's belligerent attitude and disruptiveness in Ms. B's class was more than she could tolerate. Ms. B was very angry and quite critical of John, and went on and on about his terrible behavior. This offered no solution to John's behavior, and instead encouraged John to be more rebellious in my office as he contradicted everything she said. As they both stood in my office screaming and accusing each other however rightly or unjustly, I asked Ms. B:

"When *has* John behaved for you in the past?"

Stopped in her tracks, Ms. B was puzzled and quiet. I then asked John:

"When *have* you behaved for Ms. B and what has she done in the past that helped you behave?"

Both teacher and student were quiet and became very serious as they began to tell me times when the "behavior" was better. The teacher and student both became less defensive immediately and began to talk about what could be done differently by both of them. I was amazed at how they arrived at the solution. I then asked them both:

"What can you do this afternoon, John, so that the "behavior" that brought you here is not bothering you as much?"

"What would you suggest that you try this afternoon, Ms. B, to encourage more of the behavior you find acceptable?"

They looked at each other and worked it out for that afternoon. The teacher stopped as John left the room and told me, "Thanks—I *do* need to notice the positive more often." I did not see either of them again. I didn't have to do anything. They did it all!

The vice principal became a consultant in the above case. She told me that she noticed in the student's folder that this was his first trip to the office that year. She then mentioned to the teacher how she had not complained for the first four months of the school year, so she obviously was doing something that had worked with the student. She covered the basic steps of SFBT with very little intervention on her part by inquiring about the following from both teacher and student:

1. When things were better in the classroom (Goal)
2. Who did what to make things better in the classroom (Exceptions)
3. What could both the teacher and student do for short periods of time that had worked before (Task)

The ability of an administrator to settle a dispute or discipline issue immediately lessens the chance that a problem will become overgrown through the referral process. In keeping with the philosophy of SFBT, if we "normalize" a problem and see the interactions around it as a "complaint" and not a "symptom," we open up possibilities which seem to mean: "This problem is temporary. It doesn't happen constantly, therefore, I can probably solve it and move on." Often the fear of *not* knowing how to solve a problem makes it feel insurmountable. If an administrator can assist a teacher and student with a problem, there is a good chance that the student might not need a referral to the school counselor, and will therefore see his/her problem as solvable. The administrator appears benevolent, and responsibility gets placed on the complainants. In the case of assistant principals, time is of the essence. The vice prin-

cipal who assisted the "flaming teacher" continues to relay similar successes to me on occasion, and claims her "waiting list" is dwindling.

MAXIMIZING PERSONAL COMPETENCIES FOR PROFESSIONAL GROWTH: SCALING QUESTIONS

The scaling questions developed by Lipchick and de Shazer, mentioned in Chapter 2, are another way of assisting teachers with their concerns by maximizing their competencies and defining their past successes with students and parents. Scaling questions keep the goal specific and behavior-oriented, thereby lessening blame and constructively designing tasks. The following scale was drawn during a conference between a counselor and teacher who desired to be more assertive with her fourth grade class:

Counselor: What will be the first thing you will notice when things are better for you in your classroom?

Teacher: I will be more assertive with my class.

Counselor: Where are you now, on this scale, with 10 being assertive and 1 being passive?

Teacher: About a 5.

present goal

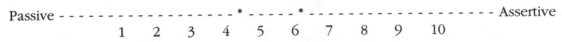

Passive - - - - - - - - - - - - - - - - - - * - - - - - * - - - - - - - - - - - - - - - - - Assertive
              1   2   3   4   5   6   7   8   9   10

Counselor: Where would you like to be by the end of this week?

Teacher: A 10, of course!

Counselor: Let's not move too fast, although I know you could....

Teacher: Okay, realistically, a 7.

Counselor: What would I see you doing differently when you reached a 7?

Teacher: Standing behind the assignments I give out and not budging when the kids complain it's too much for homework.

Counselor: Have you stood firm where other things in your class have been concerned?

Teacher: That's interesting, because when it comes to fire drills or safety rules on the playground, I always stand behind it.

Counselor: How do you do that?

Teacher: I tell myself it's for their own safety, their own good...I trust myself to know that it's important that they comply with the rules.

Counselor: Do you trust yourself that the assignments you give are important and good for their education?

Teacher: Sure, that's why I give them in the first place. I know when it's really too much and they are just complaining.

Counselor: How could you use this "self-talk" that you use on the playground and during fire drills next week in your classroom for a few days?

Teacher: I can think beforehand whether the assignments are really too much, and if I do decide to give them, think about how important they are for the kids to do.

Counselor: Great...and how about trying this for just a few days *this* week...maybe make it to a 6 or 7.

Teacher: I think I can do that; it makes sense that I already do it somewhere else. Thanks for pointing that out—it helps.

Many of us would like to think that our skills as educators lie somewhere in between too passive and too assertive, or between other such extreme descriptions. Anything in between the two extremes is, in fact, healthier than the extremes; they are simply different "grades" of skills. However, people tend to think in terms of the problem or the solution, one extreme or the other. It is more probable that someone will gain control of an anger problem by taking small steps instead of becoming docile or rarely raising his/her voice. As a teacher describes frustration, isolation, depression, crying, and so forth as problems, consider asking:

On a scale of 1–10, 1 being the problem in control and 10 being you in control, where are you now?

"Based on what you have told me has worked in dealing more effectively with other people, where are you now in terms of understanding how to get in control?"

"Where would you like to be when I see you again?" "How will you do that?"

Caution: Go Slowly!

It is important to caution students, teachers, and parents not to move up the scale too quickly. Change takes time. The best changes occur over time, where small steps are mastered again before taking larger steps. Change does not begin at one point and climb upward steadily. Consider the metaphor of an adolescent learning how to play a piano. As he/she practices a new song the mastery increases, but with each *new* song, mastery must occur again. Change also fluctuates as people learn what steps to take to achieve new goals. Encourage the person in counseling to take small steps by specifying small amounts of time to perform the new behavior and to modify the steps to the new behavior. This cautiousness lessens the possibilities of failure. It also allows the educator to become a cheerleader when the student, teacher, or parent returns triumphant! Even if someone claims that he/she dropped on the scale one point, bolster their ability to only move down *one* point.

Problem focusing is prevalent in our world. When someone claims things have not improved, assume they are still looking through gray, problem-focused lenses. Continue to ask "When, since I've seen you, have there been just a few times that were *slightly* better?" The assumption is that *somewhere, someplace, sometime* since you've met with them, things have been slightly better. Should the student, teacher, or parent continue to deny any change, ask how they have still managed to go to school, keep their jobs, take care of their children or teach their classes. The SFBT educator's job is that of a consultant, and to assist the person in noticing the exceptions to their problems or concerns, no matter how small, will be your greatest contribution to their solution construction.

TROUBLESHOOTING THE SFBT APPROACH

As parents and fellow teachers need time and patience to understand the SFBT approach, so does the student need time to believe in his/her abilities or competencies. It is a different experience (and a very pleasant one) for students to hear what they do well instead of being reprimanded. It will become the norm for puzzled looks to appear on the face of a high school junior who is told repeatedly how interesting his responses are in English class. As her teacher inquires of her humorous approach and helpful comments (even if for only one day in the week) the student fights an internal struggle to believe her and wonder what she's up to! Either way, the walls which once appeared when the teacher failed to see her competencies will begin to crumble.

My repeated reference to SFBT educators as consultants becomes more important as students begin to see themselves as competent. The book *America's Best Classrooms* describes the successful classroom as one in which something exciting is going on constantly. Excitement bears motivation. I recall my sixth grade teacher proclaiming that she had taught us seventh grade work all during the school year. As she had us stand up and sing our various drills, I remember smiling and feeling as if I could do more and more. And we did. She was not interested in being the teacher who made a difference, she was interested in *our* making a difference.

"It's Never Better!" (Watching for Exceptions)

Noticing exceptions is an integral part of SFBT. As a counselor begins to use the ideas of SFBT, he/she is often surprised that students and parents become very quiet and solemn when they are asked, "How did you do that?" Many of these parents have experienced years of being told what's wrong with their child, by well-meaning educators. This context also gave them reason to ask the *educators* to solve the problem, since *they* were the ones complaining about performance. As the SFBT educator changes the context of conferences from a problem-focused approach to a solution-focused approach, parents may need more information before they can develop their new roles.

Our world is a problem-focused world, focusing on less than successful times. As the previous quotation by Haley mentions, noticing one tree leaning in a westerly direction is not as easy as noticing how all the others lean in an easterly direction. As with any new approach, skill-building takes time. It is helpful for an educator to think of how he/she has implemented other approaches before or how he/she has explained a new approach with a parent. Perhaps duplicating the worksheet of the past few pages, making note cards, or displaying a short version such as the guidelines given early in the chapter may give confidence to the beginning SFBT educator.

It would not be fair, however, to mention that some people are simply determined to focus only on problems and are quite resistant to noticing anything besides the problem at hand. In keeping with the SFBT basic philosophy, *nothing is 100%*, and sometimes various approaches need to be taken to approach persons who seen things particularly negatively. If this occurs, an SFBT educator can *cooperate with the problem focus* (by seeing it negatively with them), since it is the person's world view and ask: "When is it the absolute worst?"

Helping a Student With Grief

The following dialogue shows a method of cooperating with a student grieving over the death of her grandmother. The student has struggled with thinking about when times were better for her, and has had difficulty moving past the grief she has felt:

Counselor: Debbie, you have obviously been through a lot with the death of your grandmother. I know it might be hard to think about this, but when is it that this tragedy bothers you the most?

Debbie: At night when my grandfather gets very sad and quiet. He still lives with us.

Counselor: So, does that mean that maybe there are other times, then, when things are slightly better for you?

Debbie: When I'm at school, and see my friends.

Counselor: Tell me what you are doing during those times that helps.

Debbie: It gets my mind off her and I think about other things. My friends really do try to help by asking me to sit with them at lunch, and do things after school with them.

Counselor: When else are things slightly better for you?

Debbie: My mom will take me out for a walk or to the grocery store, when grandfather gets sad. Also, I'll go to my room and listen to the radio or do homework to get my mind off of it.

Counselor: It's amazing, that you know how to cope so well. I am still impressed that you continue to come to school, pass your classes, and even come talk to me regularly. How have you managed to make such good decisions for yourself?

Debbie: I don't know. I guess I know I need to come to school—my mom says it's important and that it will help me get over this.

Counselor: Debbie, what will be going on for you in the near future that will tell you you are going on with your life and focusing less on this situation

Debbie: I'll get back into playing soccer again. When my grandmother became ill, my mom didn't always have time to take me to practice. She said we were going to start again when I was ready. I guess she and I will have more time together.

Counselor: Since you have told me today how you've been coping so far, what would you like to do more of during the next few days that might help?

These competency-based questions helped Debbie see that she had been emerging from the tragedy and had gone on, although sometimes painfully. These questions are very useful for students (and teachers) dealing with illness, a death in the family, sexual abuse, physical abuse, emotional abuse, or other traumatic situations. More suggestions for these situations will be given in a later chapter for students dealing with difficult situations. The premise of the questions is that people *survive* and are the most productive in the healing process when they discover what works for them individually.

Focus on exceptions

As educators begin to focus on exceptions to problems and behaviors, the thinking begins to become a way of life. The educator may notice how people see their world in generalities. Words such as *never, always,* or *all the time* begin to spell out how people perceive their lives. The educator who assists students, parents, and teachers to realize that no one is bothered by problems 100% of the time will be rewarded personally, many times over. He/she will begin to do more than just ask SFBT questions; he/she will begin to see the school setting's successes instead of deficits and use the successes to multiply into more exceptions.

"It's Someone Else's Fault": Encouraging Responsibility and Discouraging Blame

When people are accused of wrongdoings, they often become defensive and sometimes respond by blaming someone. Students, especially adolescents, often feel vulnerable to the expectations of others (parents or teachers) and respond with blame to feel less rejected. The following quotation sums up how students often respond to teacher expectations or accusations:

We first raise the dust and then claim we cannot see.

BERKELEY

Over the years as a teacher, school counselor, and school consultant, I have observed countless educators who attempted to get students to "see the light," through well-meant criticism, confrontation, or punishment to little or no avail. It didn't work—and instead tightened the defenses. The students and teachers ended up in power struggles, and usually, hierarchically speaking, the teachers "won," as the student, stirred from the discussion, said just enough to warrant punishment. In keeping with the SFBT idea of "creating an environment where people can experience competency" (Durrant), I have found it helpful to think of the following basic beliefs when presented with a student or teacher who feels "persecuted":

1. Aligning with the student or teacher in his or her complaint and pursuit of justice will lessen resistance.

   "It must be really tough to hear what Mr. Scott says about you so often; no wonder you want things better for you. How will you know when things are better for you in his class? What will I see you doing when that happens?" (Joining and goal setting)

2. Assuming that the student or teacher has a valid argument and that the argument is a defense mechanism, not an attempt to defeat someone, will "normalize" the student or teacher's view.

   "I certainly understand why you're upset and why your mom is worried. Can you tell me times when you don't feel quite as upset? What are you doing during those times that helps you to stay calm and not be as upset by this "problem"? (Searching for exceptions to the presenting problem)

3. Wondering out loud what new behaviors might change the "blamed" person's mind about the student will stop the blame and place responsibility on the student.

   "I wonder what Mr. Scott might see you doing in the near future that would really change his mind about you. I've got this feeling that he really hasn't seen the guy/girl I'm meeting with today. You seem so concerned about school. What do you think it would take to get Mr. Scott off your back? Have you gotten him to lay off before? How did you do this?" (Further exception identification/beginnings of task development)

4. Assuming that the student has accomplished such a needed, convincing maneuver before, to be successful in other similar situations will encourage his/her chance at success again.

   "You know, this is the first time I've met with you this year; that tells me you have known how to keep the teachers happy for ____ (months, weeks). How have you done this? What would your other teachers say you do in their classes that works? Based on what you just described to me, what do you think you might try for just a few days in Mr. Scott's class, to get him to back off?" (Task development)

The questions place the responsibility of change on the student and resist the temptation of the student to blame someone else. Walter and Peller (1992) redirect the wish to change someone else by asking directly: What if the other person does not change?

In the following dialogue from *Becoming Solution-Focused in Brief Therapy*, Walter and Peller explore the possibility of the other person not changing and the consequences of that happening. The solution may not contain what the student desires (such as changing the teacher or parent involved), but it opens possibilities to some change by inquiring about what the student can do alone which may cause someone else to change in future interactions.

School Counselor: What brings you in, Jack? (*Goal frame*)

Jack: Mr. Simons kicked me out of algebra class again. That jerk!

Counselor: Really! What happened?

Jack: He does this every time. The whole class can be talking and screwing around while he is out of the room. When he comes back, who does he yell at, and kick out? Nobody else but me. He says with my grades I can't afford to be screwing around. He just embarrasses me in front of the whole class. I wish I could embarrass him a few times. I wish I could get out of that class.

Counselor: Hmmm. What are you going to do? (*With curiosity*)

Jack: I don't know, he's such a jerk. He just decided the first day that he didn't like me and now he is after me every chance he gets. He should retire. He's too old to be teaching.

Counselor: Guess you figure he's too old to change, is that right? (*Clarification*)

Jack: Are you kidding? He's so crusty. He would crack at the joints if he tried changing. He shouldn't be teaching.

Counselor: Well, you might be right about his not changing. He might be set in his ways. So, if he is not likely to change, what will you do? (*Accepting his frame, asking the hypothetical solution, and presupposing that he will do something*)

Jack: I am probably going to flunk algebra.

Counselor: Oh, and then would you have to repeat it?

Jack: Yes, and I can't do that. My parents would be all over me.

Counselor: Oh, no! What are you going to do? You don't want that. (*Presupposing that he will solve the problem*)

Jack: I guess I'll just have to bite the bullet and be mute in Simon's class.

Counselor: Will that do it?

Jack: No, he will still have it in for me.

Counselor: What would he say he wants you to do? (*Hypothetical solution, reporting for the other*)

Jack: Simons? He would probably say he wants me to "cooperate" in class.

Counselor: What do you think he would say would be signs, in his way of thinking, that you were cooperating? (Hypothetical solution, reporting for the other)

Jack: But I am a cooperative guy.

Counselor: So what do you have to do to be "cooperative" in Mr. Simon's eyes?

Jack: I guess he would say that I would not be screwing around when his back is turned.

Counselor: So, you would not be doing that. What would you be doing instead? (*Eliciting a positive representation for a well-defined goal instead of the negation*)

Jack: I guess I would be doing my work or at least keeping my mouth shut.

Counselor: This is what Mr. Simons would say? (*Clarification of reporting position*)

Jack: Yeah. He would probably say he would like me to volunteer more, too. (*Further description of the move*)

Counselor: So, you think this might do it and help you pass. Are there times when you do some of this now? (*Bringing the hypothetical solution into the present*)

This interchange avoids the notion of changing the teacher and treats the teacher as just one of those unchangeable parts of Jack's circumstances. He is faced with the consequences of continuing to do what he is doing and flunking or *doing something different*. Cooperating with Jack's feeling of being victimized is a beginning. We do not, however, want to leave him there. We are sympathetic, yet ask him what he will do if the teacher does not change. He is now in a position to explore what he *will do* to pass algebra and how he will convince his teacher that he is cooperating.*

———————————

*(Printed with permission. John Walter and Jane Peller; publisher: Brunner Mazel, 1991)

COMPROMISING POSITIONS: A MEANS FOR COMING TOGETHER

Sam, 15, was referred to counseling after he was arrested by police for carrying a knife and holding a small amount of marijuana. After attending day-treatment in a nearby psychiatric facility for ten days, he and his family began family therapy. As Sam began to "bargain" with his family for recovery of his car (he had a hardship license) and other privileges, he became quite frustrated as his parents refused to comply with his wishes. Instead, they told Sam what it would take for him to recover his car and other privileges. Sam looked at me and said "See, they never compromise." I was concerned that Sam truly believed his family did not want to work things out, and saw him determined to try to get his way. I proposed the following scale to Sam:

"I'm going to draw a scale, with your goal in the middle. I'm then going to put you and your family on a scale, with you at one end of the scale and your parents at the other end, since you are disagreeing at this moment. Mom and dad, can you tell me what it will take for Sam to get back his privileges and what you are willing to compromise with? Sam, how did you say you would compromise so that you can get back your privileges?

| 1 | 2 | 3 | 4 | 5 | Goal | 5 | 4 | 3 | 2 | 1 |

Sam   Drug free   Parents

Trust

Respect

Plan: Plan:

                                                   Return his car after 3 weeks

No plan   Allow him to see nondrug friends

                                                   Privileges according to curfew

The parents continued to list what they were willing to do and what Sam needed to do to reclaim his car: clean drug screens for three months, nondrug friends, no calls from the school regarding discipline problems or skipping class, passing grades, and a respectful attitude at home.

As seen on the above scale, Sam had not defined what he was willing to do to reach the goal—he was more concerned with what his parents would do. The scale assisted him in seeing how his parents were willing to compromise, yet he was not. He became very quiet. The conversation then progressed to *what Sam could do* to move towards the goal from his end of the scale.

This scale can also be used for teachers and students who experience conflictual conversations and prefer to blame each other instead of look at themselves. In this case, the scale could be viewed as:

	1	2	3	4	5	Goal	5	4	3	2	1	
Student												Teacher

The following questions can then be used to move both teacher and student toward the goal, where they both share responsibilities for the solutions:

MAKING STEPS TOWARD COMPROMISE

Ask both:

"How will you know when things are better?" (Goal definition/middle of the scale)

"When has this happened just slightly, before?"

"How did you accomplish that?"

"Where are you now, in relation to accomplishing the goal you both stated to me?"

"What would I see you both doing differently, if you moved up just one place (or, wherever each person would like to be) over the next few days?" (Write each plan under the appropriate names)

"Who do you think will reach the middle first?" (Motivational question)

This idea of working toward a compromise encourages the competencies in each person to emerge as they both attempt a mutual goal. The idea of moving up a scale lessens "pleasing each other," and promotes personal success. Typically, in school situations, the goals are quite similar for students and teachers. Teachers want students to behave and students want teachers to like them and treat them well. Place *both* goals in the middle of the scale. Whatever the strategies are that they decide to use to move toward the middle, they will come close to *each of the goals* as they begin to compromise. A reproducible page for compromise resolution is included at the end of this chapter.

CHECKING OUT OUR COMPETENCIES

If the solutions to problems can be found within our students, so can the most helpful suggestions for helping us develop our skills as educators. I have found it personally helpful to always ask students about the process of therapy we just underwent together. The answers given to me increase my knowledge, sensitivity, *and* make sure I am giving the student what he/she came to counseling for. In a formal research project with Dr. Frank Thomas, I found that most often, the reasons for dissatisfaction and failure in counseling are not due to uncooperative people in counseling, but to the people not being heard by uncooperative therapists! The following dialogue suggests a way of soliciting "what works":

Counselor: Thanks, Mrs. Scott and Todd, for coming in today to work things out. I enjoyed the way you both came to some agreements. I wonder, could you tell me what we did here today that might have helped or made a difference?

Mrs. Scott: I guess I realize that we both have some work to do." It's funny, the way we talked about doing what worked kind of reminded me that I do need to be more positive.

Counselor: Great idea, I'm glad what we did meant something to you. Gee, Todd, would that be okay with you if Mrs. Scott was more positive?

Todd: Sure.

Counselor: Todd, what do you think helped or made a difference?

Todd: Talking about it helped. I see that I have to do some things too.

Counselor: Looks like you both have things to do, to reach the same goal. Good luck! See you in a few days.

FORMULA FIRST SESSION TASK
(ADAPTED FROM DE SHAZER)

For the next few days, notice times when you move away from the behaviors that brought you here today. Write down below what you find yourself doing that is different:

_____

_____

_____

Notice times in the classroom with (teacher) when you don't find yourself giving in to the behaviors that brought you here today. What did the teacher do that seemed to help? Write them down below:

_____

_____

_____

Next meeting date:_____

_____

STEPPING TOWARD COMPROMISE

To Both:

How will you know when things are better?
(Goal/middle of the scale below)

To each:

When has this happened just slightly, before?
(Exception identification)

Where are you now, on this scale, in relation to accomplishing these goals?

Where is he/she on this scale?

To each:

What would I see you both doing slightly differently, if you each moved up one space for the next week? Write down under each name.

Who do you think will reach the middle first?

Goal:

_____

_____

_____

_____

Name _____Name

  1   2   3   4   5   4   3   2   1

Plan: Plan:

_____   _____

_____   _____

_____   _____

_____   _____

SFBT Educator Training Exercise: Chapter 3
Creating Possibilities: Acknowledging Strengths Through Language

Below, take a personal inventory. Learning how you describe what you do to other educators can either create an atmosphere of competency for your students and yourself or keep it from happening. The questions below are designed to help describe or redescribe your competencies and help you reauthor the way you want to see yourself in the school setting.

What do you do well with students? With parents? With other educators?

How do you do that?

1.
2.
3.
4.
5.

What would your colleagues describe as your most valuable qualities?

How would you like to be perceived at school by your students, parents, and teachers?

When have you done this before, in school or in your personal life?

How did you do that?

1.
2.
3.
4.
5.

On a scale of 1–10, where are you now in accomplishing how you want to be at school?

_____

1   2   3   4   5   6   7   8   9   10

Where would you like to be by the end of the term?

Based on how you have accomplished this before, how will you do this?
1.
2.
3.
4.
5.

Task: Make five copies of the letter on the next page. Give three to your closest colleagues and two to students you admire. Tell them you are trying to concentrate on making things "work" for you better in school. Ask them to fill out the form and return it to you. In return, tell them what you have always appreciated about them.

_____

Dear _____,

I am interested in how you see my performance here at school. Your comments are very important to me; I respect and treasure your opinion.

Below, please list what you think I do well here at school. It is my hope that your ideas will tell me what I need to keep doing more.

Sincerely,

_____

Comments:

CHAPTER 4

THE "EXCEPTIONAL" SCHOOL PROGRAM

THINKING ABOUT STUDENTS DIFFERENTLY

SCHOOLS SEARCHING FOR SOLUTIONS

The ideas of SFBT presented in this manual are as versatile as individual schools, administrators, teachers, and students. Tailoring the "Exceptional" school program to the individual needs of your school is vital. As a faculty, decide upon your school's purpose, and explore how to achieve the purpose with your staff resources. *Clue:* Begin looking for what is already happening that comes close to your newfound purpose. Chances are there are many great ideas in place already. Your job now is to make them even better by focusing on what works now.

As Michael Durrant, author of *Creative Strategies for School Problems,* mentions, what remains primary is that of "creating an environment in which people can feel competent." The ideas offered in this chapter are designed to shift the gears of schools into situations where people can take responsibility for their concerns, discover the competencies within themselves, and then put the competencies into action. The ideas presented here are merely ideas with which to create an environment in which students and educators perceive themselves differently—as people who were competent all along, yet did not realize it. As always, the best ideas are yours!

Chapter 4 Focus

- The school system of the future: A fictional case study
- Acceptance, validation, and structure: Three principles for principals
- The teacher referral form, student referral form, and parent conference
- Simple interventions for teachers
- Dealing with resistant students and teachers
- Special education: The SFBT individual education plan
- Putting it all together: A case study—a 12-year-old pilot named Kris

A Fictional Case Study: The School System of the Future

The time on the digital clock reads 8:10 A.M. Ms. Rodriguez is busy putting finishing touches on her sixth grade classroom. In twenty minutes, a school-appointed colleague will arrive with a video camera, and she wants to create just the right impression and environment for her students and herself to have a good morning together. The science lab is ready with the individual groups that worked so well last week for the students. The math center is filled with toothpicks for the morning experiment. Touching and feeling items keep the interest level with these "regular" students. The library passes are ready for just the right moment when a student is curious about an idea...Ms. Rodriguez knows the importance of spontaneity. Finally, her morning story from the daily news is on her desk. She routinely talks about the news with her students and has them recall "their" news as well. This lively ten minute discussion always seems to convey the true feelings for her students and get them off to a good start with something different each day. Earlier, she had checked her lesson plans and made sure that today's plan was different from yesterday's, full of intermittent stimuli and in sync with what she and her students have decided has worked for the first four months of the school year. She is ready.

The Exceptional Educators

In Ms. Rodriguez's school district, the administration had begun a project three years ago to enhance teaching styles and encourage motivation among its educators. Elected by their individual schools, teachers were chosen as "exceptional educators" who consistently created an environment in which students felt competent, successful, and excited about learning. Instead of awarding certificates at the end of the school year, the district chose this route which benefited all staff members district-wide. The district chose from several volunteer teachers who were handy with video cameras to videotape the "exceptional educators" each semester and the videotapes were played to similar grade level/subject matter teachers in the district at bi-yearly in-services. This method of illustrating "what works with students" was welcomed by the educators, who gained "hands-on knowledge" of their colleague's expertise, and felt they were not being given information by an outsider. Instead, a teacher in the same situations as they, with the same struggles and frustrations, showed his/her way of creating a competent atmosphere. Typically, the "exceptional educator" accompanied the in-service and explained his/her strategies. Discussions were held after the tape was shown and collaborative conversations developed.

A New Approach to Team Meetings

Upon leaving the meetings, attending teachers held weekly "team meetings" in their separate buildings, where they discussed utilizing some of the ideas they saw on videotape, and added their own personal styles. In their "team meetings," which now lasted a maximum of 30 minutes each week, ideas were exchanged about "what worked" in certain assignments (each was required to bring at least one). Instead of complaining about students, each team teacher brought up concerns about particular students. The team members then discussed from their personal experience how they managed to "cooperate" with the student, helping him/her behave/be responsible in class. The team of teachers who all taught Student A might decide upon a strategy to use during the next week and to notice when Student A did better. The teachers discussed their findings in the following meeting.

Alternate Environments and Opportunities

Sometimes Student A needed an additional environment to see himself/herself differently. Sometimes he/she appeared before the administrator and the team of teachers for a "meeting of the minds." If the team and administration opted for removal from the classroom, the student attended an "in-school suspension" (ISS) for 2 or 3 days to catch up on work. The teachers in ISS were trained to notice his/her abilitiies and build on them, requesting extra credit work where they saw his/her interests. The focus of ISS included building a better relationship with school staff in addition to developing better academic skills. Upon satisfactory completion of missed work due to behavior problems and low grades, the student met with the "team" and was offered a way to "work his/her way back into school." The student's parents were contacted and the student was offered a "mentorship" with a teacher. The student would then become the teacher's assistant. Instead of being isolated from his/her class for one to two weeks, he/she was placed back into the classroom in another role. The student might be told that he/she would be helpful in dealing with other students who are bothered by troubled behavior.

> *The student photocopies class assignments, passes out papers, puts up bulletin boards and "gets to know the teacher" in a different way. He/she sits next to the teacher's desk where he/she is required to do his/her own assignments as well as attend to the teacher's needs. After school, the student assists the teacher with straightening the room and together, they "brief" each other each morning, about the previous day's good points. Student A remains in this new form of ISS unless the team deems it better for him/her to assist a different teacher. The goal of the program is to develop a new relationship with the disruptive student, building on competencies and lowering the walls of resistance.*

The school district has found ISS diminishing rapidly: for the teachers trained in the SFBT model have approached the students differently. They have tried to put aside their beliefs about Student A's bad qualities, and decided to search for his/her good qualities. The team meetings have been supportive to this idea, the leader consistently addressing the new approach. The students soon become less resistant to the teachers and more cooperative. The district has had fewer complaints by parents for their new project, as the parents saw the efforts as a means to "work with their child," not simply punish him or her over and over.

Is This For Real?

Is a school district of this kind possible? Yes. A situation where people can experience themselves as competent? Yes. The above ideas could develop without any additional cost, and only a few structural changes. Entirely designed and implemented by individual schools or school districts, the idea of creating an environment focusing on exceptional teaching enlisted *everyone's* input and competency. The ideas of "disciplining and reauthoring" Student A's school role placed him/her systemically in the middle of teachers and administrators so he/she could be seen differently by everyone including himself/herself.

THREE PRINCIPLES FOR PRINCIPALS

In today's busy classrooms, weaknesses and struggles become the focus as teachers struggle to create environments for learning in surroundings that are often quite negative and problem focused. This causes strengths of students to go unnoticed as teachers try to keep classroom order. It seems difficult to decide who suffers the most; the students, unnoticed for their strengths due to their misbehavior, or the teachers, burned out from being disciplinarians with little energy left for creative teaching. Caught in a difficult situation, many teachers respond negatively toward their students. The students in turn respond defensively and learning becomes a scarce commodity. Developmentally, adolescents thrive on *acceptance, validation,* and *structure.* My work as a teacher, school counselor, family therapist, and mother has shown the importance of these three principles with children and adolescents. Because of the changes I've witnessed when these ingredients are presented, I continue to implement and suggest more of them. Today's teacher is under tremendous pressure and can easily forget to accept, validate, and expect structure when students seem to be out of control, but like any new habit, once it pays off, it becomes easier to do.

We Can't Wait Any Longer

When schools *do* offer the three principles of acceptance, validation, and structure to their methods of approaching and instructing students, the students succeed and their resistance is low. The key is *how do we show acceptance, validation, and structure?* Past theories of educational discipline techniques and behavior modification approaches waited for students to prove to educators that they knew how to act in school. However, today's schools, volatile with peer pressure and less parental involvement, rarely support such an environment. Maybe it's time to do more than place stars on good papers. Maybe it's time to notice when students pass or come near passing and ask them, *"How did you do that?"* Educators who have used the SFBT ideas in very volatile schools report that the students who once flinched when the teacher touched their paper, now look to the teacher as nurturing.

Learning to Cooperate with Students

Steve de Shazer, director of the *Brief Family Therapy* Center in Milwaukee, mentions that resistance has little chance when we cooperate. He also goes on to state that there really is no such thing as resistant clients, only inflexible therapists. The ideas in this chapter are suggested as a means to helping educators become flexible *within a structure that encourages students to feel competent.* Where else is there a better place to encourage competency, than in our schools? As we look into effective classrooms around the world we often find teachers who are structured yet are cooperating with their students in various ways. The encouragement can come from a teacher who praises her students with words or notes of appreciation, or from a teacher who knows to team up a bright, but shy student with another equally shy student. The teacher or counselor who notices what his/her students do well, and then allows, encourages, and expects more of it, *often sees it.*

ACCEPTANCE: A NECESSARY DAILY REQUIREMENT

When I was a junior high Art teacher over a decade ago, students were often placed in my classroom when they had disrupted and sabotaged other classes. Apparently, the administrators in my school had too much faith in me because they seemed to feel that these "difficult" students simply needed a chance to be *creative.* While I have to confess that I did not always agree that art was the answer, I rarely had problems with those referred to as "difficult" students. In fact, they did so well, I began *asking* for the troubled kids (mostly in an effort to rescue them!). What went on in the Art class was: structure, validation, and acceptance. When the difficult students (whom I referred to as *challenging*, not difficult) began to act up, I found something I knew they could do—whether it was posting new art projects, handing out supplies, cleaning up around the weaving loom or throwing a new clay pot on the pottery wheel. At one point I had several classes of 40 kids, *lots* of clay pots, and very few problems.

Accepting students for who they are instead of who they are not lessens rebellion, builds self-esteem, and challenges educators to think of new ways to cooperate so a learning atmosphere can develop. Sometimes it is extrmeely difficult, especially when students have been burned by parents or teachers who push too hard. Consider the following story of Milton Erickson, MD, as told by Jay Haley (1986), as he describes how Erickson cooperated with a student after his parents had tried everything to help him learn to read:

"A boy was brought to me who was supposed to be in the seventh grade in school, but he couldn't read. His parents insisted that he could read, and he was deprived in every possible way as they tried to force him to read. His summers were always ruined by tutors. He reacted by not reading.

"I started working with the boy by saying, 'I think your parents are rather stubborn. You know that you can't read, I know that you can't read. Your parents have brought you to me and they insist I teach you how to read. Between you and me, let's forget about it. I should do something for you, and I really ought to do something that you like. Now, what do you like most?' He said, 'Every summer I've wanted to go fishing with my father.'

"I asked him where his father fished. He told me that his father, who was a policeman, fished in Colorado, in Washington, in California, and even planned to go to

Alaska. He had fished all along the coastline. I started wondering if he knew the names of the towns where those fishing spots were located. We got out a map of the West, and we tried to locate the towns. We weren't reading the map, we were looking for the names of the towns. You *look* at maps, you don't read them.

"I would confuse the location of certain cities, and he would have to correct me. I would try to locate a town named Colorado Springs and be looking for it in California, and he had to correct me. But he wasn't reading, he was correcting me. He rapidly learned to locate all the towns we were interested in. He didn't know he was reading the names. We had such a good time looking at the map and finding good fishing spots. He liked to come and discuss fish and the various kinds of flies used in catching fish. We also looked up different kinds of fish in the encyclopedia.

> *Near the end of August, I said 'Let's play a joke on your teachers and on your parents. You've been told you'll be given a reading test when school starts. Your parents are going to be anxious about who you'll do, and so will your teacher. So you take the first-grade reader and you carefully stumble through it—botch it up thoroughly. Then you do a better job on the second-gade reader, then do a beautiful job on the eighth-grade reader.' He thought that was a wonderful joke. He did it just that way.*

> JAY HALEY, *UNCOMMON THERAPY*, 1986

Sometimes students do not fit into the categories we learn about in education classes and we have to search to find ways to connect and cooperate with them. There are different types of learners and the ways to approach them are just as different. Accepting students for who they are and how they learn is at times, in the midst of chaos, a difficult task. Our job is to create an environment in which the students can show or tell us the answers. The following story was relayed to me in a counseling session with a ninth-grade teacher:

Ms. Peterson came to counseling because she was tired of "abusive, disruptive students who sabotaged her lessons." She was certain that in all her years of teaching, she had never found such difficult students. As we explored the various times in which she felt good about her day at school, she reported to me that on days when she "worked herself to death to make it interesting," her students complied. She then looked at me and said "Gee, do you think I need to do this daily?" The answer was obvious. And yes, it may take more work. Consider our competition: video games that make kids feel they are "on site," television shows, movies, music—interesting things to young, imaginative minds. It is difficult to gain attention from students today.

I asked Ms. Peterson to look over her lesson plans that evening when she returned home, and highlight which lectures, activities, assignments, and readings seemed to be more successful than others. She returned the next week to tell me that three of the five days had been good days, with students cooperating and minimal disruptions. She said she had realized that the time of day had a lot to do with attention spans and thus, cooperation. For example, she said most of her disruptions occurred in her afternoon classes, so she realized that a movie first, then an activity with an interesting discussion relevant to something they understood, calmed down the students and helped to keep their attention after lunch. She also began using some of the teacher referral forms (included in this chapter) and gave them to a few students once a week. I commended her diligence and asked her to do more of what was beginning to work...her students had the answers she was looking for.

True acceptance begins with listening to what the student needs and then aligning with those needs. Acceptance occurs every time an SFBT educator assists a student in reaching a specific goal. It occurs as teachers notice and verbalize what a student does well, and adds the ingredient of curiosity. As indicated in previous chapters, offer questions and comments such as, "Wow, I agree, it is time to get Ms. Brown off your back. What do you think you can do to accomplish that for this week?" Notice times when students do *something you can accept*. Mention it right away! Acceptance lessens resistance and increases cooperation. Cooperation is an SFBT educator's best friend.

I'm Valid, You're Valid

Cooperating with students means *validating* them. In Chapter 1, when I acknowledged Joey's ability to stop a fight by being polite, and asked him to do more of that with his mother, I validated his strategy. In Chapter 2, when I questioned Christina about her ability to keep her mom from criticizing her and learned that she did so by doing things with her mom and talking and introducing friends to her, I validated her strategy. Learning to cooperate with students and help them realize their competencies requires that teachers, counselors, and administrators perceive the students differently, and look closely at what they *can* do.

How Do We Learn to Validate?

Students feel validated when SFBT educators notice exceptions to their behaviors, are complimented on small accomplishments, and are given written lists of *exceptions*. Asking questions such as, "When was the last time you were successful at passing Algebra?" encourages exception identification that is very validating. The educator who looks at the student with a lens focusing on competency creates an environment that is both validating and challenging. When an educator does *not* solve the problem for the student and instead, tells him/her to do what he/she has done before, he/she lessens resistance, failure, and dependence, and also validates the student's strategies.

Avoid the Barbed Wire Fence

A pathological description is not validating, or welcomed, and is often merely informative. How would you like yourself to be described? Sure, people become sad, upset, and often act out their frustrations. They also get over such feelings for the most part. To label a student as having a *conduct disorder* sticks a description on his/her forehead that is hard to lose. Talking in problem-focused language perpetuates the problem. The SFBT educator is more interested in solutions than problems.

STRUCTURE CAN BE FREEDOM

Creating an environment in which students can feel competent does not mean we lower the expectations and become free-spirited teachers who allow the throes of creativity to take over our classrooms and wreak havoc. Quite contrarily, this approach encourages structure, for within that structure is safety and stability. Structure means that students can depend on the teacher's consistency, and her creativity. If someone is asked to begin a new job today, and their only instruction is to "get the job done by 5:00 or you're fired," most of us would find ourselves scrambling for some type of structure or instruction and would probably rebel. Students are the same way. The rules for the classroom are in place and are followed consistently. The rules are also of the type that work, and are enforceable. The rules are also flexible, within a structure that does not waiver. For example, notice the scenario that follows of an "exceptional teacher":

WHO KNOWS SOMETHING ABOUT WORLD WAR II?

Mrs. Thomas began the history lesson by spontaneously dividing up the class into four groups. Group A was a rather advanced group, Group B an average group, Group C a creative group, and Group D, a group of students who struggled with reading. She asked the question: "Who knows something about World War II?" One hand went up out of the entire class. "Ken, what can you tell us?" Ken began to describe the weaponry he learned about from his grandfather. He said he had developed a particular interest in the weapons since he was in the fourth grade. He had read several books and told the class a few ideas.

"Who else knows something about World War II?" The rest of the class reported small instances from a chapter they were assigned to read the night before, but generally, the class was not ready for a discussion. Mrs. Thomas assigned various topics

within the World War II assignment. Group A was to study the economic consequences, Group B, the rebuilding after the war, and Group C, a story/script for enact-
ing what it might have been like for families whose loved ones fought in the war. Mrs.
Thomas and Group D read the chapter together, Mrs. Thomas taking a one-down position by saying "I need to read this chapter again." The student who acknowledged his
knowledge of World War II was released from group work since he knew about the
subject of weapons. Mrs. Thomas told him, "You are obviously familiar with World
War II. I don't want to bore you. I'd like you to go to the library and study some more
and then present us all with a presentation on weapons, complete with pictures, in a
week. You may use the library each class period this week."

In Mrs. Thomas' class, structure was freedom to feel competent and explore within the guidelines. Because Mrs. Thomas was so confident in her ability as an educator, she could take a one-down position and ask the class initially "Who knows something about World War II?" She invited student participation and proceeded with identifying and grouping similarly competent students together. A few years ago, peer
counseling was a popular mode of soliciting "at risk" kids, grouping them together and
turning them into peer models. The program was quite successful, since many students were selected carefully by educators who thought it would give them a chance
to prove themselves. Programs such as peer counseling accept, validate, and struc-
turally require expectations and participation. It may be very helpful to look at your
individual situation and notice which groups, clubs, and activities during the past year
invited students to feel good about themselves and lessened negative behavior. Do
more of them.

ASSISTING TEACHERS WITH STUDENT REFERRALS: AN OPPORTUNITY FOR COLLABORATION

In implementing solution-focused work into school situations, it is
important that the philosophy be extended to working with the
school staff. Invariably, most teachers are successful at maintaining
many tasks and situations during their school day. Perhaps the teacher
who feels frustrated with a particular student may not notice the
other 26 children whom he/she is managing well in his/her
classroom. The teacher needs to be validated. The wise counselor who approaches the frustrated teacher with complimentary information and feedback will often find the teacher more open
to noticing the student in question differently and being more
cooperative.

THE TEACHER REFERRAL FORM

The following *Teacher Referral Form* was designed to take the responsibility of
teacher-student conflict and place it back in the hands of the teacher and student

involved. Developing the form grew from the comments of educators who began to list exceptions instead of problems on paper when visiting with students. Many educators often found themselves overwhelmed with such referrals and were expected to perform miracles. While individual work can be successful, counselors and administrators simply do not have the time to conduct in-depth sessions. Furthermore, most problems can be solved more quickly if the *system* (teacher, parent, peers, counselor, classmates) is included in the process. Most educators who have begun using SFBT ideas have found their students to be less resistant as they avidly write down the student's exceptions. The educators also found that many parents began to cooperate more when they saw the Teacher Referral Form, and perceived that the school was more interested in growth and competency building than in punitive actions.

How the Process Works

The process may begin with the referral: the counselor/administrator receives a referral from a concerned teacher, sympathizes with the teacher's concerns, credits the teacher with his/her wisdom to refer the student, then requests that he/she complete the form for a few days before seeing the student, and return it by a specific date. The key to this process' success is in the counselor/administrator's ability to compliment the teacher who is upset or concerned on his/her ability to identify the needs of the student. Additionally, comments which explain that the SFBT educator is more interested in the *times when the negative behavior/problem is not existing* is helpful. Chances are, the details of the disliked behavior have been explained to the student and SFBT educator beforehand. Initially, the first time a teacher hears a reply such as this to his/her request, he/she is likely to wince at the suggestion of being wise in referring the student! Be patient. It takes time to look beyond the fog of problems toward exceptions. Watch out for puzzled looks!

As the teacher completes the form printed on the following page and begins to identify exceptions to the student's behavior, *two new behaviors emerge*. First, the teacher begins to notice times when the problem isn't as prevalent, and as a result may see and feel differently toward the student and react accordingly. Second, as the teacher reacts differently to the student, the student may begin to *behave* differently and more appropriately in response. There is a big difference in telling a student what a teacher noticed him/her doing well and telling him/her what he/she already knows is going poorly.

Name of Student_____Grade_____Date_____

TEACHER REFERRAL FORM

Dear Teacher,

Thank you for your referral of_____. I am arranging a meeting with the student and his/her parents if that is appropriate. Below, please list the times when you notice _____doing WELL in class. These observations will be very helpful to this student and I as we talk about some solutions to the concerns you have.

Thanks,

*Please be as specific as possible. For example, "Suzie did well in class today when she chose to sit by herself while completing her assignment."

1. _____

2. _____

3. _____

4. _____

5. _____

_____
Teacher Signature

_____

The Map Will Tell Us Where to Go

This philosophy is metaphorical to that of reading a map. Maps have many routes to follow, and reach many destinations. The scenic route winds through small towns; the freeway moves more quickly and is direct. Both routes get to the same destination. The SFBT educator is the travel guide, offering suggestions and observing scenery from the "exceptions" noticed along the route. Schools rarely have time for the scenic route nor are they prepared for long-term counseling situations. Solution-focused brief therapy is the freeway. Instead of belaboring a problem and figuring out who's to blame, the model bypasses such "barbed wire fences" and jumps over them toward more pleasant pastures. The *Teacher Referral Form* is designed to notice the "exceptions" of a student's behavior which will lead to more pleasant interactions with other educators, motivation in the classroom, and self-esteem.

Children and adolescents who are referred for violent acts, tantrums, or verbal abuse to teachers can be approached with this method also. Observing *how the student acts while in the counseling or administrator's office is an exception in itself.* For example, a teacher who refers a student for acting violent or verbally offensive in his/her class yet is still able to gather the student and bring him to the office, has gained some sort of control with the student. Asking the teacher how he/she managed to bring the student, who has *stopped the behavior* enroute to the office, is a compliment and empowerment. Noticing that the student stopped the behavior on the way to the office, or in the office is an exception. Whatever answer the student or teacher gives, a point has been made that the *context has changed.*

Consider the following dialogue:

Mrs. Jones: I need you to see Suzanne. She has become so disruptive in my class this week that the rest of the class has a hard time concentrating on anything but her. I need you to see her and find out what's wrong.

Counselor: Okay, I will see her this afternoon. Before you leave, I would like to ask you something. You mentioned that Suzanne has been disruptive this week. How have things been going the last few months of school? Have you found her as disruptive during that time as well?

Mrs. Jones: Well, she's been one of those students who talks constantly—you know how eighth-grade girls are. She has all these friends and just can't keep her mouth shut.

Counselor: So does that mean she has been different and not as disruptive earlier in the year?

Mrs. Jones: Probably so. I remember one unit we did two months ago, on Shakespeare. She really liked *Romeo and Juliet.* At that time, she talked to me and participated really well in class.

Counselor: Good. When else have you noticed Suzanne not disrupting class and participating just slightly better?

Mrs. Jones: She was doing okay until about two weeks ago. This has been building steadily.

Counselor: The disruptiveness?

Mrs. Jones: Yes.

Counselor: Okay. Would you do something for Suzanne this afternoon and for the rest of the week, as a way to identify how she and I can work on improving this disruptiveness?

Mrs. Jones: Sure.

Counselor: This is a *Teacher Referral Form.* If you would, notice times when Suzanne is not allowing the disruptiveness to bother her. I'd like you to look for times when she is in control of her tendency to be distracted and stays focused. If you will put it in my mailbox tomorrow afternoon, I would really appreciate it, so I can assist you with Suzanne.

SFBT Helps Teachers Cooperate

In typical school situations, students are referred to counselors or administrators by teachers who are fed up with students and expect the counselor or administrator to solve his/her problem. My concern with such a process is that it relinquishes responsibility from the interactive parties—the teacher and student—and makes the counselor/administrator responsible for gathering reluctant parents and taking responsibility for change. Using the ideas from SFBT, the assessment and referral process considers the help of the teacher *and* the student vital in developing solutions to their concerns. The school counselor or administrator becomes the consultant then, and facilitates resolution between teacher and student.

In some problem-focused approaches, questions that search for reasons behind negative behaviors assume that the student has a serious problem and may provoke resistance and defensiveness. Blame is placed on the student and assumes failure on the student's behalf, or the parents assume it is the school's fault—that the school program is not motivating. School should be a place where students learn responsibility for their actions and also learn what works for them *individually* as well.

What to Say When People Want to Focus on the Problem

Sometimes the administrator or counselor is asked to answer *why* a student behaves as he/she does by teachers or parents. Is a divorce occurring at home? Has the child been sexually abused? Is there a teacher-student conflict? Many of these viable questions may hold answers but are not feasible in assisting a child to behave in class currently, nor are the answers always accurate as to why the behavior is occurring. A school counselor can do nothing about an impending divorce, nor does he/she have the time to deal with the issues arising from sexual abuse (besides empathizing of course, and reporting to local authorities). Besides, in many states, ethical limitations restrain educators from probing into the privacy of families. An effective way to respond to such questions would be to say:

"I'm not sure exactly why this behavior is occurring and I'm not sure the answer to that question would tell us how to help now. What I'm interested in are the times you have seen him/her do okay in your class or at home (or other applicable situation). Let's talk about that."

To gather support and cooperation from the teaching staff, the administrators and counselor can talk for a few minutes about these ideas at the next faculty meeting. This would give an SFBT educator/counselor an opportunity to share his/her plans for working with students, teachers, and parents. A well-informed faculty will respond more efficiently when asked to participate in the SFBT School Program, especially if it is approved administratively.

IDEAS TO REMEMBER WHEN ASSESSING THE REFERRED STUDENT

The assessment session after a referral is made is itself an intervention. As the student talks with the solution-focused school counselor/educator and hears the "exceptions" written down by his teacher, he/she should learn three things:

1. The school is on the student's side; the educators are here to assist him/her in being successful, not tell him/her what is wrong.

Alignment with students is very important. This does not mean that the student is looked upon as innocent, but as in need of assistance from school staff to make him/her notice his/her competency. When schools approach children and adolescents with confrontation and as "problems," the students often behave as such and respond rebelliously. When students are approached in a firm manner yet are asked to self-evaluate themselves for competencies, they are given the chance to prove that they can behave differently. When we cooperate with students', teachers', and parents' world views, we lessen resistance. Even the angriest student or teacher will calm down when he/she senses an empathetic educator. Resistance is lessened when both people are on the same side. Schools should be on the side of the student and not contribute to struggling interactions. When an educator replies that the student was wise to come to you, and that there is a problem, he/she aligns with the student. I like to think of SFBT as a model in which I become a travel guide, or consultant. I'm led by the student, teacher, or parent who shows me the way—I get to point out the scenery he/she misses while in distress.

2. Change can be attractive to the student:

Students tend to blame others—it is, after all, much easier to consider someone else at fault for our failures. Aligning with students and then asking "What will____see you doing that will keep him from sending you back to my office?" will encourage a student to make changes and cause others to change in response. Asking a student "What do you think it will take for you to get Mr. S. off your back," is a good way of aligning with a student and eliciting his/her motivation to receive some sort of relief himself/herself.

A student, parent, or teacher can also become more motivated when asked: "What will be better when _____treats you better in class, in response to your new ways of behaving?"

3. The student is already competent:

Students who progress one grade after another each year (even if they are held back once or twice) are successful in at least that way. The student who goes three days a week without being sent to the office is behaviorally competent three days a week. Pointing out these abilities to stay out of trouble three days a week builds competent feelings and reinforces the student's ability to do more of what works on those days. For a junior in high school, for example, a new geometry course may be presenting him/her too many new challenges and he/she may feel lost. By asking him/her how he/she might have handled other new situations in the past, possibilities to solutions occur. Many of us have ways of handling situations which fall into categories; *stress, anger, worry, frustration, new job, new relationships, too much to do,* and so on. By helping students and teachers realize that they have already accomplished similar feats, lessens anxiety.

Sometimes realizing that school, home, or work is better can be difficult when negative times have been interspersed as well. Note the hours, minutes, and days when you did not see the student. Ask the student "How have you managed to stay out of my office? This is great...let's go have a soft drink together so you can tell me." The role of the SFBT educator is to point out the hours, days, or other times when the student is successful. John Walter, author of *Becoming Solution-Focused in Brief Therapy* says that if a student says "nothing is changed, nothing is different," don't believe it! Be patient as the student describes his/her world view of how things have transpired. Listen for the exceptions and verbalize them. The guiding questions that follow might be helpful in assessments. Remember, you are the consultant, and the student is the expert on making it through one more week!

An example of a student assessment utilizing the guiding questions mentioned is given in the following dialogue: A reproducible form, *Guiding Questions for Student Assessments,* is also supplied.

GUIDING QUESTIONS FOR STUDENT ASSESSMENTS
THE FIRST SESSION

The following solution-focused questions offer a different way of working directly with students so they leave the first meeting seeing themselves differently:

1. How would you like things to be in_____'s class?
   (Goal must be behavioral and specific)

2. When was the last time that happened (even slightly)?
   (Look for exceptions)

3. How did you help that happen?
   (Task development)

4. When else do you find that this problem doesn't bother you in _____'s class?

5. What about other classes?
   (Noticing competencies)

6. How do you do that?
   (More task development)

7. Based on what _____has said and what you have said, I wonder what you might try just for today (or a few days this week) so that you get what you want?

Counselor: Glad to see you today, Jake. Sorry it's under such rough circumstances, though. What would Mrs. Jones say her reason was for sending you here?

Student: She says I'm lazy and uncooperative. I think she just doesn't like me. Besides, her class is a pain. I usually sleep through it, it's so boring.

Counselor: Yeah, sometimes it is tough to stay awake. Gee, does it happen all the time that you forget to cooperate and sleep through class

Student: Oh, no. Sometimes I do my work—it just has to be interesting and I can't sit by my friends.

Counselor: Oh, really. That's interesting. You know, I haven't seen you at all this year and as I look at your record here, I notice that you've been passing all your other subjects. That's six out of seven classes.

Student: Yeah. I've been passing.

Counselor: How have you done that...I mean...passed SIX classes out of seven?

Student: My old man is on me and rewards me for it. Plus, I like the other teachers. I think they like me too.

Counselor: What does that do for you, Jake, when you think the teacher likes you?

Student: Makes me feel like working. I try to cooperate a little...you know, try and help them out...they help me out sometimes too when they know I need it.

Counselor: So all you have to do is notice when the teacher is helpful towards you, do your work and cooperate, as you say, and you pass the class?

Student: Yeah, I guess.

Counselor: Tell you what, Jake, see this form? (*Teacher Referral Form*) When Mrs. Jones referred you to my office, I gave her this to fill out. If you look at it you'll notice that it asks her to watch for times when she sees you do well in class.

Student: Okay.

Counselor: She's going to send it back to me tomorrow." Until then, what do you say about doing whatever you've been doing in the other classes so she can put down some of those times you do well? For just a couple of days...what do you say?

Student: I guess so.

Counselor: One more thing, Jake. Between now and when I see you again, watch for signs that Mrs. Jones likes you.

Student: She doesn't.

Counselor: Just watch, okay...you seem like a pretty observant guy...you know when other teachers like you and need your help....

Student: That's true.

In this dialogue, the counselor stepped into the student's *world view* by not blaming Jake or his teacher. The student focused on the teacher having the problem and the counselor focused on the other teachers in Jake's day who did not have a problem with him. By assisting Jake to realize that he did indeed have success in other classes, he was more prone to do more of what worked in other classes.

FOLLOW-UP SESSIONS

The follow-up sessions after the initial assessment may be scheduled as needed but are always left to the discretion of the student or teacher as to their necessity. However, whether an educator/counselor works with students, teachers, or parents, a follow-up conversation is very reinforcing! Follow-up sessions might begin with the questions listed below and can be recorded in the reproducible *Student Success Diary* pages that follow:

"What's better?"

"If I were to have watched you during the past week (days, weeks) what do you think I would have seen you doing that was different than before?"

"Who else might have noticed you doing things differently?"

"What do you want to keep on doing that's working for you now?"

"On a scale of 1–10, if 1 means the problem is in charge and 10 you are in charge, where were you the first time you came here? Where are you now? How have you helped this to change?

The Note that Made the Educator Famous

Be forewarned: Students who admit things are better may fear that such admissions are hazardous to relationships with counselors, administrators, and so on! (They might like the attention!) Be persistent and let the students know that you will be glad to see them in a new and different context...and out of trouble. One way to keep up the new and important relationship between educator and student is through note writing. David Epston, a therapist from New Zealand and coauthor of *Narrative Means to Therapeutic Ends*, routinely sends written notes after he meets with students, teachers, and parents. He summarizes the visit, notes his impressions, adds compliments, and tasks. This could be used for a student as follows:

Dear Susie,

I enjoyed meeting with you today in my office. I was amazed at your ability to point out times when the problem did not bother you in your other classes. You said six out of seven classes went well. I was also impressed by your plan to move to the front of the room so you are not distracted, since that apparently works well in your Algebra class. Good luck! Stop by to let me know how things go. I'm pulling for you.

Mrs. Smith, *Counselor*

Name _____ Date _____

Student Success Diary

Grade:_____

What's been going better?

_____

How have you done this?

_____

_____

What do you want to continue doing that's working for you now?

_____

_____

- -

Date:_____

What's been going better?

_____

How have you done this?

_____

_____

What do you want to continue doing that's working for you now?

_____

_____

A similar note can be sent to Susie's teacher:

Dear Mrs. Thomas,

Thanks for referring Susie B. She and I appreciated your comments on the referral sheet. Susie has since told me that moving to the front of the class has been helpful. Thanks for your cooperation during this busy season at school. You were wise to refer Susie: she is a bright student! Please continue to notice the behavior that you see as effective and let her know. She has told me she likes the attention! Thanks!

Mrs. Smith, *School Counselor*

For more information regarding writing notes to teachers and students, see Chapter 2. For additional competency-based letters and notes, see the Appendix.

SIMPLE INTERVENTIONS FOR TEACHERS: DEFEAT OF THE TEMPER TANTRUM

This story was told by an elementary classroom teacher from Richardson, Texas, who has been quite successful with SFBT ideas in her kindergarten class:

"Jody, 5, was a kindergartener who typically had temper tantrums every morning between 9:00 and 10:00, before her class lined up for recess. One morning, frustrated from trying other methods of suppressing the tantrums, I noticed at 9:15 that Jody had not had a tantrum. I walked over to Jody and knelt beside her whispering "the tantrums haven't been here yet, wow...how have you fought them off this morning?" Jody winced at first, then smiled and said "I don't know." I then said "Hmmm...think you can fight them off for 30 more minutes so you can lead the class outside?" "Yep!" said Jody. After recess, at 10:30, I asked how she had fought off the tantrums during recess. Again, she gave me a puzzled look and replied "I just did, I don't know." I commended her strength for fighting off the tantrums and asked Jody how she might make it through the rest of the morning without the tantrums bothering her. Using my words, she said "I'll just fight them off, that's all." Jody made it through the morning tantrum-free. The next morning I repeated the same remarks until she finally said to me as the class let out for the day: "I don't think I'll be needing to have the tantrums anymore...I've been fighting them so much they're not going to come back."

The teacher utilized the following SFBT statements and questions:

"(Name), I noticed that you are (preferred behavior) today. Things seem to be

going better for you right now."

"How do you do that?"

"How can you continue to do this (good behavior)?"

"Can you do it for _____ minutes more? Great! I'll check with you soon!"

As Jody's teacher continued to point out to Jody the times when she was in control rather than the tantrums, Jody became aware of her abilities. Using language that relates to children and adolescents is vital to this approach. Words such as "fighting off, defeating, blocking, and conquering" are words young children can relate to. In older students, words such as "in control, succeeding, blowing it off, or being in charge" relate empowerment. By asking with curiosity how Jody accomplished her feat over the tantrums, Jody had to examine her behavior and come up with specific strategies. Should Jody fall back into the clutches of the tantrums some day, the teacher will only need to ask "Jody, what did you do last time that helped you defeat the tantrums?"

A Brief Way to Keep Score

Another collaborative way that teachers can make simple interventions and motivate their students is through weekly *scaling questions*. Ellen Boehmer, a school counselor at Terrace Elementary School in Richardson, Texas, adapted scaling questions into a simple-to-use method for teachers. She duplicated a scale on 3" x 5" cards. Upon giving them to teachers of referred students, she explained to the teacher and the students that "1" meant the problem was in control and "10" meant the student was in control. She suggested that the teacher and student collaborate once a week (the day of their choice) about where the student was moving to based on his/her behavior, grades, and participation in school. The simplicity of the card encouraged participation, for it simply meant circling a number and noticing the progress. The teacher simply had to ask "How have you moved from here to here?"

Teacher_____Class/Grade_____

Student_____Week Of_____

_____

1   2   3   4   5   6   7   8   9   10

Dealing With the Resistant Student or Teacher

Webster defines "resistance" as "an organized, usually underground, movement of fighters engaged in acts of sabotage (etc.) against occupying forces" (1987). People sometimes become resistant when they feel they are blamed, unsuitable, insecure, or uninformed. Within school settings, many systemic factors contribute to the student's resistance. Economic situations, inadequate supervision, criticism from parents, lack of acknowledgment/acceptance by teachers and peers, jealousy of peers, and so on. However, the three principles apply once again: acceptance, validation, and structure. Observe the following case study of a psychiatric nurse who I found resistant to noticing competencies in an adolescent patient I had been working with:

"Steven, 16, had been admitted to the psychiatric hospital after he was found drunk repeatedly by his mother, who also struggled with alcohol herself. Each week I would work with Steven and together we noted achievements in school (which were outstanding) and his participation in the unit group. At treatment team one week, where staff gathered to discuss more diagnosis and progress, I listened as staff discussed what Steven still needed to do according to their diagnosis. After listening to the long litany of complaints and pathological descriptions, I asked the team what he had been doing well. Caught off guard at the suggestion, the head nurse replied that he "never did anything well...in fact, he spits, he goes to the gym instead of AA and rarely participates in group." After repeating my inquiry several times several different ways, I decided to try and "cooperate" with the nurse. I mentioned to her that she was undoubtedly the most observant member on the team since she saw so much that he did not do well. I then asked her to do something for me that would really help— "watch for the times next week when Steven does something okay, and tell him about it." She responded quietly that she would try to do that. Before the end of the treatment team she turned to me and said "You know, come to think of it, he did pretty good in group this morning; there was a new patient and he sort of took him under his wing."

Don't Give Up—Keep Looking For the Exceptions

Sometimes, it is difficult to notice exceptions in others. Granted, in a violent student, failing sixth grader, or angry tenth grader, it is difficult to see competencies. The difficulties arise when the student refuses to "cooperate." When this occurs, consider that his/her behaviors serve a purpose, and do not try to change the behavior. This will lessen resistance. Instead, the following task by Freedman and Combs (1990) might help the student to check out his/her behavior or perceptions and confirm them if they are valid:

"We suggest that each of them find or create something that represents the obstacles he or she perceives."

In other words, step into the student's world view and try to understand that the behavior we observe *is necessary to the student.* I have found it helpful to ask how the negative behavior helps and then assist the student with "doing more of the same" only in a different manner:

Counselor: Don, your teacher said she sent you to talk to me because you continue to interrupt her in class. Is this correct in your point of view?

Don: Yeah, she doesn't like me and never calls on me so why not?

Counselor: Does this work for you, to interrupt her constantly?

Don: Yeah, and I'm not going to stop either—she keeps on my case all the time and I'm sick of it. I'm not going to let her boss me around.

Counselor: Tell me, I'm kind of curious—what does it do for you, to interrupt her?

Don: I don't know, I guess it gets her attention.

Counselor: Good attention or bad attention?

Don: Bad, and I don't care.

Counselor: How could you use your interrupting skills a little differently in class? It sounds like you're not willing to give them up.

Don: I don't know.

Counselor: I'm just wondering if you could interrupt Ms. Lee a little differently, you know, so she really notices you. This may take some skill though, and some real observation on your part so that you get the maximum benefit from interrupting her. Would you be willing to try something different?

Don: Maybe.

Counselor: I'd like you to interrupt Ms. Lee this afternoon in class when she is explaining something. Watch for precisely the exact moment when she would truly hear your interruption. You know, when she pauses, or is passing out papers. Then, I'd like you to tell her "I need to interrupt for a minute." Then ask a question about what she was explaining. This way you will interrupt her and we can both see what you accomplish. I'd like you to try this just twice this week. Is it okay with you if we write Ms. Lee a note and mention that you will be trying something different?

Don: Okay.

As the student attempts to use his/her method differently, it is helpful to inform the teacher that the "student is planning on behaving differently in class for the rest of the week." See the following note:

Dear Ms. Lee,

Thank you for your referral of Don G. We have met and he has told me his plans for acting slightly different in your class for the rest of the week. Please notice any differences in your class that work better for Don and jot them down. We will appreciate your observations!

Thanks!

Counselor and Don

ALTERNATIVE SCHOOL OR BUST: WHEN SUSPENSION LOOKS GOOD TO STUDENTS

I once worked with Josh, an eighth grade boy who was, in his words, "on my way to alternative school, and looking forward to it." The student was not at all worried about his future transfer; he had heard it would be less work and much quieter. As we talked, his arms were crossed tightly across his chest and his attitude was that of

pride/anger/rebellion/resistance, all rolled up into one! Diverting for a moment from the issue of alternative school, he mentioned how his father drank heavily and often had severe arguments with him in which he called him names and criticized him for everything. With this information in mind, I inquired about how he was still able to go to school with problems happening at home. I chose to be quiet for a while during our time and align closely with his world view.

At the end of the session, I asked if he might be willing to stay out of alternative school for one more week, since he obviously needed to show some people that he could do whatever he put his mind to. He agreed that there indeed were some people (dad, for one) who needed to see him differently. I then asked him "What do you hope they will soon see in you that will tell them they are wrong about you?" He replied that he wanted people to see that he was really a good kid who just wanted to be left alone. (He had been bothered by gangs.) I agreed with him and told him I suspected that staying out of alternative school for another week would probably do that. He agreed. He stayed out of alternative school permanently. His teachers reported to his mother that they had seen a vast improvement in his interest at school and his behavior. I'm still not certain what occurred in our meeting that caused such a change in Josh, nor does it matter.

Today's teachers and counselors struggle with students who refuse to take responsibility for their actions and are resistant to authority and compliance. This age-old struggle is simply a trait of childhood and adolescence, yet educators (and the world) appropriately perceive self-evaluation, responsibility, and change in behaviors as necessary for growth. A normal response to resistance is to be resistant. However, this merry-go-round of interactions rarely works. Like two boxers moving towards each other with their fists up, neither allows the other the first punch. Resistant teachers and students are the same. The ideas of intervening with *competency-based conversations* as introduced in Chapter 3 tend to lessen resistance and open up possibilities without blaming. Nonetheless, methods tried in various educational settings have seemed to focus around evaluative methods that diagnose and label students and their behaviors instead of noting times when the negative behaviors are nonexistent. As previous chapters have pointed out, this information holds little value for current strategies or solutions.

Too often, students see their efforts at solving problems as "defective" and tend to give up hope. They tend to blame the parents or teachers and sit back waiting for *them* to change. Waiting can cost them grades, their reputations, and self-esteem. The *Student Information Sheet* that follows grew from students' suggestions that their teachers simply did not know what helped them in class. Educators can offer the student an opportunity to *"Tell us what we need to know about you, you are the expert!"* The *Student Information Sheet* is a different exercise for most students, parents, and teachers and can be even more effective when done collaboratively with an administrator or parent. The counselor/administrator phrases the purpose as such:

"You know, I truly believe that we just simply do not understand what you need from us here at Smith Junior High School. You have done well during the past six months, but obviously things are changing for you that we don't have information for. Today, I'd like you to do an inventory for us, and watch as you go through your day for times when you do okay in class."

Name of Student:_____Date:_____

STUDENT INFORMATION SHEET

Dear Student,

Your teachers and I are interested in assisting you here at school. Below, please list the times when you think you do better in school. (Think about the past few months or last year.) Please be specific. This is your chance to tell us what you think will help you do better more often.

For example, "I do better in school when I think the teacher likes me; I understand the homework *assignment*, I place my assignment in my book to turn it in; when the teacher calls on me and does not ignore my answer."

1. _____

2. _____

3. _____

4. _____

5. _____

What worked for me in class this week:

_____

_____

_____

_____
Student Signature

_____

129

As the student watches his/her behavior, the probability is that he/she will change behaviors as well. Asking the student to talk to teachers about his/her needs will increase collaboration between teacher and student. A shy student may prefer placing the form in his/her teacher's box or to give it to the teacher directly. The importance of this venture is to let the teacher know that the student is attempting to change. With high school students, this form may not be necessary, but the idea is still helpful. A conference with a high school teacher might offer the student an opportunity to tell him/her what he/she needs from the teacher. Preparing the teacher beforehand about how the student will approach the conference might be valuable. Often, one on one with teachers is difficult for students. The teacher could be informed that the student wants to try a different approach to working things out—instead of talking about the problem, he/she wants to discuss what might be helpful to his learning/behaving/participating in class.

In addition, this exercise teaches students to *look at themselves differently*, as if they are able to accomplish tasks. The student has a better chance to become the expert on himself/herself and is more likely to ask a personal question such as "What works for me?" the next time they experience a problem. If we as educators can assist students with this practical way of perceiving and dealing with everyday situations, we have truly given them a gift for a less stressful life.

Students Are Curious About Teachers, Too

The SFBT school program is more than just a pile of new forms to send to teachers. It's a way of thinking about students and responding to them differently. However, with busy days and responsibilities to attend to that restrict the administrator/counselor from visiting teachers and students often, the *Teacher Information for Students* sheet on the following page can be a communicative way for students who are curious about what his/her individual teachers think of him. This form is often well-received by students of all ages (and their parents as well!). In fact, many students who have trouble remembering to bring assignments to class rarely forget this form. The responsibility of this form lies totally with the student.

The students copy off as many sheets as needed for each week, dispensing them to each of their teachers on Monday. For junior or high school students, each teacher *of concern* is given one form. For elementary students, one form per self-contained teacher. On Friday, the student asks for the sheet back and brings it to the counseling session/administrator/parent the following week. This form has been quite successful in breaking the ice with perturbed teachers and their students, lessening the belief that "The teacher is out to get me."

TEACHER INFORMATION FOR STUDENTS

Dear Teacher,

Your student _____ is interested in knowing when you notice him/her doing well in class. Your help will assist _____ in understanding how to do well in school more often. The student will pick up this form on_____.

Please be specific. *Example:* When Sue talked less in class on Thursday during lab, I felt like she was listening and I gave her more attention.

Thank you very much!

_____
Counselor/Administrator

_____
Student

1. _____

2. _____

3. _____

4. _____

5. _____

_____
Teacher Signature

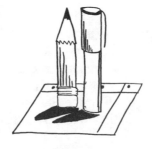

I have used this form with high school students as well as elementary students. Surprisingly, high school teachers were the most appreciative of the idea, since it was a different kind of request: positive comments for their students. Students are always curious about what teachers think of them. Administrators have also used the form as a positive reinforcement for students who were in their offices a little too frequently. Noticing the student in the hall, behaving in the lunch room, or receiving no referrals from the teacher for a week, are all reasons to write a small note or send the form to a student during homeroom class. The time it takes to jot down a few comments is just minutes; the results, according to those who have sent such notes, can last much longer.

This form works very well in parent conferences, in that it promotes teacher cooperation and student interest. It is suggested to the school counselor who chooses to utilize the *Teacher Information for Students* sheet that he/she get an administrative signature at the top of the sheet before the student passes the forms out to his/her teacher. Teachers are busy people, and one more form often seems monumental. Assistance from the appropriate hierarchical level will probably assure more cooperation from a busy teacher in completing the form. A few schools have taken the idea of the "Teacher Information for Students" and personalized it for their school and their school-age population.

The form can also take the place of *weekly progress reports* which many concerned parents request that their children solicit from teachers. Building good will between home and school is accomplished when parents receive a form describing behaviors teachers deem successful or competent. The form can be used in the form of weekly or bi-weekly information for a few weeks or an entire term. Eventually, the students may decide to listen for exceptions themselves, or be told by the teachers verbally what is working.

THE PARENT CONFERENCE: AN OPPORTUNITY FOR REQUESTING PARENTAL COOPERATION

The *Parent-Conference Role-Play* included in this section shows how the *Student Information Sheet*, the *Teacher Information for Students* sheet, and parent conference dialogue can work collaboratively to discover solutions that impact all involved. The following dialogue represents the efforts of all concerned, and creates the atmosphere of responsibility on the part of everyone to stop maintaining "the problem." For many parents, a conference entails hearing about how bad things are at school, and many parents consider themselves failures, or feel that the school has failed their child. The dialogue that follows represents how SFBT can rescue the school, teachers, and administrators from being blamed. The dialogue spreads the responsibility throughout; everyone's ideas are solicited and considered before the strategy is developed. A *Guide Sheet for Parent Coferences* is included after the role-play.

Parent-Conference Role Play

The following statements and questions are suggestions that might be useful in making parent conferences more pleasant and empowering to both student and parent:

1. Information Gathering—Parent Empowerment

Mrs._____I want you to know how impressed I am that you came to our meeting so willingly. Obviously you know that_____needs your assistance.
Can you tell me exactly what you're seeing at home or at school regarding _____that concerns you?

You know, that's really in agreement with what we're seeing in _____here at (school).

2. Searching for Exceptions

Mrs._____I'm really curious about the times when you do not see_____experiencing troubles with his/her schoolwork. Can you tell me about those times?

Which days, how many hours a week or times a week do you notice _____*not* experiencing troubles?

So, when_____ is (on a schedule, when you're right there with him/her, when you check his/her work, when he/she is not fighting with siblings, when his/her homework is done on time, when he/she thinks the teacher likes him/her) school is a little easier, is that correct?

3. Changing the Problem Thinking to Solution Thinking

That's really interesting, Mrs._____, because when I asked the teacher(s) who referred_____to me to fill out the sheets I have here (*Teacher Referral Form*) I found there were similar times to what you're describing, plus other times when_____did better. These sheets, Mrs. _____list the times here at (school) when _____does better in class. We're interested in those times here because we really want _____to succeed.

I have one more sheet to share with you, Mrs._____. It's a sheet that your child filled out for us. On this sheet again, are _____'s views about when school goes better for him/her. She/he said that she/he does better in class when (the student feels the teacher likes her, is not as tired, is not sitting in the back of the room, is not worried about you and her dad, spends time with you, and does not have to baby-sit during weeknights).

4. Developing Tasks for Solutions

Mrs._____, based on what_____has told us works for him/her, what his/her teachers have said works better, and what you have said works, what would you suggest we try with_____for a few days this week?

5. Suggesting Success

Mrs._____I appreciate your time today. Your suggestions really make sense. I guess I'd like to ask you one more quick question:
"When_____does better more often in school and you see that happening, what will you and _____get to do more of that you aren't doing now?

As the language suggests, the school, parent, and student agree that success lies in the solutions noticed by all involved. Notice the language used in the dialogue: "When_____does better..." "What will you get to do when_____does better?" This suggestion that things will improve encourages hope. Parents who have children in trouble at school often come to school concerned, feeling like failures. By offering suggestions of the teachers, students, and parents themselves, there is virtually no threat of failure. I tend to mention in training sessions that I never ask anyone to do anything that they have never done before. There is no risk of failure that way. Instead, I may suggest they do more of what worked in other situations. A mom who worries about her 16-year-old daughter's association with friends she does not know, can observe how she has set limits with her driving last summer. The daughter always told her where she was going and with whom when she drove the car or she lost the privilege for a day. By applying the same ideas for friends by requiring her daughter to introduce them, leave a phone number or address as to her destination (or she loses a night out), the mom may worry less and feel more comfortable.

GUIDE SHEET FOR PARENT CONFERENCES

1. **Information gathering:** Why are we here?

   Parent's view:

   _____

   _____

   School's view:

   _____

   _____

2. **Searching for exceptions:** Can you tell me when the problem doesn't bother your son/daughter?

   Parent's view:

   _____

   _____

   School's view:

   _____

   _____

3. **Presentation of data collected from teachers:**

   Summary of exceptions: Give *Teacher Information Forms* and the *Student Information Form* to the parent.

4. **Task development based on exceptions:**

   Parent:

   _____

   _____

   School Staff:

   _____

   _____

SPECIAL EDUCATION— A SPECIAL OPPORTUNITY FOR SPECIAL ATTENTION

Special Education teachers who hold diagnostic and planning meetings with parents (in Texas, they are called ARDs—(Admission, Review, and Dismissal), use diagnostic evaluations, teacher grades, and behavior reports. Geri Kellogg, a counselor from Burkner High School in Richardson, Texas had often attended such meetings and grew tired of the negative atmosphere. She mentioned a mother and her son, a high school junior, who sat through one such a long meeting. The counselor looked at the student and began to describe, as an addendum to the meeting, what the student was doing well and *when/how* he/she did that. She immediately had eye contact with the student. The atmosphere went from gloom and frustration to that of hope. She has since made this a routine part of conversations and has noticed how parents leave feeling hopeful, and part of a team. She then found the parents to be more cooperative in the future when adjustments to the child's curriculum needed to be made. Perhaps with this very special population, noting competencies is more important than ever.

Developing SFBT educational plans for special education programs utilizes traditional testing methodologies, required state documentation, and symptomology lists *in addition to exceptions to the pathological behavior.* The *Individual Education Plan* (IEP) described in the next few pages enlists the help of all teachers associated with the student, especially teachers whose classes the student is passing. The IEP can be accompanied by test scores and other forms relative to the Special Education program in individual states. The ideas in the IEP focus on the student's abilities and competencies, and the identification of such abilities. The SFBT ideas, noted with an asterisk (*) encourage creativity and competence on the part of the educators. Use of the teacher referral forms for the identification of effective teaching methods is helpful.

The development of the IEP on the next few pages grew from my personal experience with ARD meetings. My youngest son's short attention span was affecting his learning and efficiency in class, and together, his teachers and I wanted to do something different for him. After sitting through the ARD with his vice principal, speech therapist, and three of his teachers, I wondered, "Where do we go now?" I asked the two teachers what they thought they did that helped him remember to turn in his assignments and bring home his homework. As they described what they thought they did, his third teacher acknowledged that she might try their tactics as well. I felt very fortunate to have worked with such a receptive staff. The ideas were accepted readily and implemented. He began to do much better in class.

Name _____ Date _____

Development of the Individual Educational Plan (IEP)

Grade:_____

___YES___NO The ARD Committee reviewed achievement on the previous year's short term objectives on the IEP (applicable to all but initial ARD meetings).

A. **Present Competencies:**

1. Physical, as it affects participation in instructional settings:

   _____ No physical limitations, no modification of regular class needed
   _____ Some physical limitations, no modification of regular class needed
   _____ Needs modifications because of the following impairment:

   _____

   * In what activities does the impairment not affect the student? List specific activities:

   _____
   _____

   * Describe modifications needed, based on the above activities:

   _____
   _____

2. Physical, as it affects physical education:

   _____YES _____NO The student is capable of receiving instruction in the essential elements of physical education through the regular program without modifications.

   * If NO, list the following activities in which the student *has* shown capabilities of receiving
   instruction:_____
   _____

   * Recommendation, based on competency in listed activities:

   _____
   _____

B. **Behavioral:**

1. Educational placement and programming:

   _____ No modifications
   _____ Has some characteristics which may affect learning, although not severe enough to withdraw from regular classes:____ poor task completion:___impulsive—requires reminding to work slowly.
   _____ Distractible—may require isolation, sit at front of room, and so on. at times:___ other:_____

137

_____ * Abilities which emerge in specific learning tasks/activities and enhance cooperation in the classroom, as identified by teachers, administrators, and parents:

_____

_____

_____

2. Ability to follow disciplinary rules:

_____ Appropriate for age and cultural group. May be treated the same as nonhandicapped student. Student should be able to follow the district's discipline management plan. Use of alternative educational placement and suspension as per (TEA) regulations is appropriate. Student is responsible for school board rules and campus policies without modifications.

_____ * This student is responsible for school board rules and campus procedure. A modified discipline plan will be utilized. The following approaches have been identified as effective in working with this student through direct observation by teachers, administrators, and parents:

_____

_____

_____

C. **Prevocational/Vocational** (When appropriate): Skills which may be prerequisite to vocational education. Rate using the following scale: 1-10, where 1 = completely unskilled and 10 = completely competent:

____cognitive skills   ____expressive skills
____reading level   ____organizational skills
____performance   ____social skills
____verbal comprehension   ____following directions
____attendance   ____personal hygiene/self care
____punctuality   ____other_____

*   Utilizing all skills with a rating of 6 or above, list opportunities within the school program that seem appropriate for the listed competencies:

_____

_____

D. **Academic/Developmental:** (Grade or age levels alone are not sufficient).

1. _____ Indicate the content areas in which the student is competent and can receive instruction IN the regular or remedial program without modification:

____ all subjects   ____reading   ____math   ____social studies
____English   ____science   ____spelling   ____computer lit.
____health   ____vocational   ____fine arts   ____physical ed.
____other_____

138

2. *Based on the identified subject competencies and collaboration with the assigned teacher, list the identified subject below and a brief explanation of the teaching methods identified as effective with this student:

(Individual work, group work, isolation from peers = less distractibility, individual library assignments/projects, visual stimulation, seating arranged near the teacher, parent cooperation/collaboration, journal, rewards, dates assigned to assignments, and so forth.)

Subject   Effective teaching methods

_____: _____

_____: _____

_____: _____

_____: _____

_____: _____

_____: _____

3. Indicate the content areas in which the student's competency development needs assistance from a Special Education program:

____all subjects   ____reading   ____math   ____social studies
____English   ____science   ____spelling   ____computer lit.
____health   ____vocational   ____fine arts   ____physical ed.
____other_____

4. *List the subject areas from number 3 in which the student needs additional assistance from Special Education to further develop competencies leading to mastery. Also list appropriate, effective teaching methods from number 2 above, which would lead to more competent performance:

Subject   Suggested teaching method

_____: _____

_____: _____

_____: _____

_____: _____

_____: _____

The point of individual education plans should be to gather information which develops into direction. Explanations (barbed wired fences) only tell us *what's wrong*, and what's not working. Exceptions tell us where to go and *what works*. In the same way that directions for a new gadget tell us how to assemble the parts, special education meetings might include new ideas based on what already works with a student, no matter how minimal his/her competencies may seem. This direction will assist teachers, administrators, and parents alike to focus on the student's competencies instead of deficits, and encourages good will and systemic collaboration between parents and students.

SOMETHING AMAZING IS HAPPENING AT SCHOOL!

When I taught junior high school in the seventies, I recall a teacher suggesting at a faculty meeting that parents needed to hear good news from school. She came up with the idea of "Something Good is Happening at School" notes. She suggested that we give them to students who pass their science tests, or perform well in choir, band, or football. While I liked this idea, and sent out my share of notes, the notes made the teachers the experts in determining what was good. Educators know how class should be held and assignments completed, but I have to wonder what would have happened if a different kind of note was given to the student and the parent:

SOMETHING AMAZING IS HAPPENING AT SCHOOL!

Dear Susie and parent,

I have noticed something interesting about Susie recently. She has taken a renewed interest in her science work and is now passing all her subjects! We are delighted here at ___Junior High, and amazed at her self-motivation. Congratulations!

Mrs. Jones

What's the difference? The student is seen as totally responsible for change! It is this self-realization that he or she has accomplished a successful act solely, that increases the chance for motivation to continue and develops into self-esteem. The appendix contains some novel notes which can be reproduced and sent to students, parents, and teachers.

PUTTING IT ALL TOGETHER:
ATTACKING A SCHOOL PROBLEM WITH SFBT

Kris, age 12, came to counseling with his biological dad, Steve, and stepmom, Jean. One month before the meeting, Kris' biological mom relinquished all rights to him, and declared that she would have nothing to do with him from that day forward. The dad described his son as failing two classes at school, being angry towards his biological mom, disinterested in family interactions, and irresponsible. Kris sat in the chair with his head down and his arms clasped around a large pillow, as if hiding behind it.

Presenting Complaint

School failure, biological mom's relinquishment of rights to Kris and disinterest in family life. I asked the family how they would know when things were better for *all* of them. The following answers were given by dad, stepmom, and Kris:

Goals

- Kris' school work would improve.
- Kris would enjoy rewards, such as the flying lessons he had been receiving.
- Stepmom and Kris would enjoy more positive moments together.
- Kris would lie less.
- Kris would not be angry at biological mom.
- Kris would remember to take his homework papers to school.

The family used words such as "it's really tough"—language with which to externalize the problem. I briefly explained that it had been my experience that problems were rarely encouraged to stay around by only one person's encouragement. I wondered out loud how they all might have "maintained" the problem. At this point, Kris said it was a monster problem. Using his words, I continued talking with the family about the "monster problem:"

Problem Maintenance

Kris:
- I don't forgive my real mom for what she did.
- I get angry and say, "What the heck."

- I don't turn in my school work.
- I wake up in the morning not feeling good. and start off with a bad attitude.
- When I want *everyone* to be mad at my real mom, it bothers them.
- When I forget my papers, it's not good.

Jean:
- When I'm not willing to praise him for things. Sometimes he does okay but I don't feel like telling him it's good because he does so many bad things.
- I judge him.
- I work too hard at helping him.

Dad:
- When I get frustrated, I get hurt and talk to Kris too much, I explain too much.
- I give in too much, because I'm so aware of how hurt he is.
- I'm inconsistent with consequences I give out.
- Jean and I are not in agreement about how to handle Kris, and that causes a problem sometimes.

I complimented each family member for their wisdom and recognition of their roles in keeping the problem around. I then switched into solution-talk and asked them all, "When is the monster problem *not* around?" I asked the family to recall the times when the problem was less of an influence on their family life (White, 1990):

Exceptions

- When I worry about meetings between my parents and teachers, I straighten up at school. (*Kris*)
- Creative school work (*Kris described visual aids, movies, slides, and film strips as being very conducive to learning and holding his attention*)
- When Kris is in leadership roles (*Dad described Kris' success last summer at arranging activities for the neighborhood*)
- Kris tells himself, "This may just be something I need to get over."
- Kris said, "When I know before that I know what I'm doing."

At this point, the atmosphere changed within the meeting. Kris sat up, put the pillow aside, Jean began to speak less detrimentally about Kris, and Dad became firmer with what he expected from Kris. The session changed from focusing on Kris as having the problem, to a family focus, each supporting each other in solving the problem that was interrupting their family life. I then approached a task, based on the exceptions given during the session and I assisted the family in developing their task for the week.

Task

- Kris will turn in his homework tomorrow and for the rest of the week.

- Kris will talk to his teacher about extending his time at various "centers" since he comes nearer to completing assignments that way.

- Kris will pay more attention at home.

- Kris will know his consequences and will depend on his parents' consistency.

- Jean will judge less for a week.

- Jean will make a conscious effort to not work *for* Kris during the next week.

- Dad will be more aware of his inconsistencies in consequences, and instead, will determine consequences with Jean before delivering them to the children.

- Since the teachers are concerned about Kris, they will be given the *Teacher Referral Form* to fill out and give to Kris each Friday, for the next three weeks. This form will ask the teachers to notice when he does well in class.

- Jean and Dad will talk to the stepsister and biological sister (living with them) about how they might let go of the monster problem by changing their reactions around Kris.

Kris and his family had discussed the issues at hand both privately, at school, and during the first twenty minutes of our meeting. To continue to talk about what was not working would have enlarged the problem insurmountably. The goals of the meeting belonged to the family, not the counselor. By talking about the problem as "maintained," the family quickly dropped their defenses and attacked the problem through new behaviors. The tasks which developed from exceptions were more workable since they had been performed previously.

After the meeting ended, I composed the following letter to Kris:

Dear Kris,

It was nice to meet you. You certainly are able to see which direction to go now in removing the monster problem from your life.

I guess what most impressed me about you was your ability to visualize what will be better when the monster no longer "takes you over." You mentioned that you and Jean would have better times, the teachers would get off your back, and best of all, you would get the privilege of being a pilot. I really liked how you described landing last weekend when the pilot handed over the landing to you...such a risky thing to do! Didn't you say you did it by saying to yourself "This may just be something I may have to get over"? I think you did.

This week is a true opportunity to try some of the ideas that you told me have worked for you before. I really liked your suggestion to talk to your teacher about longer time at the centers. I also liked your responsible way of deciding to do more around the house. But most of all, I liked how you described what we did in our meeting. You said you "filed away what's been going on...and you felt better." Now it's time to take action against the monster problem. I'm cheering for you to win. I look forward to seeing you next week—good luck with the teacher forms.

Linda Metcalf

Kris and his father returned the next week with six *Teacher Information Forms* in hand. Once a student who forgot nearly every paper, he had kept up with the forms! The responses in general were quite pleasant and specific regarding behaviors which indicated that Kris had changed. However, some teachers mentioned a few negative behaviors in spite of the requests on the form for items when Kris did well. Kris' explanation for the negative comments made by teachers was: "I guess the other teachers didn't understand what we wanted them to do." He laughed slightly and said he would like to try again with those teachers.

Kris's dad reported a good week, with Kris cooperating and Jean not pushing Kris to do homework, chores, or other activities. Kris had completed the homework during the week and seemed to be enjoying his new-found responsibility which his dad and stepmom were encouraging. He was quite excited about the few positive teacher responses, and requested to take them again for the next few weeks. I asked him what that did for him, and he replied, "I just don't feel as bad when they say something good. It makes me try harder."

The school program described in this chapter developed from the various works of competency-based therapists. The idea of a competency-based approach applies to educators as well as the student. These "ideas" are offered for adapting and changing according to the needs of your students, who will inevitably teach you about themselves.

...once I had a student who worked experimentally with Tinkertoys whenever he had free time. His constructions filled a storeroom in the art studio and a good part of his basement at home.

I rejoiced at the presence of such a student.
Here was an exceptionally creative mind at work.
He had something to teach me.

His presence meant that I had an unexpected teaching assistant in class whose creativity would infect other students.

ROBERT FULGHUM, *MAYBE*, 1993

SFBT Educator Training Exercise: Chapter 4

Defeating School Problems

With the following tools at your fingertips (plus many of your own!), respond differently this week to one teacher who approaches you about a child:

- Teacher Referral Form
- Student Information Sheet
- Scaling Questions

Commend the teacher on observing that the student needs improvement. Ask them to observe again, with a different focus: a solution focus. Explain to the teacher that you are more interested in when the student does well, even if only for a few minutes, than when he/she does poorly. Resist the temptation to diagnose or explain why the student may be responding negatively. Insist that there may be another way of helping the student "do what works" in school.

CHAPTER 5

COMBINING YOUR RESOURCES

GROUP COUNSELING

GETTING GROUPS STARTED IN YOUR SCHOOL

Applying SFBT ideas to groups in elementary and secondary schools simplifies and enriches the process in groups, lessens unproductive griping and story telling, and releases the counselor from solving the problem. The students have the opportunity to tell their story initially, and are then encouraged to switch directions from a problem-focus to looking for competencies within themselves and others. Instead of just venting and complaining about teachers, parents, or friends. Students leave with "exceptions" to their problem, contributed by group members and the school counselor. Instead of the groups being labeled as "problem-student groups," the SFBT educator describes them differently to parents, fellow educators, and students. The groups might be described as:

- An opportunity to discover for yourself and from the other group members how you might have solved your problem before (or not allowed it to bother you)
- A time to develop a plan that makes the problem less of a problem
- A time to share successes and feel supported

CHAPTER 5 FOCUS

- Gathering Support and Suggestions for Groups in Your School
- Case Study: The Group as an Intervention
- Basic Ideas for Group Planning
- Developing Specialty Groups

Getting Referrals for Groups

Initially, the group is formed by referrals from teachers or parents who make suggestions regarding the kinds of groups needed, and the times for groups to meet at school. Parents are sent home information on counseling services and encouraged to call and suggest their ideas for groups. This soliciting of suggestions seems to lessen questions about what is going on in schools, gives parents opportunities for input, and makes school more collaborative. On the next page is a handout that can be given to teachers and administrators. This handout requests educator participation for two reasons: 1) Educators experience the needs of their students daily in the classroom. The input of educators is a valuable resource in determining which kinds of groups would be helpful. 2) Whenever educators are asked for their input they become part of the process and decision making. This integral principle of SFBT takes the educator's world view and lessens resistance when students leave class for group or are late from a group process.

Assuring the educator that the counseling groups will not interfere with their daily instruction is important in creating cooperation. In addition, most school districts require parental permission for a student to participate in group counseling, especially in the primary grades. Once again, cooperation lessens resistance. This opportunity for inquiry again alerts parents that the school is on the side of the student and is considering their welfare. The legal requirements are also met with a signed permission form (attached to the *Parent Consent Form*).

When to Begin Groups

The second month of the school year or semester/quarter seems to be a better time to solicit group ideas from teachers. Giving teachers an initial period in school to observe students and deal with other required documentation and planning is considerate and beneficial. They will appreciate your consideration. Group counseling, after all, is designed to accommodate students and educators. The right time, the right group, and cooperation makes for a good group counseling program.

TEACHER SUGGESTIONS AND IDEAS FOR GROUP COUNSELING

Dear Teacher,

The counseling department is interested in your ideas regarding group counseling for our students. These groups will not interfere with your class time, and will meet before school, during lunch, or after school. It is my hope that these groups will help discover competencies in our students to solve their own concerns. On the lines below, please list various concerns or issues you might be aware of with your students. Please return this to me by

_____.

Thanks!

School Counselor

Suggestions:

Example: A group for students who display inappropriate anger

_____

_____

_____

_____

_____

_____

Parent Consent for Group Counseling

Dear Parent or Guardian,

Your son/daughter,_____ has requested to attend the
_____ group at our school. The time for this group will be:
_____on_____(day). The group will not conflict with class
instruction.

It is my plan to assist the students in this confidential group with identifying their
strengths and abilities to solve their own concerns. The group will meet for _____
weeks, unless your son/daughter decides to stop attending. Your permission for your
son/daughter will be appreciated. Please feel free to call the school with any questions. Please return by:_____

Thanks!

_____, School Counselor

- detach here -

Parent Permission:

_____ has my permission to attend group counseling at
_____(school), during the _____(year) school year.

_____
       Parent Signature

CASE STUDY: THE GROUP AS AN INTERVENTION

After Judy's parents divorced, Judy's father felt that his daughter's interest in school and friends had changed. Judy, 16, told her dad that she felt alone and sad most of the time. Judy and her mother had been close, and when her mother moved away, she felt abandoned. Her father called the school counselor and expressed his concerns to the counselor about his daughter. The school counselor described a group he was currently forming specifically for students dealing with family concerns. The group was a "generic" group, which the students would name themselves, and was facilitated by the school counselor. Judy was reluctant to visit the group initially, so the counselor visited with her individually and talked with her about how she had dealt with other changes in her life before. Judy said in the past, she often talked to her best friend or to her dad. She said her dad was pretty upset about the divorce and she didn't want to burden him any more than she should with her sadness. She was ashamed and embarrassed that her mother had now moved away and was living with a boyfriend. She often wondered if there could have been something she could have done differently to keep her mom from leaving. The counselor complimented her on her sensitivity to her dad's feelings and then asked her how she would like things to be for herself, now that her parents were divorced. She said she wanted to be happy again, because things had been difficult for some time. The counselor asked Judy: "What will I see you doing some day very soon that will tell me you are slightly happier than today?"

Judy sat up in her chair, smiled a bit and said she wanted to feel like being around others again. The counselor continued to build on Judy's ability to: a) talk with the counselor about her concerns, b) respect her dad's need for privacy, and c) talk with a best friend and her dad when she felt sad. Together, the counselor and Judy decided to come up with a plan based on how Judy handled situations of change in the past and how she now wanted things to be. When described in this way, Judy agreed to try the group at least once, the same way she often tried other new situations.

The First Group Meeting

The group met the following Tuesday morning before class. The group members were referred by teachers, parents, or were self-referred. The SFBT counselor wanted the group to be constructed in an interesting, helpful, and nonconfrontive manner. He discussed his role with the group the first day and described their time together as a place to come and talk about their concerns, learn about how they had solved problems in the past, and then leave with a plan to feel better. Mr. Smith, the counselor, merely assisted the group with a few basics: time, place, and compliments on times he heard the group members do well. He found that the group made up their own rules quite effec-

tively, when he suggested how other groups had been run before. The counselor began the first group with a request and a question: "I'm interested in all of you. Could you each please tell us briefly your reason for being in our group." And then:

"Realistically, how will you know when things are better for you?"

The counselor gave each student a file folder in which they made their own "case notes" each week. He asked the group for their comments and compliments on their peers' competencies often. Thereafter, the group basically ran itself, the counselor simply asking "What's better this week?" at the beginning of each group. He marveled how quickly the students began asking each other this same question, before he had a chance! The group usually ran for about six weeks. Within two weeks, Judy began associating with the members outside of group time, became more verbal at home, and participated more in school activities. At the conclusion of the group, the counselor asked the members what "worked" during the group time and Judy told him that the process made her aware that her feelings were normal and that she no longer felt like her problems were as big as before.

BASIC IDEAS FOR GROUP PLANNING

The Group Theme

Group counseling often includes a *theme* for the group, such as *behavioral issues, sibling rivalry, anger, chemical management, or sexual abuse survivor groups, students of divorced families,* and *educational issues such as study skills.* However, some counselors in schools who feel they must not label students or groups, hold "generic" groups, or groups with students who have various concerns. These groups do well, for SFBT ideas do not necessitate concentrating on particular solutions to particular problems, and instead, focus on one's competencies in solving similar problems. Students enjoy naming their group, so encouraging them to name it with a solution-focus is particularly helpful in creating a competent environment. For example, the following group names and their "membership" are ways of *redescribing* small groups with a solution-focus:

The Anger Managers

A group for elementary students who deal with their own anger or fighting with other students. The group name can be changed to *Anger Management* for junior high and high school students.

Homework Hustlers

A study skills group for elementary or junior high students who have difficulty turning in assignments or completing homework at home. Some high schools have named such a study skill or tutoring group *Academic Chances* or *Academic Opportunities.*

Between Friends and Family

A group for family, sibling, or friendship concerns. All ages seem to like this group name.

Transitions

A group for students new to the school, returning from medical leave, experiencing changes in their lives due to the loss of a loved one, recovering from chemical use, and so on. The title is liked by junior high and high school students.

The Solution Seekers

A generic name for a generic group dealing with various issues, all of which seek refuge from the problem at hand!

The Group Has a Process

The group has a *process*. When SFBT ideas are added, the process includes *looking for exceptions, doing something different, finding out what is working,* and *celebrating success.* These ingredients become part of a successful group process, making the group more productive and not as problem-focused. The group continues throughout its designated course by searching for and identifying exceptions to the problems concerning the group members, which offer solutions toward the designated goal. The group process uses basically the same format as individual and teacher-student conferences, the questions flow similarly around defining the goal of the student, identifying exceptions to the problem, and developing a task. The use of the "miracle question" (de Shazer, 1985) as a group topic is helpful in focusing the group members on what they will be doing when the problem is solved:
"If you each woke up tomorrow and discovered that a miracle had occurred overnight, what would be different as you went through your day that would tell you things were better for you?"

Developing Goals

The *goal* of the group is to empower students to solve their own problems. Goals are set early in the group by the individual members, and are limited to specific behaviors desired by the student of himself/herself. In other words, the group is not a place to complain about someone else. Should a student want things to be better for him/her and a parent, friend, or teacher, the goal will be stated in terms of what the student might do to change the interaction. An assumption of SFBT is that there is a *snowball effect*—meaning if one person changes, the interactions eventually must change since the behaviors will not be the same. The leader helps this goal description stay solution-focused by asking questions such as:

"If we followed you around with a video camera on the day you meet your goal, and you point out to all of us that life is better, what do you think we will see you doing?"

"You know, I'll bet you've talked a lot about this problem already. Let me suggest that we talk differently about this subject for a few minutes. How would you like things to be someday when the problem doesn't bother you as much?"

Spreading the Word

Announcements about groups are also made at faculty meetings, PTA meetings, and in the school newspaper. The names of contact persons are given to make the referral easier. Students are also able to self-refer themselves to a group. Since the groups meet before school, after school, during homeroom period, or lunch period, there is little interference with school work and teachers are more cooperative. The group combines the resources of faculty, students, and educators. The entire process of developing, forming, and running the groups is done systemically and collaboratively.

Ideas for Group Leaders

Perhaps one of the most integral elements of making SFBT groups successful is the assumption held by the group leader. A counselor who runs the group employing the following assumptions will probably influence the group members to complain less and be more responsible for their individual changes. The SFBT educator-group leader assists the group members in seeing their problems as solvable:

- People are competent
- Change is inevitable
- Exceptions to the problem exist
- Change takes time
- Focusing on solutions is more productive than focusing on problems

SUGGESTIONS FOR FACILITATING THE GROUP PROCESS

The following ideas for the group process can be used in basically all groups held in school situations. It is suggested that these be *guiding questions* which can be enhanced by the individual SFBT educator's style and resourcefulness, the ages of the group members, and the issues of the specific group:

1. Setting the Mood for Focusing on Solutions:

"What brings you to our group today?"

If a student was sent to the group as a consequence, necessity, or suggestion from a parent or teacher, ask:

"What would_____say was their reason for sending you here?" "What would _____probably say he/she needs to see so you can stop coming here?"

2. Goal Setting:

"How will you know when things are better for you?"

If the student describes what others will be doing and forgets to focus on his/her own goal, help him/her by asking specific questions such as:

"What do you see yourself doing realistically?" (Mention that the other people who he/she may be concerned about are not present.)

3. Searching for Exceptions to the Problem:

"I've been listening to you all as you've told us why you're here today. A lot of your descriptions sound really tough. Let's talk now about the times when things were not as tough."

"When was the last time you were able to get away from the problem that bothers you at times and have a little of the goal you just described to us?"

"How were you able to do that? Where were you? Who was there?"

"What did that do for you so the problem was smaller or not as intrusive?"

4. Encouraging Motivation:

"Someday when the problem that brought you here today doesn't bother you as much, what will you get to do more?"

"Who in our group knows_____(refer to someone in the group) fairly well? Who's seen him/her lately when the problem wasn't bothering him/her as much? What did you see him/her doing then?"

5. Task Development:

"You have all told me some great ideas about the times when problems bother you less. Let's talk now about what you might do next week that will assist you in keeping the problem at a distance in your life, so you can do what you really want to do."

"As we stop today, I'd like to ask you each to do something that only you can do. I'd like you to watch yourselves until we meet again, and notice when the problem isn't bothering you as much."

6. Conclusion:

"What did we do in here today that made a difference?"

"What would you suggest we do more of next week?"

The Role of the Group Leader

The role of the SFBT group leader is to create an environment in which students can discover and *experience* their competencies. How the leader does this is up to his/her individual resources. For some group leaders, a more active part is taken in activating "solution talk" through questions for each week or dealing with specific issues. The leader may redescribe the problem alone or collaboratively with the group, and ask the students to talk about it differently, helping them see the problem as helpful through this redescription. Normalizing and dissolving feelings of failure can be accomplished by asking group members to watch other group members during the group time or during the week in school and notice when the troubling problems are not as influential. The leader may begin successive meetings with:

"What's going better for each of you this week?"

"Who's noticed____(name of student) doing things differently this week and not giving in to the problem that bothers him/her at times?"

The SFBT counselor's primary position is to assist the students in discovering when the difficulty is less of a problem in their lives. Again, how he/she accomplishes this will be based on the counselor's and group members' individual resources. Perhaps begin the first group session with the question: "What's something you are really good at?" would be an intriguing way of getting to know the resources of the group members. There is not a need for vast background information nor is it necessary for the leader to have an understanding of how things became so difficult to run a group effectively. In fact, many school districts today discourage a counselor from probing into a student's life outside of school. The SFBT group leader·allows the respect and distance which may be appropriate, yet stays consistent, focusing on solutions. A counselor can elicit sufficient information for group discussions by simply asking:

"Briefly, what do you think we really need to know about you?"

"What would you say is the bottom line of your concern?"

"What finally happened so that you decided to come here and make changes?"

Sometimes a student will insist on telling "war stories." It is important to listen to him/her for a sufficient amount of time (varying with each student) and then mention that this group is different. The group members are interested in hearing about his/her past experiences and are honored that the new member is so trustworthy." Then: "Now we would like to talk about moving away from focusing on the problem to a time when things will be better for you."

The SFBT counselor listens creatively for exceptions, or times when the problem is not as invasive in the lives of the student. Looking at exceptions to problems is a different approach—students will catch on to their "exceptional abilities to see themselves differently," especially if the counselor appears "curious" in the questioning of their success. Be aware of and notice if the problem bothers the students during the group sessions. Assume that things will be better. Ask them directly how they have managed to keep the problem under control during group time. Then ask "When else today have you been this successful?" If he/she can't remember, ask the group!

SPECIFIC IDEAS FOR SPECIFIC GROUPS

Terry Walkup, a counselor at Bowman Middle School in Plano, Texas, passes out manila file folders to his students as he begins new groups each school year. On the following page is an "individual diary" for each group member to staple inside his/her folder. This is a nice and very inexpensive idea for keeping track of student success and documenting efficiently in schools. He asks the students to write down their goals, reasons for coming to the group, and begins to talk about the following scale which is included on the *Individual Diary Sheet*:

1	2	3	4	5	6	7	8	9	10
I am in control									The problem is in control

Terry asks the students to mark on the scale where they see themselves in regard to their problem as they begin the group sessions. He describes a "1" as being "completely taken over by the problem" and a "10" as "being in complete control of the problem." Each week, he begins the session by asking where the student is on the

scale in regard to his/her problem. He asks the students to circle their new position on the scale they have drawn on their file folder. He then asks them to write down how they accomplished the move. He ends the session by asking "Where would you like to be when we see you again?" By asking the student "How will you do that?" he assumes change will occur and conveys that assumption to the students.

THE GROUP THAT HATED THEIR MOTHERS

Terry once worked with a group of junior high school girls who "hated their mothers." These girls were referred to him by teachers who were concerned about the students' grades, self-esteem, and comments about their negative relationships with their mothers. As he began the group, the members wanted to name the group *"We Hate Our Mothers Group."* Terry assured them that group time was not going to be about how they hated their mothers, for he was certain that they had already had plenty of discussion on that issue. Instead, he described to them that this was going to be a group where they learned to like, or at least make peace with their mothers. This simple explanation seemed to work as the members renamed the group *"To Her With Love."* Terry said that the mere renaming of the group set a new context for the girls to begin thinking differently about their mothers.

Terry developed a list of questions from SFBT ideas to assist the students in their dilemma of hating their mothers. He asked the students to focus on exceptions to the problem and on times when the problem did not interfere in their lives. Terry perceived the students' concerns, and his preparation for the group consisted of questions that would steer them in a more solution-focused direction. Your expertise and experience with your students will assist you in developing your own solution-focused questions for various specialty groups. Notice the individual student personalities, what they need to stay on a subject, and your own resourcefulness/experience in accomplishing that goal. Some students may need to write down ideas, draw ideas, or relate them metaphorically. Your resourcefulness, like Terry's, will encourage your students to be resourceful as well. The next few pages contain questions designed by Mr. Walkup.

TO HER WITH LOVE*

1. When you and your mom get along, what will be better?

2. What will you get to do when the problem isn't there?

3. When in the past has the problem not interfered?

4. Scaling questions:
   On a scale of 1–10, where were you when you came in today?

5. Where would you like to be next week?

6. What do you know now about your successes in the past that will help you achieve your goal?

Future Sessions:

7. What's going better this week? How have you done that?

8. If I asked your mom what was better, what would she tell me? (Stay specific)

---

*Slightly adapted and printed with Terry Walkup's permission.

Name _____ **Date** _____

INDIVIDUAL GROUP DIARY

Name of Group:_____

My reason for coming here:_____

_____

I will know when things are better for me when I am able to:_____

_____

On the scale below, if 1 = Your problems are in complete control of you, and 10 = You are in complete control of your problems, circle where you are today:

_____

   1   2   3   4   5   6   7   8   9   10

Group Day #1:

Where are you today on the scale?____

What did you discover today about yourself that will help you move to a different point?

_____

_____

Group Day#2:

Where are you today on the scale?____

What did you discover today about yourself that will help you move to a different point?

_____

_____

Group Day #3:

Where are you today on the scale?____

What did you discover today about yourself that will help you move to a different point?

_____

_____

Group Day #4:

Where are you today on the scale?____

What did you discover today about yourself that will help you move to a different point?

_____

_____

Group Day #5:

Where are you today on the scale?____

What did you discover today about yourself that will help you move to a different point?

_____

_____

Group Day #6:

Where are you today on the scale?____

What did you discover today about yourself that will help you move to a different point?

_____

_____

_____

Externalizing Problems in Groups

Michael White talks of externalizing problems as a means of seeing them as intrusive in a person's life. This is an excellent approach for working with the adolescent population who developmentally may handle blame reluctantly, and children, who enjoy imaginative group processes and activities. In the group setting, the idea of "removing the problem from your life" is a welcomed topic and applicable for groups dealing with study skill development, transitions, or generic groups dealing with many different types of concerns.

On the following page are questions developed from the work of Michael White, which serve to guide and assist the SFBT educator in helping students free themselves of the problems that bother them. The guiding questions for externalizing problems follow the basic ideas of SFBT:

- *Goal Description:* describing how life will be when the influence of the problem is lessened.

- *Problem Maintenance:* discovering how the problem is kept in one's life by one's behavior.

- *Problem Externalization:* picturing the problem as outside of the person—the *problem* is the problem.

- *Competency/Exception Discovery:* discovering times when the influence of the problem does not affect one's life.

- *Task Development from Competencies:* learning to do more of what worked before to lessen the problem's influence in one's life.

Assigning the Tasks

Task development and completion in SFBT groups seems most successful when the student is asked to carry out the task for a very short period of time. Again, success and motivation go hand in hand and are possible when people attempt what they are competent at doing. Suggesting to a student to "do more of what's working now" practically guarantees that he/she can do it successfully. Enlisting the help of a group member to notice when the problem isn't bothering a student and electing a group member who succeeded in defeating his/her problem for a week and giving a certificate in that honor is powerful. Receiving a note from the group leader describing his/her amazement at the courage it takes to come to group when things are tough goes a long way in aligning with a student's world view and opens the front door to change.

GUIDING QUESTIONS FOR EXTERNALIZING PROBLEMS IN THE GROUP SETTING

1. What would your life be like without the "problem?" Who would be doing what?

2. How have you allowed the problem to interfere in your life?

3. What is it like when the problem is not affecting you as much? What are you doing during those times?

4. If you could visualize the problem, what would it look like?

5. How does the "problem" trick you into doing things you dislike later?

6. There must be times when the problem "doesn't stand a chance" although it tries to bother you. How do you stop it?

7. If you could write a story or play and title it Chapter 2, omitting the problem, what would be different from your current Chapter 1? Who would be in it?

8. From your description of the Chapter 2 story or play, what are some things you could gradually do now, to avoid the problem?

9. What would the audience applaud you doing when they watch you in Chapter 2?"

10. Did anyone in the group see _____(group member)'s problem bother him/her in group today? To member: How did you do that?

SEXUAL ISSUES GROUP

Students who come for help with "sexual issues" (abuse, rape, and so on) often view themselves as victims. However, many people who have experienced sexual abuse are very successful in careers, rear healthy children, and hold good jobs. After clarifying that the abuse is no longer taking place by reporting it to proper authorities, students may approach this group as a "way of defeating the influence of what's occurred." Phrases such as "escape from the problem," or "run from the problem" indicate that there is a way out. There is peace in knowing that one can run "from pain towards gain." The group activities that follow are designed to not focus on past traumas, but instead, to focus on abilities of students who have coped with such experiences so their lives may begin to be freed of the influence of the events:

1. Tell me briefly what you think I need to know about the reason you are here today.

2. Describe times in your life when you have not allowed the sexual (issue, abus) to take control and keep you from enjoying life.

3. What's different when you are in control of the sexual (issue, abuse) and you are doing what you want?

4. Someday soon when you are no longer troubled and imprisoned by this "issue," how will your relationships improve?

5. On a scale of 1–10, 1 being impossible and 10 being totally successful, where do you see yourself at this time in controlling the effects of your sexual issue on your relationships and your life?_____

Where would you like to be in the near future?_____

ANGER GROUP

Anger plagues everyone once in a while. A method of venting feelings, it can be a healthy release. Sometimes however, anger creates problems in our lives that makes us distance ourselves from others, causes us to threaten physical harm, or makes us sabotage future plans and relationships. The anger problem is externalized and spoken of as if it is *personified* and separate from the group member.

Situations in which I let *Anger* take over:	Situations where *Anger* is not successful:
1.	1.
2.	2.
3.	3.

In what situation (today) would you like to be in control of your anger?

When was the last time you were successful at being in control?

How did you accomplish this?

What is your plan today, based on how you listed your control in the chart above?

On a scale of 1–10, 1 = impossible, 10 = successful, where are you now in your control of *Anger*?_____Where would you like to be next week?_____

Between Friends and Family Group

1. If a miracle happened tonight when you were asleep and tomorrow you awoke to find things much better with your friend/family, how would it be different?

2. Has there been a time in the past when that happened, even slightly?

3. What were you doing to help that happen? What specifically would we have seen you do that worked better for you and your friend/family?

4. How did you do that?

5. How can you do that again now?

6. When things get better for you and your friend/family, what will that free you up to do more of?

7. On a scale of 1–10, with 10 being totally successful in accomplishing what you say you want with your friend/family, where were you when you came to group today? Where are you now?

8. Where would you like to be by the time the group meets again?

9. How will you do that, just for a few days (one week)?

10. I'd like the group members to watch_____this week and notice when you see him/her more at ease and less bothered by this problem. (Use if applicable)

CHEMICAL MANAGEMENT GROUP
FOR MAINTAINING A DRUG-FREE LIFE

Discouraging "Denial:"

1. How has drinking/using drugs kept you from succeeding in your life and living the way you want to live?

Goal Setting:

2. What will you get to do when alcohol/drugs are no longer a concern for you and others in your life?

3. Who will probably notice first that you are in control?

Exception Identification:

4. What have you tried in the past to control your drugs/drinking?

   List, then mark out unsuccessful strategies while asking "Did it work?" Recognize that the unmarked strategies are working strategies.

5. When did you last find yourself in control of the problem with drugs/alcohol? How were you able to do this? Where were you, who was there, or not there?

Task Development:

6. On a scale of 1–10, 1 = being completely taken over by drugs/alcohol and 10 = being in control of not using drugs/alcohol, were would you like to be?

7. Based on all that you've described to the group today that has helped you stay in control of not using drugs/alcohol, how will you move up the scale (or stay where you are) for the next week?

GROUP NOTES FOR GROUP LEADERS
TODAY'S DATE:_____

Keep track of group members and their achievements weekly and you will have ample exceptions for compliments and writing notes. On the lines below, list the member's name, and competency/exception that developed during the group time today. Consider a short note to the group member who truly "amazed" you!

Name	Exception/Competency
1.	
2.	
3.	
4.	
5.	
6.	
7.	

SFBT Educator Training Exercise: Chapter 5
Combining Resources

Consider groups or meetings you have attended in the past that were meaningful to you. Which occurred that you appreciated? Which activities/actions made such a difference that you wanted to attend consistently? What did the leader do or say that motivated and encouraged you?

Think back to groups you have facilitated or classroom guidance discussions that were successful. Solicit ideas from colleagues who have also facilitated class or group discussions.

Drawings, music, popular movie or television excerpts are all instigators of discussions. Think of your particular style. What are your resources that would make your involvement in group work fun, motivating, and solution-focused?

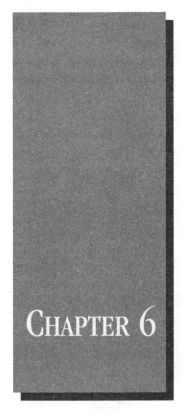

CHAPTER 6

TURNING IMPOSSIBILITIES INTO POSSIBILITIES

IDEAS FOR DIFFICULT SITUATIONS

School counselors are presented with a wide array of problems by parents, teachers, and students. Often, the problems go beyond classroom difficulties and stem from outside influences. School counselors must "stay on the fence" and not permeate too deeply into personal issues, yet still offer a supportive position to the student, teacher, or parent requesting help. Schools today must exercise caution in their strategies and not cross religious, cultural or socioeconomic boundaries. The SFBT ideas in this chapter focus on assisting educators with the more difficult situations occurring in schools today. Many of the situations included in this chapter are dealt with in a manner appropriate to the individual situation, yet avoid ethical impasses and cultural, religious, and socioeconomic differences through the SFBT questions. While all the case studies offered in this chapter differ in content, issue, and process, the basic constructs are the same: the focus is on identifying the solution, and not the problem.

Consider the ideas behind the interventive questions as individually tailored strategies, not rigid suggestions. The ideas behind each question/intervention/task solicit the competencies within the person in counseling and develop the tasks through his/her own discoveries. Our job is to assist them in discovering, even when the situation seems impossible.

171

CHAPTER 6 FOCUS:

- Case Study: A gift of hope
- Interventions for Crisis Situations
- Suicide, Loss, and Sexual Abuse: Ideas for resolution
- Additional Case Studies: Ideas for students, parents, and teachers dealing with problems in school or family issues
- Conclusive Case Study: An extremely creative and resourceful engineer

CASE STUDY: A GIFT OF HOPE

I once worked with an eighth grade girl and her mom who wanted to improve their relationship. The mom was dying of cancer, her husband was divorcing her, and she wanted to spend the remaining months of her life in a fruitful relationship with her daughter. The mom worried about her daughter's school performance yet her daughter had not listened to her mom's pleas for being responsible for herself and her school work. The daughter was failing two subjects at school and was in detention at school on a daily basis. The mom's energy level was extremely low yet she insisted on staying up until the wee hours of the morning begging her daughter to do her homework. The daughter, becoming quite tearful at her mom's descriptions, looked first at me and then to her mom and then said clearly:

"Mom, if you will let *me* be responsible sometimes and stop doing everything for me so much, I might feel like I can do something. You tell me all the time how *you* help *me*. It makes me feel so guilty that I don't enjoy any kind of privilege or want to leave you to go with my friends. It's hard seeing you so sick. I wish you would give me things to do and expect me to do them so I would feel freer to do things on my own."

Goal Setting:

I was amazed and impressed at the daughter's insight into her situation and told her so. I then appealed to mom on behalf of her daughter's wishes, that it was time to go one step further to instill in her daughter something she had tried to do for years: give her hope. Two sessions ago, individually, the mom had said to me that she wanted to give her daughter what she had never had in her life—hope. She told me her parents were very negative with her when she was growing up and that her husband of twenty-one years had never given her anything. She bought the house, furniture, and did everything for the children. She said she was determined to teach her daughters to have hope by telling them how to do well in each of their endeavors. This monumental task left her quite frustrated and exhausted as her daughter argued with her over what she wanted and needed to do in her life. I commended mom on her efforts and then asked her daughter if becoming more responsible might give her hope. She said yes. The task developed from the mom's wish that her daughter would behave more responsibly. After a few minutes of exploring how she had encouraged that before, both she and her daughter came up with what had worked before. These successes were integrated into tasks.

Task Development

1. For one week, mom was to notice as closely as possible the times when her daughter was responsible and reply "Wow, that's great." This was in keeping with mom's desire to be around her daughter continually during her final days of life, but instead of telling her daughter how to live her life, she was to observe her competencies in living it.

2. The daughter was to act responsible with the two subjects she was failing at school, and without her mother's assistance, do whatever she thought might bring the grades up to passing. She was also to bring more friends home so mom could see that her choice of friends was of a high caliber.

3. The mother, instead of worrying about telling the daughter how to live and be responsible for her school work would do things for herself that once brought her joy, before the illness progressed. I enlisted the support of her daughter and reframed it as a means of "living life in the most hopeful way."

4. I encouraged mom to give her daughter specific chores that she could complete in a responsible way. I then mentioned that the most important part of giving her the chores was in watching how she chose to do them on her own.

5. Finally, I asked the daughter to "give mom something to notice" this week that would convince her that she was becoming very responsible and that she could stop doing all of the work for her and instead, look forward to their pleasant, hopeful times together.

The daughter and mom came back the next week and the daughter reported that she had contacted her teachers and arranged for tutoring three afternoons per week. She said she had been given chores on Saturday, all of which she had worked very hard at to complete. When she finished, she was so exhausted, she was reluctant to go out with her boyfriend as promised by her mother. The mother encouraged her to get dressed and go out. The daughter reluctantly did so and had a good time. I commended the mother for making such a supportive move. We continued to talk about how mom's supportive manner seemed to work better for her daughter. I asked them both: "What do you want to continue doing during the next week that is already working?" Mom said she would like to continue to help her daughter be responsible by backing off. The daughter smiled and said she wanted more time with mom, to work at her own pace on school assignments and to make mom see her as responsible.

INTERVENTIONS FOR CRISIS SITUATIONS

Aligning with the Student:

Check out how the student, parent, or teacher has coped to this point. Ask:

"How have you managed to this point?"

"How have you kept things from getting worse?"

Goal Setting:

Ask the student what needs to be better for himself/herself? The goal is stated in specific, behavioral terms for the person with the complaint. For example:

"How will you know when things are slightly better for you?"

Discovering Exceptions to the Problem:

Identifying times when "the problem" occurs less gives strategies for lessening the impact of the problem at times it reappears. These exceptions may occur in different situations in one's life, but the skills are useful in all situations. For example:

"Have there been times when you were involved with a problem similar to this?"

"How did you handle similar situations that seemed to help?"

"In the past, how have you handled other really rough times?"

"When has this problem not occurred?"

Task Development:

"From your descriptions of what has worked before during other tough moments, what would you suggest trying for this afternoon (today, this week)? How will you do that?"

WHEN STUDENTS TALK ABOUT SUICIDE: CONVERSATIONS THAT ENCOURAGE LIFE

A high school counselor relayed the story of a 17-year-old female student who came to his office tearfully, claiming to have suicidal thoughts. She appeared frightened and very upset. The first words uttered by the SFBT counselor were: "How did you know to come here? I'm so glad you came."

The student, crying steadily, said she just had to talk to someone because she was afraid she would kill herself. The school counselor checked with the student regarding a plan. She had no plan. She said she had thought about suicide for several months, since her boyfriend had dropped her and her dad had moved out. Her life had seemed hopeless and her mother, now having to work at night to support her and her ten-year-old sister, no longer spent time with her. She talked of worrying constantly about killing herself and wanted more than anything to be happy again (Goal). The school counselor explores with the student how she has managed to stay alive:

Counselor: With all this going on, I am amazed at your ability to cope. I notice here on the attendance record that you haven't missed a single day of school. Tell me, how have you kept from hurting yourself over the past few months and stayed alive in spite of all that you're dealing with?

Student: I don't know. I guess I didn't want to hurt my mom. She has enough to worry about with my little sister at home and dad leaving her for someone else. (Exception)

Counselor: Wow, so you thought of how it would affect people. What else helped you stay alive?

Student: I guess I really didn't want to kill myself, it's just that it seemed like the only way out.

Counselor: Have there been times during the past few months when things were really hard and you found a small "way out" just for a little while?

Student: Well, my friends helped. They would get really upset and say "Oh, don't be stupid, you don't want to kill yourself. Call me if you get sad." I did that a few times, and it helped but the feelings didn't go away. (Exception)

Counselor: What did that do for you, when your friends told you to not kill yourself and to call them instead?

Student: It made me feel like I was important to someone...like someone cared. (Exception)

Counselor: How many people do you think really care about you? (Spends the next few minutes encouraging her to count her acquaintances who care)

Student: Probably my mom, my sister, my dad, even though he's not here anymore. I guess my friends, my teachers, even my exboyfriend might care.

Counselor: You certainly do have quite a team of people who care. When else have the feelings you mentioned been less of a worry to you?

Student: I have a job after school, and I'm really busy there—the feelings aren't quite as bad then. (Exception)

Counselor: Wow, so you know how to put the feelings aside so they don't worry you as much by talking to friends, being busy at work—when else?

Student: Well, at school, sometimes I don't think about it as much, or I talk to a friend and that helps. It's mostly at night, when my mom is working and I'm with my little sister that it's really bad. (Exception)

Counselor: I see, how many hours is that, would you say?

Student: From about 8:00 P.M. to 11:00 P.M.

Counselor: So, about three hours a night.

Student: Yes, until mom gets home. (Exception)

Counselor: You mentioned that mom doesn't talk as much as she used to. If she were in here today and heard some of your worries, what do you think she would say?

Student: Probably that I shouldn't think of suicide...and that I should tell her. But she doesn't know...I haven't told her.

Counselor: I get the impression that you and your mom have been close in the past.

Student: Yes, until dad left.

Counselor: How in the past have you gotten mom to be close to you, when you really needed her?

Student: I waited until a good time, like when she wasn't too busy. We used to stay up really late and watch movies together. (Exception)

Counselor: I see. If you were to use some of what you've told me today to keep yourself safe, what would you do for the next few days to get a way out from these worries?

Student: I guess talk to friends, keep busy at work and school, and tell my mom I need to talk with her more. (Task development)

Counselor: Great ideas. Tell me, what did we do here that might have made a difference?

Student: Well, talking always seems to help. Now it seems like I do have friends who do care. It's just that I wasn't thinking about that until you mentioned it—I guess I've been too wrapped up in myself.

By the time the session ended, the counselor had developed a warm and trusting rapport with the student. He informed her of school policy to call parents if a child mentions suicide or another life-threatening circumstance. Together, the student and counselor called her mother. The counselor mentioned to the mother the exceptions noted by the student, which had helped her stay alive. He then mentioned to the mom how important she was to her daughter. The mom asked the counselor what she should do for her daughter. In reply, the counselor tapped into the mother's competencies when he asked her: "What have you done in the past when your daughter was really upset like today?"

The mother replied that she typically knew when her daughter was upset but apparently had not noticed enough lately. She said she needed to take more time to talk with her and stay aware of her feelings and needs. The counselor complimented her on knowing her daughter and suggested that she do what had worked before, since her daughter had mentioned to him today how important their closeness had been.

The daughter and mom then conversed over the phone and decided to talk that night. The counselor asked the student to check back with him the next day and assisted her with making a list of her friends to call if she needed someone besides her mom to talk to when mom was at work. He saw her smile for the first time as she left his office. He took a few minutes that afternoon and wrote a short note to the student:

Dear Sandy,

Thanks for the opportunity to talk to you today. After you left my office, I remained impressed with your ability to identify several "ways out" of a difficult situation. You certainly appear to be a young lady with sensitivity and courage, not only with dealing with the changes occurring in your family, but with your needs. Hooray for you to do something that worked before by talking to someone. Coming to talk to me instead of hurting yourself proved to me how important you truly believe you are to your mom and sister. I hope you will notice during the next few days just how important you are to them. I encourage you to watch very closely their actions and words and notice the small ways they tell you about your importance to them each day. My door is open to you should you decide to come by anytime.

Sincerely,

School Counselor

The use of SFBT ideas in critical situations such as the one described above assisted the student in feeling heard, developing personal strategies, and connecting with her parent. Adolescents often see life and its experiences as extremes and neglect (as do adults) to see their competencies of coping. The scenario described previously centered in the world view of the student. Assumptions utilized by the SFBT counselor were:

Non-pathological approach

Instead of focusing on *why* the student was thinking about suicide, the counselor chose to affirm the fact that she had not harmed herself, and wondered out loud how she had coped so well with so much going on in her life.

Students define the goal of counseling

The student wanted to discontinue having the worries about suicide and feel happier. She also wanted to know that someone cared for her in her life. These concerns were addressed specifically by the counselor.

Fit with the student's world view

The counselor was quite empathetic towards the student, who described her life as hopeless and lonely. He aligned with her needs when he asked how many people would be concerned about her. He also helped her to define the number of hours she spent worrying about suicide, which again, helped her see her situation differently.

Students have complaints, not symptoms

The counselor was aware of school policy which stated that he would need to call her mother, yet spent sufficient time with the student, normalizing her feelings and encouraging her strengths. He did not see her as a person who needed his expertise to solve the problem. Instead, he acted curious about how she had stayed alive so far, in spite of the problems. Seeing herself as a competent human being enabled her to after her self-perception.

Focus on the possible and changeable

To focus on changing her feelings of worry about suicide would have been less productive than focusing on what the student could do to lessen the worries. By assisting the student with identifying times when she felt less worried about harming herself, and less anxious about no one caring, he opened up possibilities for her to do something to lessen the problem's impact on her life. Talking to her friends, concentrating on school and work and talking more closely to her mother were all tasks she could do since she had done them previously.

Preserving the Influence of a Loved One: Ideas for Dealing with Death

Michael White, in his book, *Selected Papers,* 1990, writes about persons who are experiencing "pathological mourning" and mentions that "such persons are well acquainted with the map for the grief process...they clearly understand that they have failed, in their grief work, to reach the appropriate destination. They "know" that their arrival at this destination will be evidenced by a fully experienced "goodbye," acceptance of the permanence of the loss of the loved one, and a desire to get on with a new life that is disconnected from that person. What is helpful about this process is again facilitating a context in which the student perceives himself/herself differently and writes his/her new story.

At first contact, persons experiencing "delayed grief" or "pathological mourning" look as if they have lost their own "selves" as well as the loved one. White says it can be expected that, under these circumstances, further grief work oriented by another model, or one that specifies the stages of the grief process according to the saying goodbye metaphor will complicate the situation further, rather than empower these persons and enrich their lives. Instead, White suggests more of a cooperative model in which the student, teacher, or parent appreciates the influence of the loved one on their lives and applies it currently.

Creating a New Reality: Ideas for Secondary Students

Cooperating with clients is an integral part of SFBT, which encourages success, and lessens failure and resistance. As persons grieve about the loss of a loved one, a counselor who aligns with their feelings and respects the need to talk and relive memories with the loved one, helps to create a new reality...a reality in which the loved one's influences are kept and cherished. White (1989) has developed questions to assist the person in counseling to develop a new reality. See the questions on the reproducible page that follows.

Name _____ Date _____

CREATING A NEW REALITY: DEALING WITH LOSS

If you were seeing yourself through ___'s eyes right now, what would you be noticing about yourself that you could appreciate?

_____

_____

_____

What difference would it make to how you feel if you were appreciating this in yourself right now?

_____

_____

What do you know about yourself that you are awakened to when you bring alive the enjoyable things that ____ knew about you?

_____

_____

What difference would it make to you if you kept this realization about yourself alive on a day-to-day basis?

_____

_____

What difference would feeling this way make to the steps that you could take to get back into life?

_____

_____

How could you let others know that you have reclaimed some of the discoveries about yourself *that* were clearly visible to _____, and that you personally like?

_____

_____

Reprinted with permission of Michael White.

A Different Context Creates a Different Perception = New Behaviors

This resource attempts to suggest that possibilities can unfold when people are assisted in creating a context in which to see themselves differently and recognize themselves as competent. This new way of seeing oneself, or *redescription of one's experience,* has a profound effect on how one perceives oneself as life goes on. With this idea in mind, consider how persons define and contextualize the idea of losing someone important in their lives. The recollection of time before the death is dominant and when the loved one dies, that recollection seems incorrect, for a key player is absent. The person often feels abandoned and disoriented as to which way to turn for comfort. Many models on working with death issues encourage persons to "let go" and move on with their lives. This is very difficult, and often encourages resistance which results in depression, anger, and isolation. What White suggests through his development of questions is *restorying our lives after a death occurs, integrating how the deceased person might perceive us* and perceiving ourselves in that manner. This kind, sensitive approach has brought peace to many persons.

The SFBT educator who suggests to students, teachers, and parents who mourn the loss of a loved one that "saying good-bye" is not necessary, lessens resistance, lessens anxiety, and instead helps them to restory their fond experiences with their loved one. A high school senior might be asked to recall how she thought her mother would see her graduate and go on to college. This kind remembrance and reverence for the deceased loved one offers students new ways to use "alternative stories" and live by the perceptions their loved one had for them. Michael White found that his questions inspired the creation of fuller lives—instead of fighting the urge to "move on and forget," persons in counseling relinquished to the influence of the positive and loving perceptions of the person no longer physically with them.

Externalizing Sadness: Ideas for Elementary Students

Peggy Dowell, an elementary counselor at Aikin Elementary School in Richardson, Texas, relayed her work with a young student who had lost her grandmother. The grandmother and grandfather had lived with her family for a few years, and when the grandmother became very ill, the student became closer to her. The student had daily episodes of tearfulness, to which her teacher would send her to the counselor for assistance. Peggy began by talking about the problem as "sadness" instead of as the death of her grandmother. The student began to talk about the sadness readily. The dialogue was recalled by the counselor as follows:

Ms. Dowell: How big is this sadness sometimes, when it bothers you the most?

Student: As big as this room, up above the roof and into heaven!

Ms. Dowell: ...and with it being so big, you still come to school, do okay in your class and even come here to talk to me...Wow! How do you do that?

Student: I don't know, I just think I'm supposed to.

Ms. Dowell: Are there times when the "sadness" is not as big?

Student: Yes, when I talk to my grandfather, but he's really sad too.

Ms. Dowell: When else?

Student: When I play in my room with my little sister, or ride my bike, or when I have to do my homework.

Ms. Dowell: Then, how big is it?

Student: It's about as tall as I am.

Ms. Dowell: Has there been a time lately when you could have let the sadness take over and you didn't?

Student: Well, yesterday, I cried and cried, and then I stopped for science class.

Ms. Dowell. Really, you just stopped like that?

Student: Yes.

Ms. Dowell: I wonder, how might you do that this afternoon if the "sadness" bothers you and you begin to cry?

Student: I guess I could just stop, or do something else at my desk.

Ms. Dowell: You know, you aren't crying right now... in fact, you're smiling...how big is the sadness now?

Student: I think it's kind of small.

Ms. Dowell: What's going on that's helping that to happen?

Student: Sometimes it helps to talk about it too.

Ms. Dowell: Okay, tell you what, if you want, you can stop by here whenever you want a "break" from the sadness, okay?

Student: Okay.

Peggy's use of "scaling questions" in the form of "How big is it?" encouraged the student to see the problem as something she could control with her behavior. Peggy said that the initial conversation was all the student seemed to need to begin to control the tearfulness. The student thereafter intermittently stopped by a few times and talked about the "sadness" and had many fewer tearful episodes in the classroom. This approach of "externalizing" sadness and redescribing a death as "sadness" instead of "loss" helped the young student deal with her feelings and contextualize them differently, as something she could control.

SEXUAL ABUSE SURVIVORS: DISCOURAGING THE INFLUENCE OF ABUSE

In many models, the sensitive issues of sexual abuse encourage a portrayal of people as victims, and give reasons why they cannot achieve certain levels of living. My concern over such portrayals is that the people presented as "victims" are very successful persons. I prefer to see them as "survivors" of terrible ordeals, who have stepped out of the influences of the abuse and become survivors! I am impressed with their courage, drive, and determination to succeed beyond the wildest dreams of their perpetrators.

Normalizing Discourages Victimhood

A suggestion emphasized throughout this manual is that recognizing competencies and treating students normally in spite of their difficult experiences creates a different perception of themselves. New perceptions encourage different behaviors. Teachers have long believed that *expecting* their students to perform encourages their performance. Treating a child or adolescent as a survivor rather than a victim encourages him/her to feel okay about himself/herself and behave as such. Such treatment discourages problem formation and stagnation. We do our students a favor when we don't do them favors! When we curiously ask students how they manage to cope with life's difficult times, we make them the experts on their own success and encourage that behavior to continue.

Educators, therefore, have opportunities to become strong allies with survivors and help them see themselves this way. William Hudson O'Hanlon compares two approaches to working with clients who have experienced sexual abuse on the next page: the *Traditional Approach* and *Possibility Therapy Approach*. The page that follows offers ideas for ways of approaching these survivors based on *Possibility Therapy*, a development from the solution-focused model.

CONTRASTING APPROACHES TO THE TREATMENT OF THE AFTEREFFECTS OF SEXUAL ABUSE*

William Hudson O'Hanlon, M.S.
The Hudson Center for Brief Therapy, 11926 Arbor, Omaha, NE 68144 USA

Traditional Approaches	Possibility Therapy
Therapist is the expert and has model about sexual abuse to which the student needs to submit (Colonization/missionary model)	Student and therapist both have particular areas of expertise (Collaborative model)
Client is viewed as damaged by the abuse (Deficit model)	Student is viewed as influenced but not determined by the abuse history, having strengths and abilities (Resource model)
Remembering abuse and the expression of repressed affect (*catharsis*) are goals of treatment	Goals are individualized for each student, but do not necessarily involve catharsis or remembering
Interpretation and management of transference	Acknowledgment, permission, validation/valuing and opening possibilities
Past-oriented	Present/Future-oriented
Problem/pathology-oriented	Solution-oriented
Must be long-term treatment or is seen as colluding in denial and minimization	Variable/individualized length of treatment
Invites conversations for insight and working through	Invites conversations for accountability and action and declines invitations to blame and invalidation

---

*Parts of this chart were adapted by William Hudson O'Hanlon, M.S., from "Overcoming the Effects of Sexual Abuse: Developing a Self-Perception of Competence," by Michael Durrant and Kate Kowalski in *Ideas for Therapy with Sexual Abuse*, edited by Michael Durrant and Cheryl White (1990), Dulwich Centre Publications (Adelaide, Australia). Reprinted with permission.

POSSIBILITY THERAPY WITH SURVIVORS OF SEXUAL ABUSE

William Hudson O'Hanlon, M.S.
The Hudson Center for Brief Therapy, 11926 Arbor, Omaha, NE 68144 USA

Find out what the student is seeking in treatment and how he/she will know when treatment has been successful.

Ascertain to the best of your ability that the sexual abuse is not current. If it is, take whatever steps necessary to stop it.

Don't assume that the student needs to go back and work through traumatic memories. Some people will and some won't. Remember that everybody is an exception.

Use the natural abilities the student has developed as a result of having to cope with abuse (e.g., being facile at dissociating). Turn the former liability into an asset.

Look for resources and strengths. Focus on underlining how they made it through the abuse and what they have done to cope, survive, and thrive since then. Look for nurturing and healthy relationships and role models they had in the past or have in the present. Look for current skills in other areas. Have the person tell you how they stopped themselves from acting on destructive impulses, got themselves to seek therapy, etc. despite having the aftereffects of sexual abuse.

Validate and support each part of the person's experience and self.

Use symbolic tasks and objects to help mark transitions from the past and to help externalize the problem or some experience to be worked on.

Make provisions (e.g., contracts) for safety from suicide, homicide, and other potentially dangerous situations if necessary. Make these mutual.

Keep focused on the goals of treatment rather than get lost in the gory details.

Do not give the message that the person is "damaged goods" or that his/her future is determined by having been abused in the past. Remember that change can occur in the interpretations associated with the event(s).

Gently challenge self-blaming or invalidating identity stories the person has or has accepted.

WHEN FAMILY PROBLEMS BECOME OVERWHELMING, IT'S TIME TO ESCAPE!

Case Study: "The Burdens" are after me!

Charles Thompson, a counselor at Kilgore Middle School in Kilgore, Texas told me the story of an adolescent who came to his office wanting the "burdens" in his family to stop. Apparently, the young adolescent felt as if he needed to help solve the adult issues occurring in his home, and found that his efforts were not succeeding. Saying he felt rather "burdened," Charles began to talk about "the burdens" as if they were external. He asked the student:

CT: When is it that the burdens don't bother you?

Student: Well, when I concentrate on school and not on the burdens, I do better. Sometimes when I leave my problems at home and put my mind on other things it's better.

CT: Really? I wonder how you could do that more often?

Student: What?

CT: Leave your burdens at home.

Student: (*After a very long pause*) I could write them down and leave them on my dresser.

CT: I wonder what will happen when you begin to do that?

Student: I'll probably feel a lot better.

The student went back to see Mr. Thompson a few days later and reported that he was feeling much better. He said he had gone home and written down all the "burdens" which had followed him to school (his words) and left them inside the house each morning when he went to school. The student said he made it a routine to slam the door firmly, a signal to him that the burdens couldn't go to school with him.

CASE STUDY: BEING ON TIME

Charlie Thomas of Burkner High School in Richardson, Texas, worked with a "hardcore" adolescent who had previously lived with his father after his parents divorced. The student ran into problems with his father and was kicked out of his home. The

"punishment" was to live with his mother, whom he had not stayed with for years. Distraught, the student came to the counselor because of the constant bickering and yelling between him and his mother. Charlie suggested that the student and his mom meet with him together. Mom clearly stated that she was interested in having a better relationship with her son and wanted to stop yelling at him, but his current antics were quite discouraging and frustrating to her. Charlie began the meeting with a question:

CT: How have you handled things before when you became frustrated and managed not to yell at your son?

Mother: Well, I'm not sure. It's just that he doesn't take care of himself, physically...that's what keeps us fighting.

CT: What do you mean by taking care of himself?

Mother: Doing his chores, keeping himself clean.

CT: When do you find that he *does* his chores and keeps himself clean?

Mother: You know, come to think of it, he does do a lot around the house, and for the most part, he keeps himself clean. I think the hardest part is that I have to go in and get him up every morning, and I get tired of it.

CT: I can understand that.

Student: I used to get myself up at dad's...I had an alarm clock.

CT: Oh, really? Where is the clock now?

Student: (*Looking at mother*) I don't know.

Mother: We can sure get one.

CT: Think so? Hmmm, and you think you can get yourself up by yourself like you did before at dad's, so the two of you can get along better?

Student: Yeah, I can get myself up.

Charlie saw the student a week after the session and asked him how things were going with mom. The student said: "Great...things with me and mom are great." This example of using a solution-focus with the stated goal by both mother and son, assisted them towards noticing when things worked. The successful solutions did not necessitate Charlie knowing more about the son's move to mom's home, nor the transitions mom was experiencing. He could respect their privacy in those issues yet still be extremely helpful. His role was that of facilitator, not of problem solver.

CASE STUDY: "I'M NOT AFRAID OF THE BAD WORDS ANYMORE"

Tricia Long, an elementary counselor at Corey Elementary School in Arlington, Texas, told of an elementary student who lived with her mother and her mother's boyfriend after the parents' divorce. The child had been a frequent visitor to the counselor's office and had often sadly told about the "bad words that mommy says to me." The child's case had been reported to Child Protective Services by the counselor, yet little had been done since there was no physical abuse. Ms. Long knew that she often visited her father every other weekend and asked if she had ever told him of the concerns she had about the "bad words." The student said she was afraid to tell her father because her mother would surely get angry and then things would get worse.

Ms. Long continued working with her and one day asked her how she coped with "the bad words." The child mentioned going to her room and putting on her earphones to her tape recorder, reading a book, or watching television as means of avoiding the bad words. Upon hearing the child's coping skills, Ms. Long congratulated her on her wonderful ideas for dealing with the bad words in a very grown-up manner. Ms. Long continued to see the student for a short time and within three weeks, the student happily reported that she had told her father about the "bad words," which he responded to by filing for custody of his daughter. Both father and daughter became closer and the daughter's depression lifted.

WHAT DOES BEING DISRUPTIVE DO FOR YOU?

I once saw an adolescent who was "dragged" to counseling by his mother. The junior high student was failing two subjects and the mother was certain it was due to his poor relationship with his father. His dad, an alcoholic, had been cruel to him verbally for years. The mother was contemplating a divorce, yet was currently more concerned about her son's attitude, which filtered throughout the household, disrupting "everything." The son sat, arms crossed, assured that there was nothing I could do to make him "change," and told me so. I told him I was glad that was out of the way because I felt the same way. I then asked him:

Counselor: What will need to happen so that you can stop coming here?

Student: I don't know.

Counselor: If I asked your mom, what do you think would be the first sign that you didn't need to come here?

Student: Well, probably staying out of in-school-suspension. Probably not going to the alternative school they're all trying to throw me in.

Counselor: Alternative School? Wow...what do you think about going there?

Student: Fine with me.

Counselor: What will that do for you to go to an alternative school?

Student: It's just a change...different people...I've had friends who went there and they said it wasn't that bad...better than school now.

Counselor: How would you like things to be?

Student: For people to get off my back.

Counselor: Like who?

Student: The teachers, my dad, my mom, my sister.

Counselor: And alternative school, will that do it?

Student: I don't know...probably not.

Counselor: You certainly know what you want. I'm wondering, mom said you were failing two classes. Tell me about the other five that you are passing....

Student: History, Math, Art, Life Management, and P.E.

Counselor: Wow, quite a few. What's your secret?

Student: Secret to what?

Counselor: Passing...I'm much more interested in what you're passing so together, you and I can work on getting these people all off your back.

Student: I think the teachers like me.

Counselor: I'm not surprised by that. What would they say you do in their classes that helps them like you?

Student: I don't know, I guess I don't get in trouble as much in there.

Counselor: How do you do that? I'll bet there's opportunities to get in trouble.

Student: (*Laughing*) Sure, all the time.

Counselor: Yet you still manage to pass and stay out of trouble in those classes?

Student: Yeah, I guess.

Counselor: You know, I'm just wondering if, for the next week, you might look a little more closely at exactly how you pass those five classes. I'd like you also to consider staying out of alternative school for another week, so all these people you want off your back can see you a little differently.

Student:"Okay.

Sometimes students are resistant because they feel like failures. Rebelliousness is a cover-up for insecurity. Cooperating with students and finding out what certain behaviors (negative or positive) do for them lessens resistance and rebellion. Shifting the benefits of the change to the student in the above scenario helped in this way, and gave him a chance to show "those in charge" that he was indeed competent. The teachers of the student described in this case called his mother two weeks after the first session to remark how his attitude about school had changed. He was able to bring up one more grade and was then tested for special education assistance in another subject. The student continued to do well in school. I worked with him two more times and our conversations centered around his ability to "stay out of alternative school," which always brought both a smile and sense of pride to his face.

LOOKING FOR ANSWERS IN ALL THE RIGHT PLACES: A CONCLUSIVE CASE STUDY

This chapter has attempted to present many diverse situations to educators so that the flexibility of the SFBT model could be examined. Like any way of thinking or working with people, its effectiveness in the classroom, administrator's office, or counseling office depends on applicability. Educators who have applied SFBT ideas to various school situations remark about its flexibility and adaptability to many different types of cases.

Does this Work in Really Difficult Situations?

One of the most common questions I receive when training educators or counselors in the SFBT model for schools is: "Does this work in really difficult situations?" Of course, the definition of a "really difficult situation" may vary according to one's perception or belief. To conclude this chapter and to answer this question, I would like to share a story about a very difficult situation told to me by the mother of a very ill little boy.

AN EXTREMELY CREATIVE AND RESOURCEFUL ENGINEER WHO SAVED HER SON'S LIFE

Although the child was not school age, this situation could have occurred at any age. The child was one-and-a-half years old when his mom came, alone, to the first session. As she sat down, she immediately burst into tears and told me her eighteen-month old son was diagnosed as needing a heart transplant. She told me of two open-heart surgeries he had already experienced in his young life. The doctors had told her that a tumor had grown and became enmeshed with his heart and neither tumor nor heart could be seen as separate. Her son was one of less than a hundred children (all of whom died) since the 1800s to be diagnosed with that particular tumor. If he did not have the transplant, he would die. For several moments I did not know what to say to her. I empathized with her pain and tried to comfort her as much as I could. It seemed like a hopeless situation,

Then I slowly began with SFBT questions:

Counselor: With all these concerns about Ben, what can we do here in our time together that might assist you just slightly?

Mother: I want to learn to cope with knowing he has to have a heart transplant. It's so hard every day. I'm an engineer and I have debated quitting my job and spending every second with him, but my husband and I don't think that would be good either. We're also concerned about the medical bills and whether the insurance will cover the heart transplant. I've decided to keep working.

Counselor: I know this is a very difficult situation for you, but I wonder how in the past you coped with tough times....in other words, what works to help you cope with difficulties?

Mother: Well, I do research on my job when things get tough. I'm a very logical thinker and when I get into the computer at work and do research projects, it makes me think I've got some control.

Counselor: What else helps?

Mother: My husband helps...we do a lot with Ben. I also talk a lot with my neighbor. She knows quite a few physicians. Everyone I know is looking for answers. It helps to look for answers. I've read everything I can find on the tumor.

Counselor: Since you're a logical thinker and enjoy the computer, and get comfort from reading and searching, I wonder how you might use that even more during the next few weeks as you await the donor heart. I wonder...are you on many databases at work?

Mother: Yes.

Counselor: We have two medical schools in our area (she was from the northeast), two nursing schools, and a large university. It might be interesting for you and I to check into which databases they might suggest for you to consult with to learn as much as you can, since you said that works.

Mother: I like that idea. The more I know, the more I feel prepared.

That day, she and I called the various medical schools, nursing schools, and universities in our city to inquire about medical databases which might give her information. She went back to her job that afternoon. A week later I received a call from the mother. She told me she had located the surgeon who recently separated Siamese twins. He requested information which she faxed to him. He then referred her to a physician in Los Angeles, who requested the complete medical file on Ben. A week later, the family was on their way to Anaheim. Their first stop: Disneyland. Their second stop: a physician who would make a difference in Ben's life.

Ben underwent surgery in Los Angeles and the surgeon removed the tumor which was intruding on Ben's life. The operation was a complete success.

Ben is fine today, and is expected to have a normal life.

He will visit Anaheim every two years for a while, but the physician expects no complications. Somewhere there is a little boy who will grow up and hear the legacy of his loving and creative mother who basically saved his life. His mother taught me the value of the SFBT model in being able to be a part of solutions that can make radical differences in people's lives. Yes, this model can be of use in difficult situations.

The magic of this model lies in its flexibility, respectfulness, and determination in those who utilize it, to broaden their perspectives and beliefs in the students, teachers, and parents they attempt to help. Looking deeply into our students', parents' and fellow educators' abilities in the other avenues of their lives, we can assist them also, with discovering the solutions they have within themselves. As Robert Fulghum, a former educator, explains about life and our desires to know our destiny:

> *If I were absolutely certain about all things, I would spend my life in anxious misery, fearful of losing my way. But since everything and anything are always possible, the miraculous is always nearby and wonders shall never, ever cease.*

> *I believe that human freedom may be stated in one term, which serves as a little brick propping open the door of existence: Maybe.*

> ROBERT FULGHUM, *MAYBE (MAYBE NOT)*

SFBT Educator Training Exercise: Chapter 6
Our Own Possibilities

Many of us have experienced unhappiness and even extremely difficult situations as we have walked the paths of life. Today more than ever, celebrities and other notable people in our world are coming forward to tell of their unfortunate experiences. The stories are full of sadness yet the people who survive the experiences emerge triumphant through their personal successes.

Consider a situation(s) from your life that seemed, impossible to solve at first. How did you get through it?

When did you take control and lessen the impact of the problem on your life?

How did you do that?

CHAPTER 7

TURNING ATTITUDES INTO RESOURCES

IDEAS FOR CLASSROOM GUIDANCE

Classroom guidance is a valuable option for schools. Today, teachers are faced with children and adolescents whose experimentation with drugs, sex, and violence are brought into the classroom and interfere with learning and motivation. These serious issues leave teachers feeling helpless due to the constraints of the community, school board, and religious groups, and their concerns to "not impose values." Once teachers and schools were looked upon as "pillars of wisdom," yet today they find themselves limited and frightened regarding how they can/cannot intervene with serious situations. The ideas presented in this chapter are designed to assist in some of the dilemmas commonly found in schools today in an approach that is respectful, nonbiased, and competency-based.

This chapter addresses the very young student and his/her need for creative interventions such as stories and metaphorical experiences, and adolescents, who tend to resist suggestions but do well when addressed as competent persons with valuable opinions. Ideas for group discussions have been written to lower resistance and encourage ideas to develop for students to assist them in making decisions in their lives. It has been my experience that educators can lower resistance and inform students of safety simply by their method of delivery. This chapter will suggest ways educators might approach such delivery and adapt their own ideas to their individual situations.

CHAPTER 7 FOCUS

- Facilitating Classroom Discussions
- New Activities for Classroom Guidance: Ideas for dealing with AIDS, dangerous situations, identifying what works in school, study skills, and student opinions
- Metaphorical Stories and Funny Medicine: Ideas for all grade levels
- Choices and Resources: Ideas for planning a high school career

FACILITATING CLASSROOM DISCUSSIONS

Preparing students for real life has often been full of obstacles. Don Juan Casteneda mentions the following about master and pupil relationships and sheds some light on how teachers should influence their students:

"The first act of a teacher is to introduce the idea that the world we think we see is only a view, a description. Every effort of a teacher is geared to prove this point to his apprentice. But accepting it seems to be one of the hardest things one can do. It is the single most important technique that an apprentice can learn."

When students learn to view their world differently, negative feelings, behaviors, and personal interactions often change. A teacher who redescribes an idea, changes the meaning of an interaction, or talks of a behavior as "normal" encourages a new view of a situation. The next page suggests a way of dealing with such serious issues as sex, drugs, and violence.

The group activity and questions presented in the exercise can be given to randomly selected groups of six high school students in a health sciences/biology class. Among the topics to be covered during the six-week term might include safe sex, AIDS, and gang violence. The teacher/counselor's goal is to create an atmosphere in which the students can write their own description of a dangerous situation and set the context for the topical discussion. The teacher might then focus more on the students' ideas of danger and personal safety than educating them about such topics. Later, the teacher/counselor can integrate the group's descriptions of danger "criteria" into later discussions about sex, AIDS, and gang violence. Soliciting their opinions first makes for a more cooperative way to introduce information. How the individual students deal with the information and how they use it in their lives is up to them.

The teacher might tell the groups that she is giving them a hypothetical situation in which they are invited to participate. The results will be tallied, written up, and presented during their next class period. The various ideas can then be discussed in terms of AIDS, safe sex, and gang violence. The tally will give the educator ideas as to what works to get the attention of her students regarding these important topics.

Questions such as the ones offered on the next page are only suggestions for discussions that encourage the competencies of students through their processing of hypothetical situations. Talking *at* students and/or giving them guidelines for decision making is only one way of approaching difficult topics. The exercise involves looking at the *character* of the groups and noticing what works with them in typical class periods. What is important is the *fit* between classroom guidance and student.

Name _____ Date _____

WHAT IF...YOU WERE IN A THREATENING SITUATION

You find yourself in a threatening situation. You want to participate so that you won't appear odd or foolish, but you feel afraid, anxious, and nervous because you have heard that other people have been hurt or have died in similar situations. You feel pressure by your peers to participate. In your groups, discuss this situation with the following group questions.

Group Discussion Questions

Hint: Choose a discussion leader and a recorder to write down the answers on another piece of paper.

1. Describe a frightening situation that you have experienced in your own life. How did you know that it was a truly threatening situation in *your life*? What facts told you that it was threatening? (Each group member describes a situation)

   _____
   _____
   _____

2. Describe a situation recently when you were afraid of being hurt or threatened, yet you saved yourself and/or others from danger or other negative circumstances.

   _____
   _____
   _____

3. How did you do that? What were your strategies for taking care of yourself? (Thoughts, actions, words)

   _____
   _____
   _____

4. What would others say they have seen you do in the past to protect yourself or others you care about from danger?"

   _____
   _____
   _____

5. How would you like others to describe you in regard to how you deal with/avoid dangerous situations?

   _____
   _____
   _____

On the back of this paper, write down what you liked about this exercise.

What's Working in School?

A classroom guidance program in an elementary school in Irving, Texas, turned into an intervention after the sixth grade class became rebellious and resistant to school. The teachers complained to the school counselor that they had tried everything to get the students motivated: new projects, rewards, and positive reinforcement. The teachers had also taken on similar characteristics of their students; their attitudes were negative and their responses had become cruel. The next week, the school counselor took 3 x 5 cards to each sixth grade class. She announced that she was certain that the teachers and students at school were simply not hearing each other. She asked both teachers and students (separately) to write down on the 3 x 5 card an answer to the following questions:

> When does school work for you?
>
> When was the last time that happened?
>
> What did that do for you?

After the cards were completed, she asked the students to place them in a suggestion box. The counselor said she received a few negative suggestions and some silly suggestions such as "more amusement park field trips," but she also received a large number of excellent suggestions such as:

- video movies for history class
- competitive math and spelling games
- more sports in physical education
- activities in science class
- more explanations and one-on-one time with the teacher
- when the teacher says something nice to us
- guest speakers and different kinds of assignments

The teachers came up with their own lists of "what worked." The counselor found that asking the sixth-grade class for its opinion was not only age appropriate but useful to the teachers who were struggling to provide quality education. The teachers also felt more heard by the students. The results were published in the school newspaper and the rebellious attitudes diminished considerably.

THE STUDY SKILL MYSTERY SERIES: IN SEARCH OF THE "GOOD STUDENT"

In the book *Students Teaching, Teachers Learning* (Branscombe, Goswami and Schwartz, Editors, 1990), Patricia Johnson writes of a new way of dealing with the development of study skills. She had looked over the curriculum for developing good study skills in her class and found them dreadfully boring. She reviewed the workbook chapter. She realized that the purpose of these blanks and checklists and outlines was for students to understand what a good student is and does and thinks and how one behaves. Why not, she thought, look to the resources that surround us? Why not look to our families, classmates, teachers, and coaches to find an example of a good student? Instead of completing worksheet pages that would not develop any real thought, the students were given a research question on the sample handout on the next page which served as a guide only. The teacher might begin such a project with a question to the class such as: "What makes someone a good student?"

The class might discuss the question for a time and then the teacher would give them the idea for the project at hand; find the "good" student. Johnson noticed that it did not take long for the students to come up with ideas to interview and research their topics. The students in Johnson's class became motivated and excited as they interviewed virtually everyone from teachers to parents. They were often surprised and intrigued to learn about their parents and their football coach and realize that they too, had once been students.

The students in Johnson's class discovered their own competencies as they identified the attributes they wanted to exemplify in themselves. The students became so involved in the project that Johnson continued throughout the year to assign such topics for book reviews as "What makes a really good book?" and "How did this book score with your descriptions of a really good one?"

Name _____ Date _____

THE FIFTH GRADE MYSTERY SERIES: IN SEARCH OF THE "GOOD STUDENT" A HANDOUT

Search for, be on the lookout (!), and select someone who you feel is a "good" student. Come up with a list of qualities you feel this person has and share the lists with classmates. Write them down however you like.

Then, come up with a list of questions you would like to ask the "good" student to find out what the "good" is all about. Interview your chosen "good student." Ask him/her a question such as: "How do you manage to be such a 'good' student?"

Using your own ideas and the ideas of your "good" student, design a presentation to show your class that tells all about your "good" student.

TEACHERS LISTENING, STUDENTS TEACHING EACH OTHER

Lack of interest and little motivation to learn or discuss subjects at hand plague all educators at least once. When Sara Allen felt her teaching was not reaching her high school seniors, she took the advice of her department chair and turned over the teaching of the subject to the students. She told the class that she was sure they could take the topic at hand, talk and listen to each other about it, and report to her. She in turn would simply observe *how they did it.*

Allen's "student-sustained discussion" brought the class to life as the teacher resisted any urges to "instruct" the students on their readings. Instead, she walked around and noticed what the students did in their discussions. She found also that if she did ask a question, it was related to *their* question.

Allen's ideas fit nicely into SFBT classroom guidance. Imagine asking students to discuss topics such as cultural differences, drug and alcohol abuse, safe sex, and AIDS prevention. The following questions for discussion might lead to some interesting student-sustained discussions that may also lead to personal application:

Sample Discussion Questions (Choose 1 per class period)

"Discuss the idea of cultural differences and what that means to you."

"When does alcohol use become abuse?"

"Is there such a phenomenon as safe sex?" (Yes or no, defend your answers)

"Could the outbreak of AIDS affect your life?" (Yes or no, defend your answers)

The teacher might give out one question for discussion by all groups, and suggest that he/she will only be listening for discussions at each table, making notes of what is discussed and who does the discussing. The teacher adamantly expresses to the students that he/she is switching roles—he/she wants the students to teach him/her about themselves. The students can draw, write, or present their findings in whatever format they choose: an enactment of a situation between a boyfriend and girlfriend for "safe sex;" a comparison of various cultural differences and similarities and how they can collaboratively "work" with relationships; information on alcoholism and how alcohol affects people. Encourage the students' *own* suggestions—allow their creativity to work with their own resources. The athlete, the cheerleader, the artist, and the debate team winner all have abilities to use in the project.

Encourage this! If a group asks how to present the topic to the class ask: "How have you presented topics in other classes that worked for you?"

The grade for the project will be based on participation. The highest grades will be given to those students who respond to the question with an application to his/her own life. The teacher will listen for various student ideas that indicate a sense of involvement and meaning to the student. The teacher may write his/her impression of the student's involvement on a 3 x 5 card or use the forms provided after the exercise on the next few pages. The compliments are to be passed to the student discreetly at any time.

Dear Calvin,

I am very impressed with the way you listen to others in your group and really respect their opinion, even when it's different from yours. Your strong beliefs about culture are exciting to hear. Your group is lucky to have you in it!

Ms. Impressed

Allen says that when students do the real talking, they feel a responsibility that goes beyond simply being allowed to express their thoughts. One student she taught discovered a new sense of authority, which led him far beyond "right" and "wrong" answers. The students responded because they were the ones in control, were being observed, and had the opportunity to teach, learn, speak, and listen. There was no one person who had the last word, the *right* word that others would be judged by. *The student was the expert on him- or herself.* Everyone was treated equally.

STUDENTS TEACHING, TEACHERS LISTENING

Your teacher will give you a discussion question. Discuss and answer the question in regard to your personal feelings about the subject and how it applies to you. Your teacher is very interested in what you will teach him/her about yourself through your responses in the group and will be listening closely!

Give him/her something to notice!

Concluding questions:

- What did you learn about yourself through this class experience?

- Who impressed you with their responses in your group? How so?

- As this class topic ends, how would you want the other group members who participated in this discussion to describe your feelings on the subject?

- What behaviors would keep this description of you "alive" in their eyes?

YOUR IDEAS ARE IMPRESSIVE...

_____

_____

_____

_____

_____

- - - - - - - - - - - - - - - - - - - detach here -

YOU'VE TAUGHT ME A LOT ABOUT YOU!
...HERE'S WHAT I'VE LEARNED

_____

_____

_____

_____

_____

_____

METAPHORICAL STORIES

In *The Republic,* Plato states that educators must "turn the mind's eye to the light so that it can see for itself." How an educator connects with a student in that manner lies in how the educator perceives what he/she is trying to do. If the educator has a lesson plan in mind and wants to imprint it in the mind of a student, he/she takes a chance that her idea might not make sense to the student. However, if the educator "fits" with the world view of the student and turns the mind's eye to the light through strategies and ideas, he/she might "fit" with the student's needs and interests and information will be received.

As we grow into adults, many of us recall stories told to us as young children and the context in which they were told. Stories are ways of delivering messages that develop new ways of thinking about one's life or behavior. When a metaphorical story is told to someone troubled by a problem, a connection is often made that gives relief. This method of working encourages the person to be in charge of his/her own solutions and to develop them within his/her own competencies.

Combs and Freedman, authors of *Story Symbol and Ceremony,* suggest several questions to ask ourselves that help us find stories to access emotional states and attitudes:

"What does the state or attitude remind me of? How can I elaborate within this realm to evoke the state?

When have I experienced the state or attitude?

When has someone else experienced the state or attitude?

When could someone experience the state or attitude?"

COMBS & FREEDMAN

ROLEX, THE WATCH DOG: A STORY FOR SIBLING RIVALRY

As an elementary counselor, I once told a story to two siblings who were at war with each other. The older sister, 14, was tired of dealing with her 8-year-old brother's antics when she baby-sat him after school. Her strategy was to kick him and then run to her room and lock her door. In hot pursuit, he followed her and banged on the door intermittently until the parents came home from work. The siblings seemed to enjoy certain times together, such as playing board games or video games, but other times found them at each other's throat. I told them the following story:

Have you ever become the proud owners of a new kitten or puppy? Well, I have, and I certainly learned a lot about how to care for them. I bought a new golden retriever several years ago. His name is Rolex, by the way, since he's a "watch dog." Rolex was a great puppy, but I worked all day and when I came home at night, he would paw, cling, and scratch at me until I picked him up. It was okay some days when I had time, but other days when I didn't have time, he was a real mess! He would chew socks, garbage, and even furniture. He just wouldn't stop!

One day I came home early, and he was asleep in his bed. I walked over to him and picked him up, played with him for a few minutes and as he lay on my lap, he went right to sleep. I was so surprised to see him fall asleep so easily after we played! He looked so quiet and content, that from then on, whenever I could, I petted him when he was attacking a sock or garbage can and we played. He's much bigger now, weighing in at 90 pounds, but he still likes to hop up on the couch and lay his head in my lap when I remember to sit down with him.

As Combs and Freedman suggest, recalling certain instances that remind us of situations we face at school are a powerful means for resolution. I recall many times in rearing our three children, when a recollection of my own childhood experiences calmed them when they were upset and helped them resolve their own issues.

CASE STUDY:
CALMING A PARENT AND GAINING COOPERATION

Freedman recalls a family referred to family therapy because Jeffrey, a second grader, was withdrawing and disinterested in completing his school work. The mother was not sure about counseling and said, "I think I should tell you that I don't want to be here. I don't believe in this. I think people should solve their own problems. I grew up on a farm. We always worked hard. We expected to. It was part of life. When something was wrong, we just worked harder. We didn't call in anyone else. It was our farm. If it was just up to me, we would just work harder, not come to talk to someone else."

I (JF) responded, "I used to work at a residential treatment facility for kids. I thought it was a really special place. The staff worked hard, and we loved the kids...One thing that really rankled me and was hard to get used to was staffings. Every Wednesday, we would spend an hour staffing each kid. The houseparent would talk about how the kid was doing socially, the teacher would talk about how the kid was doing in school, and the therapist would talk about how the kid was doing in therapy. But then the psychiatrist, who had spent one hour with him, would tell us all what to do! I knew that no degree was more important than knowing a kid" (*Combs & Freedman, 1990, p. 166*).

The mother sighed and said, "It's nothing personal. And as long as we're here, let's see what can be done."

Freedman was reminded of her own experience and constructed a story to lessen resistance, and connect and suggest resolution to the situation at hand. The story placed the mother in a prominent position, one she seemed to initially feel was insignificant. Stepping into the world view of the mother gave ideas for constructing a story that was meaningful.

FUNNY MEDICINE
(as suggested by Keeney)

Bradford Keeney, PhD, talks about "funny medicine," his terminology for children's ideas which suggest ways to help other kids while helping themselves. Keeney says, "All we can do is create an accident to fall into." This simply means creating a context in which students can discover for themselves the solutions to their issues, whether the issues are serious or developmental steps of life. Creating the environment for them to tell us how to solve a problem is more meaningful than lectures. Keeney also talks of understanding why things are as they are—he suggests that we move from understanding to making differences.

Complimenting Students and Asking for their Solutions

One way to make differences with the children we work with in elementary schools is to hook into their resourcefulness as well as our own. Children have wonderful ideas to share with us. This manual has described many situations in which teachers and counselors alike simply asked a child, "How did you manage to keep the temper tantrum away?" or, "How did you keep the sadness small?" The resources were there; the educators simply helped them emerge. When we as educators are resourceful, we foster resourcefulness in our students (Keeney, 1994). According to Keeney, an elementary counselor might enter a room of kindergarteners and ask: "Has anyone in here ever been afraid?"

After receiving some response the counselor might add:

"I have a project I need help with. I know a child who is very afraid of something and I need all of you to help me. I want you to tell me how you might convince him/her that he/she does not need to be afraid. You can come up with an activity that might help. You can draw something, tell a story, or do anything you think might help. For the next few minutes, I am going to write down what you tell me and together, we're going to help him/her to not be scared anymore."

Learning to Run from Problems

Elementary SFBT educators have opportunities to explore what students bring to the classroom through assessing their competencies. For example, an educator attempting to educate her students about avoiding sexual abuse might ask a kindergarten class, "What are the kind of touches you should run from and tell someone about?" Then, the teacher could ask the children to practice these responses by running around the school yard and shouting. Elementary students can also be asked to draw a picture (class project) of what being on drugs might be like. Have everyone participate in drawing a very ugly monster (externalizing the problem). Then ask the children "How can you keep the monster from bothering you? What will you say? What could you teach a friend to say? How have you avoided or ignored (use their words) other people who have bothered you before?" Make a new poster with all the responses. Display it next to the monster and call it "Monster Tamers."

The same idea of "funny medicine" may be utilized in secondary schools as teachers observe the character of a particular class and suggest activities that might fit with its resourcefulness. The idea of funny medicine is just that—a clever, funny method to develop or express ideas or solutions. The important factor is that the students then develop their own projects, plays, and writings to describe a "cure" for a certain issue.

The idea also applies to the educator. If you like artwork, consider working within an artistic mode and presenting the problem as such with the suggestion that it be solved artistically, or through singing, if you prefer music, for example. Solution-focused ideas encompass everyone within the school "system," and are most effective when *everyone* is encouraged to use the resourcefulness within themselves.

To grasp the meaning of a thing, an event, or a situation is to see its relations to other things: to see how it operates or functions, what consequences follow from it, what causes it, what uses it can be put to.

JOHN DEWEY

Carol Stumbo writes of her visit to an elementary school in an old section of town where she encountered a teacher who just finished videotaping her students reading pieces of their writing. Stumbo recalled how the teacher had been touched by the story of one child in particular. The teacher had asked the children to imagine what it would be like to be an animal of their own choice for one day. The class consisted of many students, one who had a fatal muscular disease and was confined to a wheel-chair. In the exercise, the child wrote about what it was like to be a bird. In a simple voice, she talked about how difficult it was to come to school in her new form. She couldn't reach her food in the cafeteria. She had to avoid some friends because they would "squeeze" her too hard. Even though it was hard, the student wrote that she still felt "human" inside. Near the end of the piece, the child wrote "It's all right though because I can fly away when I get tired, and go home."

Shirley Brice Heath once said: "Do not focus on what the students do not know but what they *do* know and the knowledge they bring to the classroom. Some will never learn what's in the textbook." Through various questions, activities, stories, and discussions knowledge can occur when it is tailored to the individual student. The students have our answers for tailoring the assignments; we just need to observe.

CHOICES AND RESOURCES:
IDEAS FOR PLANNING A HIGH SCHOOL CAREER

The next pages contain ideas for high school career planning. Some of the ideas were developed from a booklet offered by the Arlington Independent School District in Texas. I am grateful to Ella Starnes, a good friend and school counselor at Barnett Junior High School for the many ideas we have shared over the years. The ideas use SFBT language and assumptions, competency-based ideas, and are less structured than typical career planning programs. I solicited ideas for the following projects from an expert eighth grader...my son, Roger, who "showed me the way" to interesting activities. The suggested questions and exercises may be adapted to the individual needs of the teacher and students. The "goal" is to assist incoming high school students with discovering their abilities so they can make good decisions in choosing elective courses in addition to required ones for their high school "plan." The activities utilize the assumptions of SFBT and are developed for self-discovery and positive peer reinforcement. The teacher/counselor merely starts the activities and lets the students discover the rest!

LABEL SMASHERS

During the spring term before high school, many students are given course selections by which to choose the first year of high school. The courses are intriguing at best, and often intimidating. The new high school student may have difficulty choosing an elective that will get him/her where he/she wants to end up. Adolescence is often a confusing time in regard to self-image, self-identification, and abilities. Worksheets and lists are sometimes not acceptable ways of learning about oneself. Using the most powerful of all influences—peers—"Label Smashers" (developed in collaboration with Stephen Chilton, M.S.) is an enjoyable and informative activity to use all year. The activity provides the students with ample information from many sources, so that when they look at course choices for high school, match-ing abilities with courses is simplified.

It starts in the beginning of the school year

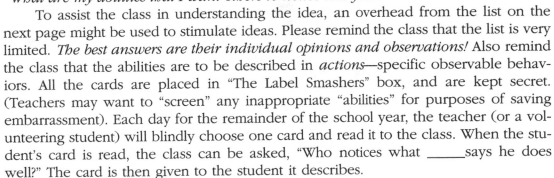

An appropriate class in junior high or middle schools to conduct "Label Smashers" is the "homeroom" period, English, or Language class, the second month of school. The teacher gives each student four Label Smasher Cards, and keeps one card for himself/herself. The student takes one card and passes out the other three to three peers of his/her choice in class. The teacher and three classmates answer the following question about the student: *"What special abilities do you notice in _____?"*

The student answers the same question in a slightly different way, and keeps his/her answers in his/her notebook: *"What are my abilities that I want others to notice this year?"*

To assist the class in understanding the idea, an overhead from the list on the next page might be used to stimulate ideas. Please remind the class that the list is very limited. *The best answers are their individual opinions and observations!* Also remind the class that the abilities are to be described in *actions*—specific observable behaviors. All the cards are placed in "The Label Smashers" box, and are kept secret. (Teachers may want to "screen" any inappropriate "abilities" for purposes of saving embarrassment). Each day for the remainder of the school year, the teacher (or a volunteering student) will blindly choose one card and read it to the class. When the student's card is read, the class can be asked, "Who notices what _____ says he does well?" The card is then given to the student it describes.

It ends at the end of the year...

Again, the same question applies, only with a different focus: The week or so before course selection arrives, the teacher passes out three cards to each student, who gives the cards to the same peers as in the beginning of the year, and the teacher keeps one. (If students have moved, students may give a card to a different peer).

"Which of _____'s abilities have really impressed you during this year?"

Use the next page, "Label Smashers," as a handout or overhead. "Abilities" can be used either way in connection with "Label Smashers."

The student then collects his/her cards and makes some conclusions about his/her abilities and what they might indicate in course selection. The teacher might assist this process with a few volunteer students, reading the cards aloud and suggesting courses that might apply. Utilizing the peer influence, his/her self-esteem gets a boost and so do his/her choices for high school.

"What's Important to Me?" is a list of hobbies, values, and dreams that students can check off as they apply. Asking the following question can lead to productive discussions: *"What will I see you doing in the near future that will accomplish these ideas?"*

Name _____ Date _____

LABEL SMASHERS

What special abilities do you notice that I have?

_____

_____

_____

_____

_____

Name _____ Date _____

LABEL SMASHERS

What special abilities do you notice that I have?

_____

_____

_____

_____

_____

Name _____Date _____

ABILITIES

Below are samples of abilities that might apply to you or the person you are describing. Add other abilities that describe what you (or someone else) does well:

_____ Selling products or services, motivating people to do something

_____ Understanding and expressing ideas using computers

_____ Understanding and expressing ideas in words

_____ Working with light, color, composition to create works of art

_____ Thinking through complicated problems

_____ Repairing or working with machines, appliances, tools

_____ Organizing things for school activities

_____ Helping others make decisions and solve their problems

_____ Making things—woodworking, sewing, pottery, carpentry, leatherwork

_____ Performing for others in music, drama, dance, comedy

_____ Doing research through a computer database

_____ Performing in sports activities

_____ Writing or enjoying poetry

_____ Communicating ideas and working well with others

_____ Compassionate and good with animals

_____ Enjoying helping others who can't help themselves

Name _____Date _____

WHAT'S IMPORTANT TO "VALUABLE ME"?

Check off the values below that apply to who you are and what you want to accomplish in your life. Add others as you discover them!

_____ Being an honest person

_____ A long and healthy life

_____ Good and meaningful relationships

_____ Enjoyable leisure time

_____ Financially comfortable life

_____ Secure and positive family life

_____ Accomplishing something worthwhile

_____ Equal opportunities and freedom for all people

_____ Learning and gaining knowledge

_____ Feeling self-confident in school, work, or home

_____ Unlimited travel and cultural opportunities

_____ A physical appearance you can be proud of

_____ Being helpful to the sick and disadvantaged

_____ Enjoyment of nature and beauty (any form)

_____ Chances to be creative

_____ Being a good and trusted friend

_____ Being kind to people less fortunate

_____ Other:_____

215

Seven Out of Ten
An Activity for AIDS Education

This activity is appropriate for an adolescent population. The ideas presented here were developed collaboratively with Stephen Chilton, M.S. This activity is dedicated to helping adolescents understand the deadly consequences of contracting the AIDS virus. *This activity is presented in memory of Chris Snodgrass, who died of AIDS.*

The teacher begins with a lively discussion of students' future hopes and dreams. He/she then divides the class into groups of 10 and passes out 3 x 5 cards to the students, asking them to write down what they want to be when they grow up. The teacher then collects the cards and places them in a stack on the desk.

The next discussion begins with information and a statement: "Recently, a person died of AIDS who had lost seven of his ten friends to the virus." The teacher then passes out 10 folded pieces of paper in an envelope to each group. Seven of the ten pieces of paper have an "X" marked on them. The teacher instructs each student to choose a paper and keep the contents secret. The teacher then continues the discussion about the many ways that AIDS creeps into people's lives who don't ask for it—people who are conscious of it but do not take its threat seriously. Then, the teacher opens the classroom door and asks for the group members who have an "X" on a paper to leave—saying that these people have "just died." The teacher then reaches for the stack of cards filled out by the students. Counting out the appropriate amount, he/she asks a student to read who just "died" (doctor, lawyer, metal worker, accountant, parent). The discussion continues with asking the "just died" group to rejoin their group. Then questions are posed to the groups:

"What was it like for those of you who died so suddenly without ever reaching the goals you wrote as you came in today? Face your survivors and tell them."

"What was it like for the rest of you left behind to watch your friends suddenly disappear, not complete their goals, or be in your life? Face those who died and tell them."

The teacher then continues with "how people die from AIDS is a tragedy, and the loss of your loved ones could be significant in your lives...it could happen any time, like in this role play. If you were to teach other students and friends about the importance of taking precautions against AIDS, how would you do that?" From this point, the class (or individual groups) may decide on a message to fellow students in the school, or develop a program or poster to represent their experience. A follow up to this experience might include viewing the films *Philadelphia* or *And The Band Played On,* available through video rental stores.

WHO'S THE MOST POWERFUL OF THEM ALL?: SUGGESTIONS FOR DISCOURAGING GANG INVOLVEMENT

What does belonging to a gang do for some adolescents? Acceptance, validation and a sense of belonging. The nature of adolescence is to find a place to feel important. Moving through their lives with fragile egos, adolescents look to various groups for a sense of belonging. For some, the group is violent, for others, more acceptable. If we are to change the enormous trend of joining gangs we must first begin creating environments in which adolescents experience *through nonviolent situations* the feelings of acceptance, validation, and belonging. Why not start with school? This entire manual has stressed repeatedly how searching and discovering competencies in individuals changes their perceptions—which then change behaviors.

One way of lessening the glamour of gang involvement is to create situations in which students develop their own opinions of exactly what the "glamour" is about. The films *Boys In The Hood, Mo Better Blues, Stand and Deliver,* and *Lean On Me* are stories where people emerge as powerful, and who resist the violence they find themselves near.

A suggested activity (developed collaboratively with Stephen Chilton, M.S.) might be to show one of the films mentioned and then have a group or class discussion in which the following questions are answered and discussed:

"Who has the most power/respect in this story?"

"What did he/she do to gain this power/respect?"

"If you could write a sequel to this movie, with the "most powerful" characters included, what characteristics would they keep so they appeared the "most powerful"?

Assignment: Write the sequel as a group and present it to the class.

THE MIRACLE BOARD

A central concept throughout this manual has been to "notice when school works." This idea is often overlooked as we go through our days obstructed by actions, events, and interactions that intrude and mask our perceptions of when "the world works." The "Miracle Board" is an idea for a bulletin board in any age-level classroom. The board is filled with "miracles" that children or adolescents clip from newspapers, magazines, or record from family or peer observations. The very young child can involve his/her parents to seek out or recall a miracle that touched their lives. This board can be started when school begins, and referred to daily. The student who brings in the miracle might be asked:

"What was it about this story that told you it was a miracle?"

"How was this different from similar situations?"

To the class:

"What do you think would be different in the world if more people did what the person in the miracle did?"

"How can we begin to do that?"

The positive aspect of this board is directed at changing how students envision their world. As in the ideas expressed through this manual, thinking differently about the world in which we live influences our behaviors to be different as well.

(DEVELOPED COLLABORATIVELY WITH STEPHEN CHILTON, MS)

Positive People In Our Lives

There are many "turning points" in our lives. For many, it is a teacher, an aunt, a coach, even a co-worker who made a difference in how we saw the world. This positive person made an impact in our lives. Often fond memories rekindle pleasant thoughts and bring brightness to our day. The equipment needed for this project include:

> An inexpensive Polaroid camera
>
> Enough film for two pictures per student

Early in the year, the teacher simply announces that a bulletin board has been designated for "Positive People." Each student will take a Polaroid camera on loan or use their own camera from home to take a picture of a person who has a positive influence in their lives. This person might be a parent, sibling, aunt, uncle, or neighbor. The students are told that the person they choose should be someone they admire, who makes them smile, and see the world differently—so differently, that they feel good and "positive" when being around them. Then the dynamics begin!

The teacher might lead a discussion on "Positive People" with these suggested questions:

1. Who do you know that is a positive person in your life?
2. What do they do that makes them a positive person?
3. What does that person do that makes him/her seem positive to you?
4. How does knowing a positive person change your life?

As the students take their pictures and bring them to school, they each present the picture (assign dates to present) and tell the class why they chose that person for their "Positive People" board. Then the class might ask questions about the person and how he/she was chosen. After the discussion, the student pins the photo on the board. As the year progresses, if students struggle with decision making, grades, or peer problems, asking the student what his/her "positive person" might advise will give the student a new way to think about his/her concern.

This project can be conducted year-round in school by all grade levels. Perhaps the idea of the student searching for a positive person in their life will inspire parents, grandparents, and siblings to *be* more positive and compete for the position as well. This idea was developed collaboratively with Stephen Chilton, M.S.

SFBT EDUCATOR TRAINING EXERCISE: CHAPTER 7
TURNING YOUR ATTITUDE INTO RESOURCES

In the same way that students bring their world, their resources, and abilities into the classroom, so do educators and administrators bring their resources to school with them each day. Looking at students differently and redescribing their behaviors takes practice; it's a new way of thinking and a very different focus.

Sometimes it helps to begin thinking differently about students if we begin to think differently about ourselves and our loved ones. For the rest of the week, keep a notepad handy and write down the names of those you love and your name, one name to a sheet. As you go through your busy week, notice, notice, notice, what you and those you care for do well. Keep it a secret until the last day of the week. Tear out the note below, and sign it, love,_____. Watch the reactions. Learn from your own discoveries what "works" for you at school. Stop doing the things you dislike and tailor them to your own likes and abilities. A coach who teaches math might adapt a sports game to a math project. The former counselor turned administrator might think of running a group for teachers once a month...talk about collaboration! An art teacher who finds herself teaching social studies might consider a mural for the school. You get the idea...we as humans are in our "element" when we can practice being who we really are.

- detach here -

YOU MEAN SO MUCH TO ME

that I just had to tell you...

_____

_____

_____

_____

_____

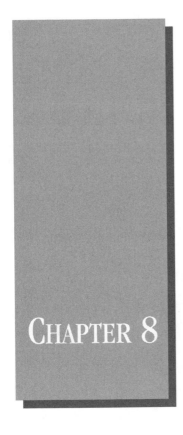

CHAPTER 8

BEHAVIOR TRANSFORMATIONS: DISCIPLINING DIFFERENTLY

TAKING A NEW LOOK AT OLD BEHAVIORS

Effective discipline has been a concern of educators for decades. Behavior modification approaches, corporal punishment, in-school suspension and expulsion have been a few of the "solutions" educators have tried to gain the attention of students so they might change their behaviors. Looking at today's schools full of violence, rebellion, and disruptions, these approaches have turned into boxing matches with students, parents, and special interest groups.

It's Time for a New Approach

The ideas in this manual are not designed to attack any specific behavior problem. The SFBT approach encourages educators to develop and implement a new atmosphere for students that discourages problem behavior and encourages competencies. This chapter suggests new ways of dealing with compulsive behavior problems of students who have dealt with long-term behavior disturbances. The ideas presented are suggestions for helping students who are bothered by disturbances to begin seeing themselves differently, as their educators do.

CHAPTER 8 FOCUS

- Case Study: "The Target"— a new description to an old school behavior
- Redescribing problem behavior: Creating opportunities for change
- Creating mentorships between teachers and students
- Lessening the power of being disruptive through compromising
- Team-teacher meetings: New ideas, interventions, and strategies

REDESCRIBING PROBLEM BEHAVIOR: CREATING OPPORTUNITIES FOR CHANGE

The following dialogue was written and contributed by Brian Cade,* a colleague from Sydney, Australia, which shows how thinking differently about a problem and redescribing behaviors to a young man threatened by expulsion challenges him to change.

The Target

Jack, age 13, was brought to see me by his parents because he was constantly in trouble at school. He was endlessly battling with his teachers, and was also regularly fighting with his peers and with older boys. He had been suspended from school several times and recently, had been threatened with expulsion. This would then be the third school from which he would have been expelled in just over two years: He was running out of options.

As his parents outlined the problem, he sat looking disinterested and bored. After a short time, I asked the parents to wait outside and saw Jack on his own. He seemed quite happy to tell me about what was happening at school. He agreed that he was in trouble constantly, but expressed no concern about it:

Aligning with the Student Against the Situation

Counselor: What made you decide to be so helpful to everybody?

Jack: What do you mean?

---

*(Printed with permission, Brian Cade, 1994.)

Counselor: Well, I am sure that there are other kids in your class that play up. Isn't that right?

Jack: Yes.

Counselor: Do they get into trouble as much as you do?

Jack: Not usually.

Counselor: That's what surprises me about you. You seem to have become so helpful to them. Whatever they might do, you seem to be the one that the teacher picks on. It's as though you have become such a big target that the other kids can hide behind you and get away with things. How did you decide to be so helpful?

Jack: I don't know what you mean.

Counselor: It sounds as though your classmates can get away with all sorts of things because you have such a reputation as a troublemaker that, when the teacher turns around, you are the first person he or she looks towards. You then get busted, and the others seem to get away with it. Isn't that what happens? In fact, I bet there are lots of times that you get busted for what the others have done even though you have done nothing wrong.

Jack: Yes. So?

Counselor: So, nothing. I am just impressed with how helpful you are to your classmates. Have they ever thanked you for it?

Jack: No. (*He looks puzzled*)

Counselor: What? Do you mean to tell me that you often take the rap for all these other kids and they don't even thank you for it?

Jack: Of course they don't.

Counselor: Good grief! (*Then, after a thoughtful pause*) Have the teachers thanked you?

Jack: What are you talking about?

Counselor: Well, you make it so much easier for them. Surely they have expressed their appreciation.

Jack: What do you mean?

Counselor: You save them the trouble of trying to work out who it was that was mucking up. The teachers can just turn around and bust you and thus save themselves all the bother of trying to work out who the hell it was that really made the noise, or whatever it was that attracted their attention.

Jack: You're crazy!

Counselor: Are you sure that the teachers have not thanked you for your help?

Jack: I'm not helping them.

Counselor: You're not? But haven't you found that the other kids in your class are often mucking up but the teacher always looks at you first, even though you might not have been doing anything wrong? And haven't you often been busted for things that the others have done? The real culprit then just keeps quiet and gets away with it?

Jack: Sometimes.

Redescribing the Problem

Counselor: So, how come you keep acting like such a big target so that whoever mucks up or whoever starts the fights, you are the one who is the center of attention and gets busted?

Jack: It just happens.

Counselor: Do you mean you don't do it deliberately?

Jack: Of course I don't.

Counselor: Would you prefer it to be different?

Jack: I don't care. (*Profanity*)

Counselor: So you are happy to get busted for what the others do? I'm impressed. How come you're so generous? Why do you put yourself so much on the line to be so helpful? I bet none of them would do the same to help you...(*Silence*)

Counselor: Are there other ways that you help them by being such a big target?

Jack: I'm not helping them. You're nuts.

Counselor: I don't understand. By being such a big target, whenever there is trouble, you draw to yourself the attention of all the teachers. They expect you to be the troublemaker and so they automatically look towards you. Isn't that right?

Jack: I guess so.

Opening Up Possibilities for Goal Setting

Counselor: But, what would happen if you stopped?

Jack: What do you mean?

Counselor: Wouldn't you feel responsible that, by keeping out of trouble, you were the cause of them getting into trouble?

Jack: No.

Counselor: Are you sure you'd want to be responsible for the other kids getting into trouble?

Jack: I don't care. (*Profanity*)

Counselor: You'd be happy to try to stop being such a marked man, a big target, even though it meant that the other kids would have to take the rap for what they do?

Jack: Yes.

Counselor: Are you sure you want to take that degree of responsibility?

Jack: (*Holding his head between his hands*) This is crazy!

Counselor: Sure, but what about the teachers?

Jack: What about them?

Counselor: Their job will be much harder if they have to work out for themselves who it actually is who is mucking up.

Jack: So?

Counselor: Are you sure you want to be responsible for making your teacher's job harder?

Jack: Of course I am. Why would I want to get myself busted all the time to help them?

Counselor: That's what I was thinking. Why would you?

Task Development

Counselor: I don't know, but I guess you'd need to find ways of being a smaller target, of keeping a lower profile, of keeping your nose clean. Do you know what I mean?

Jack: I guess so.

Counselor: It won't be easy. Everyone expects you to be a troublemaker, kids and teachers.

Jack: So?

Encouraging Student Competency to Solve the Problem: Making It His Agenda

Counselor: It could take a while to turn it around. How will you handle it, for example, if you manage to become a smaller target, if you manage to keep your nose clean, and yet you still get into trouble either because some of the kids set you up or because the teacher assumes it must have been you. Will you be able to take your medicine, however unfair it might be, without fighting back so that you avoid being pushed into becoming a big target again?

Jack: If I wanted to, I guess I could do it.

Counselor: Look, I don't want to kid you. If you decide to do this, it could be really tough. I would advise you not to try it unless you are really sure that you want to do it and that you can carry it through. Do you know what I mean?

Jack: Yes.

Counselor: Would you prefer to think about it for a week or so?

Jack: No. I guess I can give it a go.

Counselor: Are you sure?

Jack: What do you want from me, for me to sign it in blood?

Counselor: No, it's not that. I just want you to be sure what it is you'll be taking on. After all, the teachers and the other kids won't know what your new plan is, and they'll be treating you as though you are the same as you were the last time they saw you. They'll be seeing you as a troublemaker, as someone who is easy to wind up and get into trouble. In a sense, you'll be on your own with no one to help.

Jack: I don't need any help.

Counselor: Well, if you're sure, I wish you the best of luck. Don't be too disheartened if it doesn't work out straight away. You might find that there are going to be lots of times when you'll be struggling against the urge to fight back. What I'd like you to do, if you don't mind, is to take particular note of all the different ways that you can find of resisting the urge to do the sorts of things that both your teachers and the other kids will be expecting you to do based on the past. Will that be OK?

Jack: I guess.

Counselor: Also, if it is not too much to ask, would you be prepared each day to draw a picture of a target that represents what size of target you think that you were that day? If you were as big a target as you have ever been, draw it about this size (I demonstrate by drawing a large target on a piece of paper). If you manage to

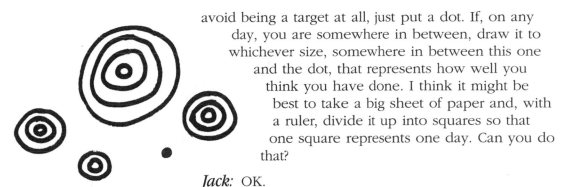

avoid being a target at all, just put a dot. If, on any day, you are somewhere in between, draw it to whichever size, somewhere in between this one and the dot, that represents how well you think you have done. I think it might be best to take a big sheet of paper and, with a ruler, divide it up into squares so that one square represents one day. Can you do that?

Jack: OK.

Cade mentions that during the conversation it was important that there was no hint of challenge in his voice or his demeanor. All of Cade's responses reflected curiosity tinged with puzzled incomprehension. A challenge would doubtless have represented just a more-of-the-same kind of approach that had clearly not worked in the past. It would have reflected a change in behavior as being the counselor's agenda, not Jack's in the same way that, up until then, it had been his teachers' and his parents' agendas, not his. In Cade's experience, people only change in ways that reflect their own agendas.

Enlisting Help from Parents and Teachers: Noticing What's Better

Cade continued to see the parents in therapy for a short while, yet saw Jack separately. He took the parents' concerns seriously but also asked them if "they would be prepared to back off and, for a while, leave things to Jack to try to sort out." Cade felt it important that they did not ask him at all how things were going, to avoid it from becoming again their agenda, and not Jack's. They agreed. In the event of them getting further complaints from the school, he asked that they be prepared to take the position with Jack that they were sorry that he seemed still to be having troubles and that they hoped he would finally be able to sort things out; period; end of response. They were prepared to do this.

Cade suggested that the parents contact the school and let them know that they had sought professional help and to ask the staff if they would be prepared to look out for any signs, however small, that Jack was making efforts to improve his behavior. Cade also suggested that they let the school know that it was the counselor's opinion that whatever his intentions, it might not be easy for Jack to change such an entrenched pattern of problem behavior in just a few days or even a few weeks. Would they be prepared to give him the benefit of the doubt for a while in order that he not be too quickly discouraged? Cade often calls schools personally, but in this situation, he felt the parents, who were highly motivated, would do well being more involved in resolving the problem. "It is easier to back off if you have an alternative thing to do."

	MON	TUE	WED	THUR	FRI
1					
2					
3					
4					

CONCLUSION

At the next session, Jack did not find it easy to stay "cool" or conceal a degree of pleasure when he showed Cade the diminishing size of the targets he had drawn on his chart. The parents received feedback from the school that his behavior had clearly improved. With delight, Jack told Cade several stories of how some of his classmates had been in more trouble over the last couple of weeks than was usually the case.

Over the next few months, the ongoing therapy concentrated not on times when Jack "relapsed," but on the different ways he found day-by-day to avoid the urge to rise to the bait, and the ways he got back on track after the lapses. It was important that changing the pattern at school remained totally Jack's goal. When Cade encouraged Jack, he did so following Jack's lead. "It is rarely helpful for a therapist to appear more enthusiastic for any change than the client. The slightest hint of that would have undoubtedly led to resistance on Jack's part."

At a six-month telephone follow-up, Jack's parents confirmed that while Jack was certainly still no angel, he had settled down considerably; his grades were improving, he was no longer constantly receiving detentions; and his possible expulsion from school was no longer an issue. During the call, Cade spoke to Jack briefly and Jack gave the following explanation:

"It's easy, I just keep my head down behind the couple of big targets that are sitting near to me. They're too stupid to see what's happening."

CREATING MENTORSHIPS WITH TEACHERS, ADMINISTRATORS, AND STUDENTS-IN-TROUBLE

Nan Lovelace, a vice principal at Barnett Junior High School in Arlington, Texas, has been so successful in her work with students facing expulsion or in-school suspension that she's commonly referred to as "mom," by her students who visit her long after their junior high career ends. What's her secret to "enlisting" the troubled adolescents who show up at her door? "I ask them 'what do you want in your life?' " She remarks that many students are quite often "put out" by being expelled or in suspension and at first, resist her assistance. She doesn't give up, however, when she meets such resistance: "I ask them if they know where they want to go in life. Typically they don't know. I then explain to them that if we went on a trip to Florida, and didn't have a map, how would we (herself and the student) get there?" The students often become quiet and reserved at that point. Lovelace then tells them that she's there, and if they are interested, to come back and talk. "I'm not going to call you from class; you can come see me. I'd love to get to know you."

This approach, as Lovelace describes, beckons many similarities to the SFBT approaches presented in this manual:

Goal: How do you want things to be in your life?

Exceptions: What are your abilities and strengths that will get you there?

Problem Influence: What might keep you from getting there?

Task Development: How will you watch out for future problems and solve them with your abilities?

As a vice principal, Lovelace said she has many opportunities to "open the door frequently, but never go in until they invite me." Her observation that the students need to be ready to work before she begins her mentorship has proven correct time and time again, as she encounters less resistance and more success with her approach. The following dialogue is an example of how Lovelace might approach a student facing suspension:

Vice Principal: Do you have a plan for your life?

Student: No.

Vice Principal: Would you like to have one?

Student: No.

Vice Principal: So, you like being expelled, in trouble like this? Looks like a crummy way to live. Man, I'd much rather see you in different circumstances. We could probably have a pretty good time.

Student: (*Silence*)

Vice Principal: Tell you what, I'm here for you. You seem like a neat kid. I'd love to get to know you and together, work on a plan. Let me know.

Lovelace says her invitations are rarely turned down. Her students obviously sense her hope for their lives, her interest, and curiosity in their abilities and strengths. She does not send for the students to come to her office, even if she has an inkling that they are interested. She waits, often until the second time they come back, making sure they are invested in their own change process. Later on, when the student decides that he/she is ready, Lovelace begins with a new dialogue, goal-oriented and focused on competencies:

Vice Principal: Let's pretend you just won the lottery. How much did you win?

Student: $50,000,000.

Vice Principal: Great! Let's go on a trip, okay? You and I. Where would you like to go?

Student: California.

Vice Principal: Why California?

Student: I've never been there.

Vice Principal: Great. Good reason for going there. You have good ideas. I love California, but you know, my car is really crummy. It has real problems. Let's buy a new one with some of the lottery money.

Student: Okay...a Ferrari.

Vice Principal: My kind of companion. I need cool clothes for a car like that. Let's go to the mall on the way to the car dealer.

Student: Okay.

Vice Principal: Now, we've got our car and clothes and we're off. Where's the map?

Student: I don't know.

Vice Principal: It's kind of hard to get there if we don't know where we're going. Let's see, where could we find one?

Student: The library.

Vice Principal: Now that we have a map and we're on our way, everything has been great until we get to the desert and we have three flat tires. Three! I'm hot, thirsty, hungry, the vultures are flying. Help!

Student: What?

Vice Principal: Help me, I don't like it here...what will you do for me? I'm old, I'm hot, and I don't like it here.

Student: I guess I can go for help, and come back to get you.

Vice Principal: Great idea. Get going.

Lovelace then talks to the student about how this metaphorical account of a trip is similar to goal setting and that life is full of "flat tires." Lovelace then compliments the student on his/her problem solving (flat-tire pumping) in the trip description. With this renewed hope, the student and Lovelace create a "Goal Sheet" similar to the one on the next page. The student then concentrates on learning how to "fix the flat tires" in other areas of his/her life, using his/her abilities. The metaphorical description of problems as flat tires connects the student with reality and lessens resistance through belief in his/her ability.

The *Student Success Diary* has been added to Lovelace's goal identification, to collect and compile the successes of students for later visits. The diary is repeated here for clarity. Lovelace inspired my development of this diary when she described routinely writing notes to her students and "recapping" the student's successes, adding her compliments. The notes often end up pasted on mirrors, refrigerators, and so on. Her colleagues who remark at her effective, brief approach have tried her ideas even more "briefly" to discover that words of kindness and hope by an administrator makes tremendous differences in the lives of their students as well as their own! Less stressed, the administrators at Barnett Junior High School have time to walk down the hall and, as Lovelace said, "greet the kids and say: Wow, nice to see you out here and not in my office!" Lucky kids...and colleagues.

Name _____ Date _____

MY GOALS

My goal: (Stated in the positive: I want to graduate from college, become an electrician, and so on.)

_____

_____

_____

What I've done before that might keep me from getting there:

_____

_____

_____

My abilities that *will* get me there:

_____

_____

_____

How I'll "pump up the flat tires" (Ideas from my ability list)

_____

_____

_____

How will that change my life when I begin to do this, on a small scale?

_____

_____

_____

Name _____Date _____

STUDENT SUCCESS DIARY

Grade _____

What's been going well?

_____

How have you done this?

_____

_____

What do you think you might keep on doing that's working for you, to reach your goal?

_____

_____

Grade _____

What's been going well?

_____

How have you done this?

_____

_____

What do you think you might keep on doing that's working for you to reach your goal?

_____

_____

_____

TEACHER-STUDENT MENTORSHIPS: THE OTHER SIDE OF THE DESK

Teachers have always perplexed students. Many teachers will report the surprised looks on students' faces when their students see them in the grocery store, at the mall, or at the park. Do teachers really exist in other places besides behind their desks? The "teacher mystery" can be utilized perhaps in a mentorship role with students-in-trouble, by inviting them into the teacher's world. In

Chapter 4, I mentioned the "School System of the Future," where a student-in-trouble might find himself/herself in a mentor position with a volunteer teacher, experiencing teacher duties, responsibilities, and frustrations. Perhaps this experience should do more than just "consequence" students like in-school-suspension. It might open the eyes of the student to a) see the teacher as someone who works hard to provide an interesting class session; b) see the teacher as someone who is not an enemy but an ally; c) provide the one-on-one nurturing a student may be craving, from the very population that may not be noticing.

A Trip to the Other Side of the Desk

The process might begin with the disciplinary process already in effect. However, instead of sending a child to an in-school classroom where he/she is isolated and "labeled" as bad, he/she is placed in a position similar to an office aid, with responsibilities that grow as competencies do. Teachers are chosen on personality similarities. The teacher with whom the student was disruptive or disrespectful is not initially chosen as the mentor. This relationship may take time. Instead, at the initial faculty meeting the principal might announce:

"This year, we are providing a mentorship program for our at-risk kids. This program means that you will be asked to be a "mentor" for three students, unless you desire more! When a student is placed in your care, you will meet with the student and the counselor or administrator initially to learn how your personality and his/hers are matched for mentorship. Thereafter, the student will become your personal "aide" and will do whatever you need him/her to do. He/she will not be identified as carrying out a "sentence," but instead will hopefully blend in with other office workers. This process will take place no longer than two weeks, based on the in-school suspension time he/she would put in otherwise. The student will be told initially that he/she has a choice to participate, or be placed in a cubicle for the duration of the suspension."

Each week, the mentor teacher will utilize the scaling question card (see Chapter 4), and along with the student look at the progress to set a goal for the next week. Upon completion of the goal, the student will return to class. Thereafter, the teacher will ask the student to stop by and check in weekly, so that separation does not occur, but instead, a friendship develops. The importance of this exercise is in developing a rapport with an educator, the population the at-risk student tries to resist. By lessening resistance and showing care, validation, and attention, the teacher has the opportunity to be perceived differently. Again, when perceptions differ, so do behaviors.

LESSENING THE POWER OF BEING DISRUPTIVE: THE CONTEST OF COMPROMISE

An elementary counselor relayed a case of two young boys who were constantly brought to the principal's office for fighting and cursing. The boys not only fought other children, but also each other. The counselor was discouraged by several staff members from working too hard with the children, for they had quite a reputation for being defiant. She paid little attention to reading the past "history" waved at her and sat down with the two boys, drawing a line, placing the words "freedom from fights" in the middle, and their names on each end of the scale:

freedom from fights

| 1 | 2 | 3 | 4 | 5 | | | 5 | 4 | 3 | 2 | 1 |

Jimmy   David

The counselor explained to them that they were losing a lot of freedom by staying in the office; they were losing time on the playground and were missing out on some fun activities in school. She called this the "problem." She then set up a competition for the two students, framing it as a contest. She asked the students:

Counselor: Where are you, Jimmy and David, on this scale? Number 1 means you are totally under the problem's control and can't get away from it at all...you are in its clutches! Number 5 means you get total freedom to do all the neat things at school with your classmates and stay out of the office.

Jimmy: I'm at a 3.

David: Probably a 2.

Counselor: Wow, so Jimmy is ahead? How, Jimmy, have you managed to be a 3?

Jimmy: Well, I'm not fighting all the time, just on the playground at lunch.

Counselor: And David, you're a bit behind Jimmy but how have you managed to at least move to a 2?

Jimmy: I'm not sure.

Counselor: Where would you both like to be by Friday? Go slow, okay?

(Friday is two days in the future. The counselor wisely chooses this small number because of the boys' ages. She knows that by keeping the time span short, success will be more likely to occur and the students will have a better chance of "fighting" the problem...and winning.)

Jimmy: I want to be at a 4.

David: Me too, a 4.

Counselor: Wow, this is almost like a contest. What fun. I can't wait to see who wins first. How will you do that, Jimmy? David?

Jimmy: Stop fighting at lunchtime.

David: Me too.

Counselor: What else would the teachers say might put you at a 4, so you get to do fun stuff here at school?

Jimmy: Not get in trouble in class.

David: Yeah, not push in the lunchroom line.

Counselor: Good ideas. What will you do instead?

Jimmy: Do my work, I guess, and raise my hand...I forget to do that.

David: Stand in line. Maybe I can ask if I could lead the lunch line, if I'm good.

Counselor: I think that's a great idea. Have you asked for that before?

David: Nope. She doesn't let me lead anything.

Counselor: How about I write down what you and Jimmy are working on. You can take it to your teacher and work a "deal" with her when you start this contest.

David: Okay.

Counselor: Okay, hey, I wonder which of you will reach the middle first? Hmmm.

(Both boys smile, David crosses his arms and Jimmy points to himself.)
The counselor later learns that David has lived in a poverty-level home with seven siblings, and has been supervised by his fourteen-year-old brother while his divorced mom works two jobs. She does not bring up these facts to David, but makes sure whenever she sees him, that she gives him a hug. She also gives each of the boys' teachers a *Teacher Information Sheet* from Chapter 4, trying to gather positive comments for future meetings with the boys. She has made a point to speak to David's teacher about line leading. During the next few weeks, both boys improve dramatically. Her need to see them decreases and her future meetings are simply check-ins

on the contest. The agendas were the boys, not the counselors. Their winning over the "problem" became their triumph, and the contest disappeared as they became best friends.

TEAM TEACHER MEETINGS: COLLABORATIVELY DESIGNING INTERVENTIONS AND STRATEGIES

The concept of team teaching has been an educational wonder for students and teachers alike. The comradeship often experienced in the team approach has kept many educators from burning out, and instead, opened up opportunities for creative teaching. In addition, the teachers who work together, planning their lessons, know the students they each encounter every day. This common knowledge about students offers some marvelous opportunities for team teaching to go one step further—in its planning and discussion of handling student behavior problems differently.

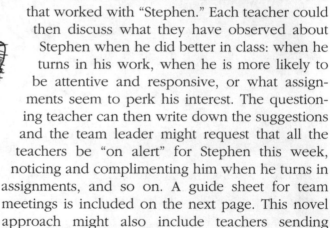

For example, a team of teachers might in their weekly or biweekly meeting scan the team for concerns about a particular student. The teacher concerned could ask what others have found that worked with "Stephen." Each teacher could then discuss what they have observed about Stephen when he did better in class: when he turns in his work, when he is more likely to be attentive and responsive, or what assignments seem to perk his interest. The questioning teacher can then write down the suggestions and the team leader might request that all the teachers be "on alert" for Stephen this week, noticing and complimenting him when he turns in assignments, and so on. A guide sheet for team meetings is included on the next page. This novel approach might also include teachers sending Stephen a note during the next week or two, describing to him what they have noticed him succeeding at.

An additional way of assisting students with the team approach is to have the student attend the team meeting. This is especially valuable if a student does not understand what the teachers are concerned about. Should this occur, the dialogue might begin as follows:

Teacher: Stephen, we're glad you're here. Do you know why we asked you to come?

Student: No, but I guess I'm in trouble?

Teacher: Actually, no, we're interested in making school work for you, and we've noticed during the past six weeks that you are forgetting papers, and so on.

Student: Yeah, I do that a lot.

Teacher: We're each going to go around the room and tell you what we *did* notice about you and your work that impresses us.

(Each teacher shares a positive experience with the student, complimenting him/her and asking what he/she thinks would make things even better.)

Teacher: How will you know that school is working for you?

Student: I guess when I hand in all my papers each day.

Teacher: How will that help?

Student: I'll probably pass my classes and my mom will be happy.

Teacher: In whose class has Stephen turned in his work for this week?

(Teachers respond, team leader counts the number of classes in which he has turned in his work.)

Teacher to all Teachers: Well, four out of the six classroom teachers can see that you know how to do it. Great! How did you turn in papers to four out of six of your classes?

Student: I finished them in class and put them in the assignment box.

Teacher: How does that help?

Student: I don't take them home and then I don't lose them.

Teacher: So, putting the papers in a certain place after you do them works, right?

Student: Yeah.

Teacher: I wonder, now that we've talked about a certain place for papers, you might try to turn in maybe one more classroom assignment tomorrow, in one of the other two classes.

Student: Well, if I put it in my book I don't forget to hand it in. Yeah, I can do one more class.

Teacher: Okay. We all have a task. For the next two weeks, why don't we all notice *when* Stephen turns in his work. Let's keep a very close watch as to how he does it. Let's meet here in two weeks, Stephen. We'll be waiting to hear how it goes.

(At this point, a copy of the Teacher Information for Students *(Chapter 4) might be given to team members. The* Team Strategies for Students *might also be completed in the next meeting from the teacher information sheets, and given to the student and sent to parents.)*

Name _____Date _____

TEAM STRATEGIES FOR STUDENTS

Team Member: Strategies for Behavior:

_____

_____   _____

_____

_____

_____

_____

_____

Team Members: Strategies for Learning:

_____

_____

_____

_____

_____

_____

_____

_____

Seeing discipline "problems" differently and responding to them differently, can be half the battle of "transforming" negative behaviors into solvable behaviors. The teachers in Stephen's team meeting could easily have discussed the problems Stephen had, wondered about his family life and exaggerated the problem beyond resolution by asking "Why?" Instead, by placing the problem in Stephen's hands, yet showing him the support of the teachers in the team meeting, he became part of their effort to help.

REVERSING THE PRESSURE: ENCOURAGING A STUDENT TO INFLUENCE OTHER STUDENTS

A 14-year-old female student relayed to me this wonderful intervention that occurred for her one day at her junior high school:

Student: "I guess I had not been doing as well as I was before this last six weeks. I'd kind of gotten lazy. One day last week, all my teachers called me into the conference room. I knew I was in deep trouble. Instead, do you know what they said? They said they were concerned about me. They said I was a good kid and that other students really looked up to me and that I could really help them out. I was shocked. Then, they went around the room and each of them told me something good about myself. I've never had anything like that happen to me at school."

Counselor: Wow, what else happened then?

Student: They told me my grades had dropped but they had my folder there and showed me how I had done so well early in the year. They asked me if I needed anything from them so I could improve. I couldn't believe it. It was real cool. I told them I didn't know right away but I would think about it. They told me they were going to watch me very closely and ask me if I needed them again.

Counselor: They must really believe in you.

Student: I guess so. It was awesome.

The student went from 70s to 80s and 90s in six weeks and her behavior improved drastically. She had previously dropped out of several activities and after the conference, began to tutor and join new activities. Her mom was very impressed with the initiative of the school to call this conference with her daughter. The daughter felt a positive pressure to improve and a sense of support that she had not recognized before. The teachers who were clever enough to devise such a conference gave this student a belief in herself that she needed during the troubled time she was going through. The teachers also changed their image in the student's mind and the student "paid them back" by being more supportive of the teachers during classtime.

How wise of the teachers to approach the student in this way! The conference was a respectful, compassionate, and very empowering experience for the student.

The student felt supported and saw herself as important to the teachers. The conference took ten minutes from class preparation before school one day and the results lasted the rest of the term. Focusing on when the student did well, mixed with concerns, empathy, and compliments for a plan of action, equaled student success and impressed the parent as well. A guide for conducting such a conference is included on the next page.

The sheet *We Believe in You* can be filled in by teachers who cannot make the conference—but beware—there is power in numbers. If the student has been working with an administrator, ask for his/her comments as well. Remember, the sheet identifies exceptions to problems. Anything else is more of the same, and might not create the context for the student to change behaviors. The team of teachers might want to make copies of the *We Believe in You* page to give to students after the conference.

Name _____ Date _____

WE BELIEVE IN YOU!

1. Our concerns:

_____

_____

2. What we've noticed about you and your successful times at school:

Teacher:_____

_____

Teacher:_____

_____

Teacher:_____

_____

Teacher:_____

_____

Teacher:_____

_____

Teacher:_____

_____

Teacher:_____

_____

_____

SFBT Training Exercise: Chapter 8
Thinking Differently about Discipline

This week, as you teach, counsel, or work with students who struggle with behavioral problems, transform your thinking by *redescribing* the behavior differently to yourself and the student. Remember, definitions or descriptions do not lead to solutions, abilities do. Avoid the "barbed wire fences." Instead, verbalize a new description of the behavior and align with the student to fight the behavior so it frees the student to lower his/her defenses and see you as an assistant, not the enemy.

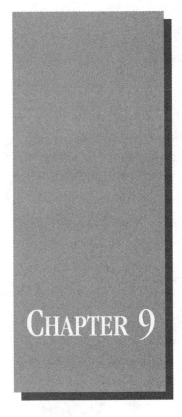

A SOLUTION-FOCUSED SCHOOL STAFF: CREATING THE ATMOSPHERE

CHAPTER 9

A TEAM EFFORT

Many new techniques developed over the years in education have promised to change behaviors and increase motivation. Many of these ideas have been developed with good reason but were created by people outside the schools. This chapter is about assisting and enlisting the entire school staff to become SFBT educators as a team. Creating team work and an atmosphere of competency in schools is the most successful when the school staff is informed of the "Exceptional School Program," and has a part in its development and implementation. It is helpful to begin such a program by reviewing what has worked within the individual school. In the same way that SFBT approaches attempt to elicit the competencies in students and parents, developing a school program among staff utilizes the same approach. Faculty members compose a rich source of resources, and the most effective SFBT school program approaches the staff with this in mind.

Many schools in America today have lost their purpose. Phillip C. Schlechty mentions in his book *Schools for the 21st Century*, that the way leaders conceptualize the purpose of their organization determines how their organization will run. This chapter will offer information and instruction for:

CHAPTER 9 FOCUS

- Developing a purpose for your school: Suggested questions for staff
- Experiential exercises for training staff in the *Exceptional School Program*
- Exercises for staff development to further the understanding of SFBT ideas through personal experience
- Overview handouts of the *Exceptional School Program*

BE A SCHOOL WITH A PURPOSE

As with the Cheshire cat in *Alice in Wonderland,* we as educators must know where we are going in order to get there. A possible way of beginning to know "which way we're going" is to ask the following questions before staff training and during each faculty meeting:

"What is our purpose here as the faculty of
_____ High School?"

"When have we accomplished that in the past?"

"How did we do that?"

"How might we do more of that as a team?"

"Where shall we begin, on a small scale?"

If these questions sound familiar, they are. These basic steps described in previous chapters for working with students apply to parents, teachers, administrators, coaches, nurses, and all other school staff members. Understanding the purpose or goal of a school gives direction in which to travel with students. The goal development process should include setting a goal agreeable to faculty members, helping teachers and administrators identify past successes, encouraging teamwork and collaboration, and a plan of action on a small scale (such as one month at a time).

Training Exceptional Educators

The next pages will include reproducible outlines for training staff members. Guidelines for making the training fun and personal are also given in the form of role plays and personal exercises. The most effective training occurs in small increments each week. The training exercises after the initial meeting might begin with:

"What's going better in school?"

"Who's noticed colleagues doing things with students that seem to make a difference?"

These guiding questions allow teachers and administrators times to evaluate and "brag" about their personal successes and remark about individual students in whom they see changes. Success is very motivating to educators and hearing their peers describe their experiences encourages others to try the new ideas.

SUGGESTIONS FOR TRAINING EXERCISE #1 A PROBLEM-FOCUSED APPROACH

Conduct Step A before giving out handouts

STEP A

The next page should be reproduced in the form of a transparency. Divide the educators-in-training into groups of three or four. Ask them to choose the following participants:

- one person is to represent a teacher, counselor, or administrator
- one person is to represent a student with a problem
- one person is to observe the process and watch for "what works"

Cover the bottom, "Solution-Focused Approach," with a piece of paper, exposing only the top, "Problem-Focused Approach" on the overhead projector. Read aloud the instructions under "Problem-Focused Approach." This exercise is the most effective *when conducted before the handout is given.* The purpose of the exercise is to show how difficult it is to convince students that they have problems (it often increases resistance) and how much more productive it might be to focus on solutions:

- lessens resistance
- decreases conflict
- encourages responsibility
- is more productive
- is less stressful on the educator

Ask the observers and students "What was accomplished?" Then proceed to Step B.

STEP B

Ask the trainees to return to their original groups. Using Transparency 1, show the "Solution-Focused Approach" and cover the "Problem-Focused Approach." Again ask the trainees the same problem, to try using the questions which focus on solutions. Arrange the overhead screen so that it is visible only to the educator, not the student. After the groups talk among themselves, ask the observers:

"What did you notice (if anything) that was different during this discussion? What did____(educator) say/ask that made a difference?"

After the discussion, pass out Training Exercise #1 and discuss all pages together.

A PROBLEM-FOCUSED APPROACH
(OVERHEAD)

Educator: A student has come to you complaining about another teacher. The student is convinced that the problem is the teacher's fault. Convince the student that he/she has a problem and needs to work on it.

Student: You are tired of the way Ms. Smith treats you. You try to behave but she is making it impossible. You are really angry.

A SOLUTION-FOCUSED APPROACH
STEP B

Educator: Ask the student the following questions:

1. This sounds awful...I'm surprised things are not worse! What will *you* be doing when things are better for you?

2. When was the last time just a little of that happened for you, even in other situations? How did you do that?

3. For the next few days, based on what you've just told me has worked for you before, what might you try?

Changing Our Thinking to a Solution Focus
Training Exercise #1

You cannot solve a problem with the same thinking that created it.

Albert Einstein

The *Exceptional School Program* asks you to begin thinking differently about students. Instead of focusing on problems, the program suggests noticing when the problems are not as dominant in the student's life. The following "steps" are an example of this model of thinking and the strategies are designed to focus on solutions with students, assisting them to develop responsibility and competency:

1. *Goal Statement:* After a student complains about a problem, ask the student a question similar to:

   "How will you know when things are slightly better for you?"

Stated in the words of the student, not the educator, the goal is defined according to what the student wants to work on. Students cannot change their parents, friends or other teachers. They can, however, change their behavior which will result in interactional changes. A student who complains about a teacher may be asked:

   What will it take to get Ms. Baker off your back?

2. *Exception Identification:* When the student states his/her goal, ask the student questions similar to:

   "When was the last time (the goal) happened slightly?"

   "What did you do to make that happen?"

   "How did you encourage (another person) to respond to you in that way?"

   "How did you do that?"

Identifying exceptions to problems takes time. Perhaps explore other situations in which the same goal was desired and define how the student performed in those circumstances. For example, a student who passes 6 of 7 classes and wants to pass Algebra, might be asked what he/she did before when a class was troublesome.

3. *Task Development:* Examine the goal, exceptions, and other impressions with the student which indicate their abilities and competencies that have solved problems in the past. From the exceptions, assist the student in formulating a task and encourage their participation by drawing the scale below:

250

| Problem is in control | | | | | | | | | I am in control |
| of me | | | | | | | | | of the problem |

| 1 | 2 | 3 | 4 | 5 | 6 | 7 | 8 | 9 | 10 |

Ask questions in relation to the scale such as:

"On this scale of 1–10, 1 being the problem is totally in control of you and 10 you are in control, where are you now that we have talked today?"

"Where would you like to be tomorrow (this afternoon for young students) or next week?"

"Based on what you have told me today that has worked before, what will you do to get there?"

GUIDELINES FOR THINKING DIFFERENTLY

1. Discover and notice the resources within yourself and your students. Evaluate daily what "worked" in school for *you*—the lesson plan that kept their interest, the touch on the hand of a rebellious student, or the kind remark to a shy child. Consider repeating what worked and discarding what did not work.

2. Jump over the "barbed-wire fences" that label and restrict growth and solutions! Escape from labels that serve only to describe problems. Instead, search for new descriptions that sound more solvable.

3. Learn to cooperate with learning styles, differences, personalities, and interests, and ask students for that information. Resistance occurs less when we cooperate with the population we serve. This does not mean overlooking disruptions, it means stopping disruptions before they begin by noticing that they have not begun. Ask students how they manage to discourage "disruptions" (as if it is external to them) and assume that they can do more of it.

Learn to ask this question in critical situations: "What will you be doing differently when things are better for you?"

Exercise: Today, notice at least one student who doesn't allow his/her problem to take over his/her behavior, even if only for a few minutes. Comment on the absence of the behavior and ask the student if he/she could be stronger than the "behavior" for an additional hour (afternoon, day), and so on.

Notes:

RULES FOR PRACTICING THE EXCEPTIONAL SCHOOL PROGRAM
TRAINING EXERCISE #1

1. Using a nonpathological approach makes problems solvable.

2. There is no need to attempt to understand or promote insight to solve problems.

3. It is not necessary to know a great deal about the complaint.

4. Students, teachers, administrators, and parents have complaints, not symptoms.

5. Students define the goal.

6. There is a ripple effect, a snowball effect when one person changes.

7. Complex problems do not necessarily require complex solutions.

8. Fitting into the student's world view lessens resistance.

9. Motivation is a key ingredient for change.

10. There is no such thing as resistance...when we cooperate.

11. If it works, don't fix it; if it doesn't, do something different.

12. Focus on the possible and the changeable—on specific behaviors, not emotions.

13. Go slowly, building on skills and successes.

14. Rapid change is possible; notice when specific behaviors change and ask students for their strategies.

15. Change is constant and inevitable—watch for it and verbalize your discovery.

16. Every complaint pattern contains some sort of exception.

17. Change the time and the place, and you change the context toward a solution.

18. Look at problems differently; redescribe them in more solvable language.

CREATING POSSIBILITIES THROUGH LANGUAGE
TRAINING EXERCISE #2

We believe that persons generally ascribe meaning to their lives by plotting their experience into stories, and that these stories shape their lives and relationships.

MICHAEL WHITE, DAVID EPSTON

Discuss the following pages together, and apply various situations to the explanations.

ASSUME THAT CHANGE WILL HAPPEN

1. Talk about the experiences as if they were in the past, available for reference, but also workable enough for redesigning in the future.

2. Encourage and invite young children to imagine describing their story to a child in need of a solution. Help change their negative experience into a successful triumph over their problem.

3. Redescribe behaviors which sound "pathological" into behaviors that seem "solvable" and "normal."

4. Normalize behaviors for students. Help them feel as if their situation occurs commonly and that they do not have a severe, unusual problem.

5. Pretend that the student's life is considered to be "Act 1" in the Play of Life. Now, construct "Act 2" with the student. Change the characters, change the interactions and behaviors into a new scene in which the student does things differently. Ask the student how his peers, teachers, or parents would probably like to see the "play" change.

6. Assume change will occur or has already occurred.

A way to change the focus from doom to dream is by "redescribing" the presented problem of a student into "solution-talk." Ask the educators to get into groups of four. On the lines below, list the problem behaviors you see in your students every day under "problem-talk." An example might be: anger, ADD, rebellion, and so on. When finished, read the last sentence on the bottom of the next page. Discuss with your training leader.

Problem-Talk   Solution-Talk

_____

_____

_____

_____

_____

_____

_____

_____

_____

_____

_____

Now, on the right side of the sheet, rewrite the problem behavior into solution-talk. For example, anger might become "upset," and depression might become "sad," hyperactivity might become "energetic." Work together to discover some new descriptions. The point of this exercise is to change "problem-talk" into "solution-talk" so the problem sounds less impossible and more solvable.

GUIDING QUESTIONS FOR STUDENT CONVERSATIONS

Connect with the Student (Parent, Colleague):

"This sounds really awful. In fact, I'm surprised things aren't worse! How have you managed to cope so far?"

Problem Definition:

"What would be helpful for us to talk about? (Be specific—keep it to what the *person* can do, not what someone else needs to do)

Goal Setting:

"How will you know when things are better for you? What will I see you doing when things are slightly better?"

Or:

If the student (parent or colleague) references that someone else will respond differently to them, ask: "If I asked Ms. Jones what it would take for her to (get off your back, call on you more often, be less angry at you) what do you suppose she would say?"

Search for Exceptions:

"When does a little of this (goal) happen? When in the past have you been successful at doing this elsewhere?"

Task Development:

"Based on what you have told me today has worked for you slightly in the past, what do you think you might try until we talk again?"

*For a kindergartener or first grader, set the task for one day; for an older child/adolescent, no longer than a week. This gives a better opportunity for success—success motivates more change.

Reproduce the next page and use as a guide for these questions. Make a copy for the student (together) and congratulate him/her on excellent ideas. Keep a copy.

Name _____ Date _____

MY SOLUTIONS!

Problem:

_____

How things will be when the problem is solved:

_____

_____

Times when the "problem" is less of a problem for me (exceptions):

1.___ _____

2. _____

3._____ _____

4._____ _____

5._____

Task for today (this week, and so on) based on the above exceptions:

1._____

2._____

3._____

4._____

5._____

Ask: Did we talk about what we needed to talk about? What did we do that helped?

_____

SCALING PROBLEMS DOWN TO SIZE
(ROLE-PLAY)

Lipchick and de Shazer talk of *Scaling Questions* as therapeutic tools used to measure the effects of a problem on a person's life. See Ellen Boehmer's 3 x 5 card idea in Chapter 4. When working with students, teachers or parents can rate on a scale of 1–10, the following: "At 1, the problem is in total control of your life and at 10, you are in complete control of the problem."

The student, teacher, or parent is then asked to tell where he/she is as the meeting begins. As the meeting progresses, he/she is then asked to tell where he/she would like to be by the next meeting. For many students who reply "I don't know," this approach allows them to think small and come up with small tasks that move up the scale. For example (consider reading aloud with players):

Administrator: Mom, you say that you are having a hard time trusting your daughter Sarah since she has failed three classes and skipped school three times this term, is that correct?

Mom: Yes, it's hard to trust her at all (*scowling at Sarah*). I would like to trust her again, but it will take a long time.

Administrator: Sarah, where would you say you are right now, on a scale of 1–10, where 1 means you are not trusted at all by mom and 10 means you are totally trusted?

Sarah: About a 2.

Mom: That's even lower than I would have said!

Administrator: Sarah, where would you like to be by the time I meet with you again?

Sarah: At least a five, but I don't know if that will make a difference to her.

Administrator: Mom, would that make a difference?

Mom: Anything will make a difference.

Administrator: Sarah, you say you are at a 2 now, and want to move up to a 5 by next week. What would you suggest you do to move up 3 places?

Sarah: Probably come home and do homework so she sees me trying, at least. Not skipping school would probably help.

Administrator: Mom, would that make a difference?

Mom: Maybe.

Sarah: See, she's so negative.

Administrator: I guess that happens sometimes, when the trust level goes down. What I'm interested in though, are your ideas, and the fact that Mom has been able to trust you before. Have ideas like this helped to gain Mom's trust before?

Sarah: Yeah, sort of. I think she trusted me last year when I studied at home and didn't skip. She spent time with me too.

Administrator: Is this true?

Mom: Yes, I remember last year was a better year.

Administrator: Looking back, where would you have placed Sarah on the same scale we've been talking about last year?

Mom: Probably an 8.

Administrator: That's great. What did she do then to be that high on your trust level?

Mom: She did study, and her grades were good. She came home when I asked her, her friends came over and I got to meet them instead of wondering who they are.

Administrator: So, Sarah, you already know how to do this.

Sarah: I guess.

Administrator: Go for it. Sounds like a 5 is a very reasonable idea for this week. I want you to keep thinking, too, where you want to end up on that scale, okay?

Sarah: Okay.

Administrator: Mom, I'd like you to pay particular attention this week to specific things that Sarah does to make your trust level with her rise, okay?

Mom: Okay.

THE *PROBLEM* IS THE PROBLEM NOT THE PERSON
TRAINING EXERCISE #3
(ROLE-PLAY)

Thinking about problems as "external" from persons frees them from feeling as if they are indeed the problem. This pathologizing only inhibits people from seeing hope and raises resistance with everyone who tries to help. Instead, this new approach from Michael White "objectifies or personifies" problems and attempts to identify the influence of problems on people's lives. Read the following role-play aloud. Choose a person to play the teacher and one to play the counselor. Discuss how the questions assist the teacher in seeing the problem of "depression" (her description) differently:

Counselor: How has this depression interfered with your ability to teach effectively?

Teacher: It keeps me from enjoying my students, being creative in the holiday activities I used to love doing, and from looking forward to the next day.

Counselor: How have you let the depression take over sometimes and intrude in your life, keeping you from these things that you just described to me?

Teacher: Well, I go home and I just sit, or I go to school and think about how bad things are since Bob left me, or I think that things will never get better.

Counselor: How many hours a day would you say you let the depression bother you?

Teacher: It's worse in the morning for about an hour and then at night, for about three hours.

Counselor: So, four hours a day?

Teacher: Yes.

Counselor: What about the other waking hours of the day—how many would that leave?"

Teacher: About eight, I guess.

Counselor: How do you keep the depression from bothering you during those hours?

Teacher: I'm here at school or doing things for my kids at home.

Counselor: How do you keep the depression from bothering you so that you are able to do things here at school or for your children? That's incredible.

Teacher: I have to...I have to do certain things to survive.

Counselor: That's great! With all this going on, you still think ahead, of what you need to do, about surviving—because you know you have to.

Teacher: Yes, the kids depend on me.

259

Counselor: What does that do for you?

Teacher: Makes me feel important, needed, wanted.

Counselor: Who else does that?

Teacher: I guess the teachers here, friends, my family.

Counselor: So you have quite a support system—who needs you, wants you around, sees you as important?

Teacher: I never thought of it that way, but yes, I do.

The "depression" quickly ceased to be the focus in this dialogue. What did you notice when the "depression" became an object to defeat or avoid? How did you see the teacher change from hopeless to surviving?

USING NARRATIVE STRATEGIES TO DISSOLVE PROBLEMS

David Epston of New Zealand (and Michael White of Australia) support and further the competencies of clients through letter writing and certificates. An example of a note to a student dealing with "energy" (labeled ADHD by others) is given below:

Dear Joey,

I wanted to write you this note to tell you how impressed I am that you have been in control of the "energy" for the past two days. Wow. It's nice to see you in charge for a change instead of "energy." I noticed that your classmates treated you much differently. Did you? Let's talk soon about how you've done this so well, okay? I am very impressed with you!

Ms. Smith, your teacher

You will find another strategy on the next page in the form of a certificate. Consider using this certificate or developing one with your school logo.

Certificate of Success

is awarded to:

_____

for:

_____

This was accomplished by:

_____

_____

signed, this_____day of_____19__

_____

teacher

Name _____ Date_____

EXCEPTIONAL SCHOOL PROGRAM
TRAINING EXERCISE #4

What is needed is an environment in which people can feel competent.

CREATIVE STRATEGIES FOR SCHOOL PROBLEMS,
MICHAEL DURRANT

Review the ideas in Chapter 4, the *Exceptional School Program*. Discuss with the trainees how influential they can be as they begin to notice competencies of students and not their deficits. Discuss how knowing "what's wrong" rarely comes equipped with strategies. The *Exceptional School Program* is designed so that coaches, teachers, nurses, school psychologists, counselors, and administrators notice "what works" and discover this information with the students they work with. Emphasize how difficult this "switch of thinking" is. Ask the trainees to consider the following:

"What went really badly last week for you?"

"What went so well last week here at school, that you would like to do it again?"

Ask them to notice that it is easier to point out the problems. Problems, as described by Michael White, are like hurdles we must leap over: the important thing to remember is that there are spaces between the hurdles. Ask the trainees to notice the times in between the hurdles.

Copy the following sheets from Chapter 4 and discuss with the trainees that these sheets will now be used in the school for their benefit: better managed classes, more efficient referrals and follow ups for increased student self-esteem and better behavior. Compliment the staff on what they already are doing well. Remember, the program begins with the staff. Noticing their competencies is a vital route to increasing their cooperation with this program. It may be helpful to begin this session with passing out 3 x 5 cards and asking each to look around the room and jot down someone who seems to make a difference in students' lives or their own lives as colleagues. Place these in a box and read a few before the meeting begins and then when it ends. Consider publishing these in a faculty newsletter and distribute immediately after this training session.

After this last training session is over, during regular faculty meetings, begin with "What's better here, at _____school"? Again, pass out the 3 x 5 cards. Remember, change is difficult, and noticing when people do things well is a change of thinking for many people who work very hard in school settings. This is not a deficit, it is the way educators have often been trained: to notice deficits and design skill building curriculum to change the deficits. Patience is important. The reproducible sheets in the appendix of this book may be used on educator's doors to classes to remind them that "There is always an exception . . . we just have to find it."
For further assistance with your school program, consider contacting the author for consultation over the phone or for in-service training.

Items to Give to Teaching Staff:

Teacher Referral Form
Student Information Sheet
Teacher Information for Students
Parent Conference Role Play
Guide Sheet for Parent Conferences
Notes to Send to Students, Parents, and Colleagues (see appendix)

In addition, give the following to Diagnosticians and Counselors:

Development of the Individual Educational Plan (IEP)

APPENDIX

ADDITIONAL REPRODUCIBLE FORMS

NOTICE:

When School Works!

Solutions Discovered
here...
come in !

You've turned SCHOOL around!

_____

_____

                        _____

Your son is INCREDIBLE!

_____

_____

                        _____

THERE'S NEVER BEEN ANYONE QUITE LIKE YOU!

_____

_____

_____

LOOK what I've noticed about you!

_____

_____

_____

I'm so impressed with you!
WOW!

_____

_____

                          _____

I can't believe how you've changed!

_____

_____

                          _____

Your daughter is INCREDIBLE!

_____

_____

_____

YOU KNOW EXACTLY WHAT TO DO!
- YOU'VE ALREADY DONE IT!

_____

_____

_____

You're doing what?

... amazing me

_____

_____

_____

It's TOO incredible to believe!

_____

_____

_____

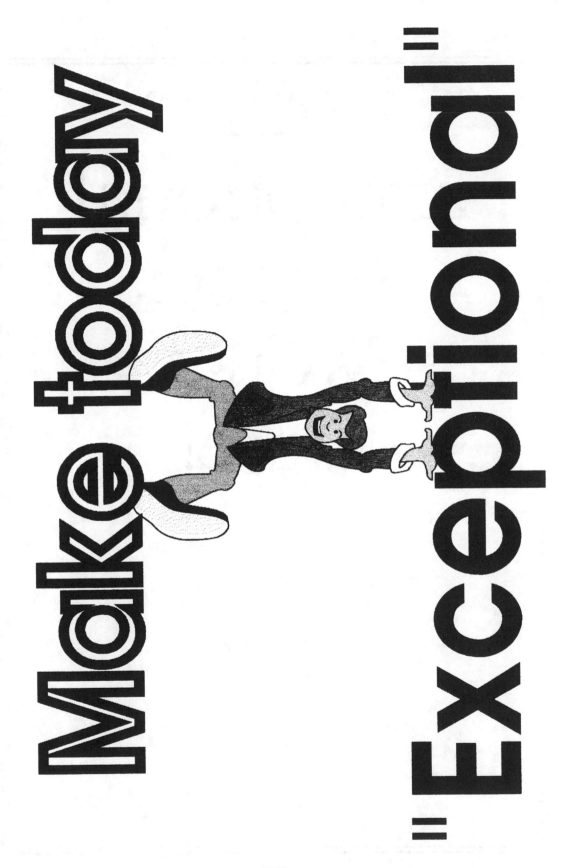

Make today "Exceptional"

An Exceptional Teacher Works Here!

(School logo here)

An Exceptional Counselor Makes a Difference Here!

(School logo here)

An Exceptional Administrator Helps Here!

(School logo here)

Exceptional Classes Meeting Here!

(School logo here)

If it works, do it.

If not, do something different!

Create an
environment
in which
students,
teachers, and
parents feel
competent!

REFERENCES

Allen, S., In: Branscombe, N., Goswami, D. and Schwartz, J. *Students Teaching, Teachers Learning.*, Portsmouth, NH: Boynton/Cook-Heinemann (1990), p. 82.

Cade, B. and O'Hanlon, W. H. *A Brief Guide to Brief Therapy.* New York/London: W.W. Norton & Company (1993).

Cade, B. *The Target.* Sydney, Australia: Written exclusively for this publication (1994).

Combs, G. and Freedman, J. *Symbol Story and Ceremony.* pp. 165-166. New York/London: W. W. Norton & Company (1990).

de Shazer, S. *Keys to Solutions in Brief Therapy.* New York/London: W. W. Norton & Company (1984).

de Shazer, S. *Clues: Investigating Solutions in Brief Therapy.* New York/London: W. W. Norton & Company (1988).

de Shazer, S. *Putting Difference to Work.* New York/London: W. W. Norton & Company (1991).

Durrant, M. *Creative Strategies for School Problems.* Sydney, Australia: Eastwood Family Therapy Centre (1993). (Forthcoming publication by W. W. Norton & Company, 1995.)

Epston, D. *Collected Papers*, pp. 75-77. Adelaide, South Australia: Dulwich Centre Publications (1989).

Epston, D. and White, M. *Narrative Means to Therapeutic Ends.* New York/London: W. W. Norton & Company (1990).

Fulghum, R. *Maybe (Maybe Not)*, p. 5. New York: Villard Books (1993).

Haley, J. *Advanced Techniques of Hypnosis and Therapy*. New York: Grune & Stratton (1967).

Haley, J. *Uncommon Therapy*. New York/London: W. W. Norton & Company (1973).

Haley, J. *Problem-Solving Therapy*. New York: Harper & Row (1976).

Haley, J. *Therapy: A New Phenomenon*. In J. Zeig (Ed.). *The Evolution of Psychotherapy*. New York: Brunner/Mazel (1987).

Keeney, B. Conference Remarks, Fort Worth, Texas (1994).

Keeney, B. *Aesthetics of Change*. New York: Guilford (1983).

Lipchik, E. and de Shazer, S. Purposeful sequences for beginning the solution-focused interview. In E. Lipchik *Interviewing*, pp. 105-117. Rockville, MD: Aspen (1988).

Metcalf, L. and Thomas, F. Client and Therapist Perceptions of Solution-Focused Brief Therapy: A Qualitative Analysis. (At Press). *Journal of Family Psychotherapy* (1994).

Metcalf, L. Therapy With Parent-Adolescent Conflict: Creating a climate in which clients can figure what to do differently. *Family Therapy Case Studies*, 6 (2), pp. 25-34 (1991).

O'Hanlon, W. H. and Weiner-Davis, M.. *In Search of Solutions: A New Direction In Psychotherapy*. New York/London: W. W. Norton & Company (1989).

O'Hanlon, W. H. Informational Sheets. Omaha: The Hudson Center For Brief Therapy (1994).

Peller, J. and Walter, J. *Becoming Solution-Focused in Brief Therapy*. New York: Bruner/Mazel (1992).

Schlechty, P. *Schools for the 21st Century*. San Francisco: Josey Bass (1990).

White, M. *Selected Papers*. Adelaide, South Australia: Dulwich Centre Publications (1989).

Whittgenstein, L. *Philosophical Remarks* (R. Hargreaves and R. White, trans.). Chicago: University of Chicago Press (1975a).